GUTS &
GUILE

ED PHILLIPS

GUTS&
GUILE

TRUE TALES FROM THE BACKROOMS OF THE PIPELINE INDUSTRY

FOREWORD BY RICHARD J. DOYLE

Douglas & McIntyre
Vancouver/Toronto

Douglas & McIntyre
1615 Venables Street
Vancouver, British Columbia V5L 2H1

Canadian Cataloguing in Publication Data
Phillips, Ed, 1917–
    Guts and guile
    ISBN 0-88894-707-0
    1. Petroleum industry and trade—Canada, Western.
2. Petroleum—Canada, Western—Pipe lines   3. Gas industry—
Canada, Western.   4. Gas, Natural—Canada, Western—Pipe lines.
5. Westcoast Energy (Firm).   I. Title.
HD9574.C22P49   1990   338.2'728'0971   C90-091406-8

Editing by Brian Scrivener
Typeset by The Typeworks
Printed and bound in Canada by D. W. Friesen & Sons Ltd.
Printed on acid-free paper ∞

Publication of this book has been assisted by Petro-Canada.

CONTENTS

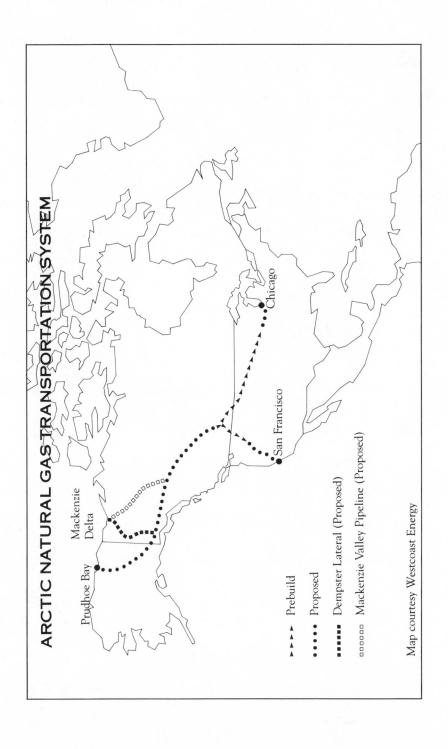

ARCTIC NATURAL GAS TRANSPORTATION SYSTEM

Prudhoe Bay

Mackenzie
Delta

Chicago

San Francisco

➤➤➤ Prebuild

••••• Proposed

▬▬▬ Dempster Lateral (Proposed)

□□□□□□ Mackenzie Valley Pipeline (Proposed)

Map courtesy Westcoast Energy

FOREWORD

When he packed up all his care and woe and moved from Chatham, Ontario, to his glamour job with Consumers' Gas in Toronto, I felt the need for one last talk with Ed Phillips. And so we met in the Victoria Room of the King Edward Hotel and had lunch. (Back in 1947, lunch was still something you "had," rather than "did.")

The question I posed Ed was: should I accept the offer I'd had to succeed him as advertising manager of the Canada and Dominion Sugar Company?

Phillips furrowed his brow (no easy task in his thirtieth year) and confessed that advertising wasn't what he had managed at C and D. "I'm a lobbyist," he said. It had been his job to pull together the distinctly different desires of the producers, processors and consumers of sugar in a time of uneven supply, international poker and—in Canada—government control.

"Managing," said Ed, "means connecting with politicians." He modestly confessed to having a useful connection I might want to cultivate. Did I, by chance, know Mr. Diefenbaker?

The machinery, of course, wouldn't work without the press. "You've got to be certain that when there are confrontations the public will get the facts." Ergo, there had to be no doubt that C and

D was the lone possessor of the truth. "Give those guys (the reporters) the gears once and they'll leave you out to dry come the next time you're in trouble. And ever after." Every step of a process had to be measured to make sure it could stand the sunlight.

What Ed was talking about was "minding the store." If I could master that, I'd be alright.

Perhaps what made my mind up about taking the job was Phillips's unlikely conviction that the tycoon and the news reporter could produce, between them, an offspring endowed with integrity. Especially if there was an understanding midwife handy. I was even younger than Ed and, with proper guidance, could see points of light long since invisible to my cynical elders at the Chatham *Daily News*.

I stayed exactly one year at C and D, developing, as Ed had before me, great admiration for Al McIntyre, the senior vice-president who, as my immediate boss, continued the discussion of Truth as a business tool.

Ed Phillips stayed much longer at Consumers' Gas than I did with the sugar barons. Attached as assistant to the general manager, he became immersed in the search for new supply to fuel an urban system that, in its pioneer days, had depended on hand-bored cedar pipes to carry manufactured gas for heat and light in the neighbourhoods of Ontario's capital.

I was at *The Globe and Mail* in the 1960s when Ed called one day to complain about our coverage of a strike that had hobbled Trane Company of Canada. Doyle: "How do you know what's going on in the union at Trane?" Phillips: "I work here. We told your guys the truth about the strike. They didn't print a word of it." Doyle: "Are you sure you told them all the truth?"

His voice was softer now. "I ought to know what we told 'em. After all, I'm president of this outfit."

In 1968, Ed was ready to return to the west coast where he had grown up. He sought and got an interview with Frank McMahon, the legendary swashbuckler of the North American pipeline business. After four martinis (Frank) and two Dubonnets (Ed), McMahon brought in a clutch of Westcoast Transmission executives. "This," he said, "is Ed Phillips. I've hired him today as vice-president to help build the pipelines from Alaska. Find something for him to do." Phillips writes that his colleagues would not have been more surprised if he had declared his jockey was going to be the next president of the company.

Thus begins the Edwin Phillips chunk of the marvellous adventure of pipeline construction and operation that has increasingly fascinated entrepreneurs and engineers throughout this last century of the millennium. From the point of view of the storyteller, we are where we were a hundred years ago with the romance of the railways. We know there is a saga to be recorded; the question remains: where to begin?

Perhaps the start of the beginning rests with what might be described as the fear of pipelines and their social and environmental implications. A long and agonizingly sensitive treatise by Judge Thomas Berger delayed the building of a pipeline in the Mackenzie Valley for at least ten years. *The Past and Future Land,* Martin O'Malley's loving account of Berger's journeying, wears the same glove.

Still to come are full accounts of the experiences of the men and women who have taken the risks and built the existing network of short and long pipeline links in so many parts of Canada. The ramifications of the industry's ventures remain to be assessed.

Ed Phillips starts at the top—in the board rooms, on the company jets, in the hotel suites where dreams are costed and snapped up (or spit out) by people accustomed to losing as well as winning fortunes.

Blackmail. Terrorism. Bluff and betrayal. All with pinstripe niceties rarely abused. The book keeps the promise of its title as it lingers over the politicking of pipelining. The failure to build the all-land line for Alaskan crude has its sequel with the Exxon spilling of 41 million litres on 1,127 kilometres of shoreline. Another shocker: the foolish loss of mega-projects just to indulge Bill Bennett's scunner against federal partnership in title to B.C. resource initiatives. Ed Phillips, forty-three years on, is still telling the truth as he sees it and cheerfully anticipating the best of this life in return.

Ed and I have met only a few times since the Chatham days. I have no difficulty recalling each reunion and remembering the pleasure I pin to it—no occasion, I might add, more memorable than when we met through this manuscript.

Richard J. Doyle

INTRODUCTION

The rationale for writing these reminiscences is as obscure as the writer's chronicling talents. Experiences galore, but storytelling ability? We'll see.

An upbringing in Hollywood, and early experiences in that celluloid city, may have equipped me for the incredible drama of pipelines and politics. My microscopic role as an extra in a crowd of kids in Cecil B. de Mille's classic film *Kings of Kings* may have helped me in later years to recognize an imperious, whip-cracking boss when I saw one in the man who is the most-mentioned personality of the account to follow. A similar unnoticed movie role in the 1926 silent version of *Ben Hur* also taught me that history, like the movies, will distort the real story as surely as Ben Hur's chariot race was fixed. Something should be put on the record about northern pipeline development by a witness who has at least the scars and some laurels as his credentials for accuracy.

Commercial expectations did not move me to put together this account, because my first business enterprise proved that sex sells literature, and the combination of pipelines and politics is more testy than sexy; in other words, a hard sell. The locale of my first business venture was outside the gates of the original Warner Bros.

movie studios, a block from my home: my product, the *Los Angeles Times*. Oil, gas and real estate were booming, leading up to the crash of '29, but newspapers were not selling that well until evangelist Aimee Semple McPherson fled her pulpit and hit the headlines. Aimee must have had the divine gift of prophecy; she portrayed the detestable role of a certain type of television evangelist more than a decade before the electronic medium was invented. The unscriptural caper of faking an ocean drowning, so that her mother could collect life insurance and Aimee could shack up in Carmel with her organist, inspired as many as four extra editions of the *Times* a day. Her hat floating ashore on the Santa Monica beach was enough for a new headline and a new edition without any really new information. "Extra, extra!" I shouted about another news tidbit, "Read all about Aimee's stocking found in the seaweed."

At a nickel a copy, with a 66-percent mark-up, the daily take was enormous. Motorists often threw a dime out the window, not waiting for the change. That boosted the mark-up to 233 percent, with no income tax to pay. That sex saga lasted for weeks and I couldn't afford to take time off to go to school. My parents did not discover that I had been playing hookey until I had to explain I had not robbed a bank for the pocketsful of money I had accumulated.

My newspaper earnings and tips in those glory days exceeded my father's modest salary as minister of a downtown congregation. However, I made a mistake. I soon returned to grade four in school instead of staying in the news business. My mother was the problem. Like all L.A. parents at the time, she forbade her kids to read the newspapers. I pleaded unsuccessfully: "I don't read 'em, I just sell 'em!" Not a fit occupation for a minister's son, was the final decree. According to family legend, my mother confessed to her Sewing Circle at the church: "My Eddie was making money out of sex before he knew what it was."

So there it is. More than sixty years after that financial success as a news mogul, I am devoting otherwise idle time to compiling some personal experiences garnered in a more pedestrian career as a pipeliner with Westcoast Transmission. Neglected, for this account at least, will be my recollections as a preacher's kid, hockey and lacrosse player, cowboy and air force pilot; and my experiences with four other good employers—Loblaws, Canada & Dominion Sugar, Consumers' Gas and the Trane Company. Those years involved going to eight schools and living in two states and five provinces, but they do not relate in a significant way to pipelines and politics, which are the confines of this record.

By a perfectly logical process, Westcoast Transmission Company Limited (now Westcoast Energy Inc.) became interested in both oil and gas pipelines in the Canadian arctic. The same can't be said for this writer, and that circumstance should be explained at the outset. There was a certain irony in the involvement of a Toronto gas man with arctic pipelines.

In 1947, I was hired by The Consumers' Gas Company of Toronto to coordinate feasibility studies for the two alternatives of building a new coke-oven plant in Toronto or introducing natural gas to that marketing area to replace the hundred-year-old manufactured-gas system. With the title of assistant to the general manager, I had the consulting assistance of Stone and Webster for the coke-oven plant, and Ford, Bacon and Davis for the natural-gas proposal.

We soon abandoned the coke-oven idea and concentrated on bringing natural gas to Toronto. Our first idea was to purchase gas in Texas at 12 cents per million cubic feet (mcf) and move it to Buffalo, New York, through the unused capacity of the big-inch pipeline operated by Tennessee Gas Transmission. Gardiner Symonds, Tennessee's chairman, was a great supporter and I admired him as an outstanding corporate executive in charge of the world's largest gas-pipeline system.

The only significant capital cost for this practical proposal would be an 80-mile pipeline from the U.S. side of the Niagara River to the Toronto city gate. The Honourable C.D. Howe soon killed that proposal because he idealistically wanted an all-Canadian route for a pipeline shipping only Canadian natural gas. With his political muscle, a bit of guile and typical resourcefulness, he simply declared the Niagara River was a navigable waterway, the famous Horseshoe Falls notwithstanding. Accordingly, the federal govern-

ment, through the defence department, would not permit a pipeline to cross it. I was learning quickly that pipelines, politics and
logic don't mix.

I was tipped off by an Ottawa source that part of our problem was
C.D. Howe's personal dislike for consultants Ford, Bacon and
Davis. We caved in, dropped that engineering firm and engaged
Stone and Webster to advise us on a natural-gas pipeline route that
would be more pleasing to his eminence.

As a compromise, Consumers' Gas next proposed a pipeline designed by Stone and Webster. It was to start in Alberta but enter
the United States at Emerson, Manitoba, and continue around the
bottom of the Great Lakes before crossing the border into Ontario.
Considerable volumes of Alberta gas would be sold from this new
pipeline in Minnesota, Wisconsin, Illinois, Indiana and Michigan,
effectively reducing the landed cost of gas at the Toronto city gate.
Intractable C.D. Howe didn't like this idea either.

Paradoxically, the all-American oilman Clint Murchison pre-
vailed with his all-Canadian route through the rock of northern
Ontario, under the name TransCanada Pipelines Limited. This
firm was cosmetically Canadianized by the appointment of Alberta's respected energy minister, N. Eldon Tanner, as president.
Another Canadian, Ross Tomlie, Q.C., was central in organizing
the company, aided by the financing skill of Dean Nesbitt, but it
was really run by Charles Coates and Frank Schultz, two competent
American colleagues of Murchison.

All of the remarkable political manipulation involved in this undertaking was the cause of celebrated parliamentary debates, Black
Friday closure on 1 June 1956 and the consequent defeat of the federal government. The ugly drama also portrayed a judge being
defrocked, an energy minister disgraced, other convictions and a
Vancouver senator's son going to jail.

The media were hungry for still more scandal. They sniffed
around C.D. Howe's tracks on his frequent trips as a guest at Murchison's ranch in Texas. They were scrambling for a scoop on a big
pay-off to the minister and did not find the evidence, simply because it did not exist, in my opinion. The optics of Canadian lead-

ership in TransCanada Pipelines clouded over abruptly with the early resignation of Tanner, the Albertan. He cashed in all his considerable TransCanada entitlements and later moved to Salt Lake City to become a member of the Council of Twelve Apostles and General Authority of the Mormon Church. I like to think all pipeliners go to heaven, but the rest of us have to wait until we die.

The elements of the pipeline battle of the 1950s were different from those of the contest of the 1970s in which I was to play a larger part. The former involved fewer bidders, and much less money was at stake, but it was a good lesson in the realities of competition in the pipeline business. As a newcomer, I was personally disillusioned with the guileful nature of the earlier process, whereas the later scramble for the arctic pipeline left me with nothing but admiration and respect for the guts displayed by the imaginative participants.

During the foregoing evolution of the cross-Canada pipeline, my employer, Consumers' Gas, was in heated competition with the oil-and-gas pioneer Frank McMahon's plan to send surplus Alberta gas to the west coast of the United States. I was too junior in the scheme of things to be involved directly with the famous Frank McMahon. However, it is a bit ironical that it was that same man who re-introduced me to pipelines twenty years later. From an obscure eastern opponent, I became his western employee—a vice-president, no less—and for the next decade became intimately involved in Frank's dream of a pipeline bringing arctic gas to market.

In 1968, I decided to resign as president of Trane Company of Canada Limited and move my family to the Pacific coast where I had been raised. To my Toronto business friends, this zany decision manifested my mid-life crisis. True, I was exactly fifty, expecting to live to be a hundred. To my wife and family, it was just another phase requiring their unquestioning support; to me it was a new career adventure.

The oil and gas industry exhibited remarkable imagination and initiative in this most expensive and high-risk quest. The stakes were incredibly high. The entrepreneurial skills that emerged during this extended period were unquestionably worthy of the task. When these vast energy reserves in the arctic are ultimately connected to consuming markets, the accomplishment will be judged by business historians as an outstanding epoch in corporate enterprise.

Although the focus of this book will be narrow and confined to the years after 1968, mine will be a long tale, reciting some of the little-known inside stories about pipelines, personalities and politics. Candour will be my style. Flowery language will be abandoned when I recall events that featured unmistakable guts and guile.

Because these are personal notes and neither a history nor a novel, there will be little mention of the well-known facts that can be found in any number of books and, additionally, in the tonnage of recorded testimony of regulatory hearings and governmental inquiries. The emphasis will be on human-interest accounts, personalities and strategies.

The structure of this record is intended to be both fair and balanced. There will unavoidably be special emphasis given to the events with which I am most familiar. But there are no predetermined targets for either acclaim or abuse. If an unplanned moral emerges, it will likely be that perseverance has a reward of its own in the executive suite.

My hope is that this account will be both interesting and constructive, particularly the latter. It is my conviction that the desirable functioning of business and politics will continue to improve only so long as their practitioners are subject to a liberal and fair mix of fearless criticism and praise where either is clearly deserved, and the net effect is to the benefit of their respective publics.

It is customary to acknowledge assistance in an undertaking of this kind. The instruments I drew upon in composing this memoir were merely my memory, annual reports and my dictating machine. The real effort to be recognized was months of transcribing by my daughter, Carol Phillips-Legh. Through many starts, stops and interruptions, she carefully massaged my conversational dictation, often hesitant and indistinct, into polished copy.

····· **1** ·····

WILDCATTER
IN THE
BOARDROOM

After deciding Vancouver would be our new home, I went to see Frank McMahon about returning to the energy business. I was astonished at his immediate and enthusiastic response. "Oil and gas have just been discovered on the north slope of Alaska," Frank said, "and I'm going to build both a gas pipeline and an oil pipeline to move those products through British Columbia to the lower forty-eight states." He then offered the opinion that the three producers, Exxon, Arco and Sohio, would want to sell their Alaska gas to Japan in the form of liquefied natural gas (LNG) and would prefer to tanker their crude oil down the west coast by the "whale route." According to him, both were dumb ideas and he was going to use the "geese route" straight across Canada, with twin oil and gas pipelines in the same right-of-way.

After four martinis and two Dubonnets, the latter being my intake, Frank invited me to join him and take my chances. We shook hands on a deal. Quite typical of Frank's deals, the specifics were missing. He merely said, "You won't get much of a salary but you should get rich on the founders' stock." He was half right.

After our extended lunch, Frank introduced me to Doug Owen, Westcoast's president; Charles Hetherington, executive assistant to the president, and D.P. McDonald, senior vice-president and general counsel. All he said was: "This is Ed Phillips. I've hired him today as a vice-president to help us build the pipelines from Alaska. In the meantime, find something for him to do." I thought the three executives would be stunned, if not offended, by this announcement, but they seemed totally sanguine. I learned later this was classic Frank McMahon. His colleagues would have been no more surprised if he had declared that his jockey, Johnny Longden, was going to be the next president of the company.

Frank McMahon, the Wildcatter, had built an international reputation that was pervasive enough to capture me as a fan long before I met him. As I worked for him, my admiration continued to grow and my respect for him gained. I knew the man was special the day I started work when his secretary, Edna Resky, said: "Mr. McMahon would like to know your wife's first name because he wants to use it when he meets her." Frank was a first-name kind of guy, although I noticed that Edna could never get any closer than referring to him as Mr. Frank.

It was surprising, but he and I hit it off from the first meeting. Quite apart from an age spread of fifteen years, we were from different worlds. I had been groomed into the corporate conformity and personal discipline of sophisticated companies in eastern Canada and the midwestern United States. Frank didn't fit any mould in either his personal or business conduct. It was a good thing for the oil and gas industry in Canada that he was totally unconventional. Who else would have gambled as wildly as he did to be such an effective pioneer for our business?

My boss was genetically programmed to be both different and special. His Irish parents must have realized that their little scamp would never grow up to be a human cipher but would be either a scoundrel or a great success. Fortunately for us all, he became the latter. Although I was appalled at Frank's disregard for accepted administrative procedures, I marvelled at what his intuition and dogged perseverance managed to achieve.

Nothing ordinary or routine ever happened to Frank McMahon. His father was a drifter who survived the 1906 earthquake and fire

in San Francisco, then returned home to safety in British Columbia, only to abandon the family again when his boys were just children. Frank's own eldest son, Frank Grant McMahon, was killed in
a tragic car accident at only twenty-four. Later, his mother was
murdered. No wonder a little knock on the head, such as drilling
ten dry holes in a row, or going millions into personal debt, could
never bring him to his knees.

One disaster was transformed into a bonanza with a wave of this
contrarian's wand. Or was it blind Irish luck? In 1948, his Atlantic
III well on the Rebus farm in Leduc blew out of control, quickly becoming Alberta's most dramatic wild well. It gushed crude for six
months and caught fire just before it was brought under control.
While most despaired, McMahon scooped up more than a million
barrels of the prairie mess and sold it for his first sizable cash flow.
Previously, most of his money had come from brave bankers and
speculative shareholders, but after Atlantic III he never looked
back. Relating the story to me, his keen memory recalled that my
brother Al and his boss Cap Tracey had been on the crew fighting
the blowout for a torturous six months.

In later years, as Frank's voice grew husky with emphysema and
gin, he acknowledged that he had abused himself physically all his
life. He was most sincere after the funeral of his youngest brother,
John, when he mused: "Life was never guaranteed to be fair. You
have to grab it and shake it to survive. What is fair about living the
way I have and end up having to bury two younger brothers?"

For all his Irish determination, foresight and success, Frank was a
shy man, quite unsuited for the life of a jet-setter he led with his
second wife Betty. His racing stable featured the famous Majestic
Prince, winner of the Kentucky Derby and the Preakness but missing the Triple Crown by placing second at Belmont. Frank's oil
fame developed friendships around the world, including formal and
varied partnerships with publisher Max Bell, Bing Crosby and other
notables. He knew Hollywood as well as Broadway, where he financed the long-running hit *Pajama Game* from which he received
payments of residuals for decades.

Our first conversation about horses was fascinating for me. All I could brag about was a thoroughbred, named Fervency, given to me by Austin Taylor. He could speak with pride about one of the biggest racing stables in the United States, most notably about his chestnut yearling, Majestic Prince, for which he had paid a million dollars, a record figure for that time. Frank recognized the name Fervency and quickly explained that my horse had been raced under the joint ownership of Austin Taylor and Peter Bentley and had been the best two-year-old in British Columbia in his year. I knew that story, but Frank's detailed knowledge of such equestrian trivia truly amazed me.

Commenting on my previous employer, the Trane Company, Frank said that his son Bill had gone to college with Frank Trane, a son of the company's famous founder, Reuben Trane. My countenance must have displayed how impressed I was because he continued: "Let me tell you about my friend Reuben Trane. He gave me a bundle of money to drill a few holes in the States, quite willing to risk it all because it could be tax-sheltered. Damn-it-all, I drilled six holes with his money and struck a bit of oil with every one." I could tell Frank was regretting that this wildcatting hadn't been done with his own money. He continued: "Worst of all, Reuben wasn't very grateful. All he said was he now had more taxes to pay than ever." To balance that success story, over the years many people have told me they put money into a lot of drilling programs by the Wildcatter that produced nothing but dry holes.

Frank's idea about the twin Alaska pipelines did not go very far at the time. The U.S. government declared national security considerations would prevent moving that amount of their vital energy supply across a thousand miles of foreign territory. Indeed, some Canadian political voices were just as negative in screaming that they did not want the equivalent of another American-controlled Panama Canal dug right across Canada to accommodate the oil and gas pipeline.

The dramatic Alaska discoveries of oil and gas, together with exploration success in the Mackenzie delta of Canada's Northwest Territories, were to unleash a rush of pipeline proposals for the Canadian arctic. God must have been a pipeliner. He, or she, deposited these vast energy resources thousands of miles from the continent's major energy-consuming regions, thereby creating the need for our industry to link the two with profitable transmission systems.

Representative of Frank's unconventional management and decision-making was an important subsidiary of Westcoast, Pacific Northern Gas Ltd. With an intriguing basis for existence, it was just getting under way when I joined Westcoast in 1968. Having cut my teeth in the energy industry as an employee of Canada's largest gas-distribution utility, I was appalled at the flimsy economic justification for this impulsive venture of Frank McMahon. But as he always said, if it's a good idea the money doesn't matter. He was correct, as usual, but it took us a long time to get our feet in the stirrups.

Frank's executives had informed him of a pending problem about having purchased more well-head gas than his gas-distribution customers could use, and it had to be paid for whether taken or not, according to contract. His spontaneous solution was to start his own distribution company to use that surplus gas. Thus, the new company, PNG, sought and obtained franchises to pick up natural gas at Westcoast's mainline near Prince George and sell it to the small communities between there and Kitimat and Prince Rupert on the coast. Despite good potential for industrial sales at Kitimat and Prince Rupert, it was daunting to everyone but Frank McMahon to contemplate the negligible sales opportunity along the 435 miles of new, expensive pipeline between Prince George and Prince Rupert, a sparsely populated region with a hostile terrain. There were only 50,000 inhabitants in the fourteen communities on the entire system. Premier W.A.C. Bennett had hinted to Frank that this region needed some economic stimulation. Grateful for the province's granting him the first drilling rights in British Columbia, Frank accommodated Bennett.

The project's main economic justification came from an ambitious cost estimate for the pipeline's construction. The companion support was an enthusiastic, to say the least, market-development study. The former was prepared by Red Tyler, Westcoast's chief engineer; the latter, by his assistant Don Duguid. Both of these experienced engineers were competent in their respective fields, but I had to wonder if they produced a go signal because that was the only recommendation Westcoast's risk-taking chairman would accept. Whatever genius was behind their favourable conclusions, the subsequent construction cost overrun and sales shortfall crippled the enterprise at birth.

The patient was slow to recover for the obvious reason that the big-inch, high-pressure pipeliners, who were attempting to save PNG, had neither the experience nor the enthusiasm to do an energetic job hooking up little houses with three-quarter-inch pipe and reading meters. Consequently, the big-inchers were excused from a task they didn't relish and Ron Rutherford took over.

A former gas-distribution executive, Ron became president of PNG in 1970 and had the assistance of Don Duguid. Soon, Bob O'Shaughnessy assumed that task. Bob was an engineer with Westcoast, who conveniently had gained distribution expertise with a gas utility in Hawaii. When Rutherford was transferred, the PNG team included Roy Dyce, also from Westcoast Transmission. Bob and Roy had been highly regarded engineering assistants to Dr. Charles Hetherington, then a vice-president of Westcoast.

The B.C. Utilities Commission would not permit PNG to charge its customers rates that would recover all its costs. As a result, Westcoast had to subsidize this uneconomic undertaking by not collecting the full price for gas sold to it. This discounting by Westcoast continued for five years, on a contract that required the subsidiary to repay that accumulated pricing crutch, progressively, over the ensuing five years. To our disappointment, the BCUC would not permit PNG to claim that debt repayment in its cost-of-service, meaning they were not allowed to collect it from their gas customers. On that basis, Westcoast chose not to press PNG for several millions in deferred payments.

To Frank's credit, he was generous in the amount of support and freedom he gave his subordinates. His visionary enthusiasm often inspired those who had the privilege of working with him, at times, as with PNG, overwhelming their professional discretion. His very genius for the bold venture mitigated inevitably against his long-term survival in a corporation heading towards the goal of stable, profitable operation.

In the last years preceding his departure from Westcoast, Frank quietly acquiesced as the management group attempted to intro-duce administrative procedures required to transform that company from a speculative pipeline venture to a mature operating utility. He didn't see the need to waste all his time on what he considered trivial details because he was totally absorbed in initiatives for oil and gas pipelines from Alaska, copper mining in California, manu-facturing in eastern Canada, plywood manufacturing in B.C. and other projects constantly hatching in his fertile mind. I would gladly swap my reliance on mission statements, organization charts, ten-year plans, research and development, critical path analysis, risk-reward ratios and committee terms of reference for the way that man could simply smell an opportunity.

THE ENFORCER

Frank McMahon's successor, Kelly Gibson, is the most complex individual I have ever known. I am not capable of any valid clinical assessment of the friend who cemented my career as a pipeliner, so I will merely describe the man and his actions to see what the evidence suggests.

For some years before I joined Frank McMahon's group, Phillips Petroleum of Bartlesville, Oklahoma, had been the controlling shareholder of Westcoast Transmission, through their Canadian subsidiary, Pacific Petroleums in Calgary. They had a great fondness and admiration for Frank as the founder but had become impatient with his management style. This was particularly evident after he arbitrarily demoted Bob Stewart, who had been Westcoast's president. Bob was a senior Phillips executive from Bartlesville who had been sent to Vancouver to introduce some sophisticated administration into the company. He could have done a good job but Frank simply didn't like him. Bob was summarily replaced as president by Doug Owen. Doug was recruited from C.D. Howe's Ottawa staff by director Frank Ross, former prime minister John Turner's stepfather. Doug Owen, Charles Hetherington and D.P. McDonald could have handled the management task as a good team, but

Frank persisted with his wildcatter style and casual indifference to traditional corporate discipline. Finally, Phillips Petroleum lowered the boom. They had Pacific Pete buy all of Frank's stock, and awarded him a lifetime annual allowance, secretarial service, office and car.

Kelly Gibson was a favourite of Phillips Petroleum because of the tight ship he ran at Pacific Petroleums. Pacific's success, however, was mainly due to the large straddle plant to extract liquids from the gas stream in TransCanada's pipeline at Empress, Alberta, an initiative of the parent in Oklahoma. Other veterans tell me that John Getwood, Pacific's president and chief executive officer, was the Bartlesville expert who is credited with that masterstroke with TransCanada. Nevertheless, Phillips placed Gibson in charge of Westcoast with a mandate to put the company into shape. I had never met Kelly. The first time I saw him was when I was called into a board meeting, in October 1969, to be told that Kelly Gibson and I had been elected as new directors of Westcoast Transmission. It was an unexpected and thrilling development, of which I had no prior indication.

The warmest greeting I received in the boardroom that day came from Kelly. He took me aside to say that my election had been on his advice and he was looking forward to working with me on the tough job of reorganizing Westcoast. I recall telling my wife, with great enthusiasm, that I was going to be working for a warm and competent oilman, and we were certain to become good friends.

The first hint that my early assessment was a bit off the mark came the day after the newspaper announcement about the changes at Westcoast. My brother Al, owner of United Directional Drilling Limited, telephoned to say: "I have known Gibson ever since he came to Stettler for BA Oil. Watch your step because he is one tough oilman. As a matter of fact, he is the only customer I visit with a Doberman pinscher at my side." Incidentally, Big Al is 6 foot 3 and weighs 220 pounds.

Over the next nine years I had many an opportunity to form the judgement that brother Al was not unduly off the mark. But over that same time Kelly was actually generous with me, promoted me rapidly and never broke a single promise made to me. For my part, I

was loyal to him and risked damaging my reputation in some in-
stances in carrying out his unorthodox orders. Through all that period, I whispered not one word of complaint to the directors until
nine years later when he abused me just one time too many.

Kelly had been told by Phillips Pete to shake up Westcoast. He certainly did that, but his ingrained style couldn't put it back together
again. His approach to corporate organization was neither subtle
nor delicate. He preferred a frontal attack simply because it was
faster. In the resulting shakeup, miraculously, I was the only one of
the top executives resident in Vancouver who remained with the
company. Kelly and I had many arguments but he never fired me
and I was too stubborn to quit. The extent of the departure of the
other executives escaped public attention. Unavoidably, it was not
helpful to the new chairman's reputation internally. This did not
particularly disturb Kelly because he was earnestly pursuing the
mandate of shaping a company, not winning a popularity contest.

To his last day at Westcoast, Kelly boasted that he had never
fired an executive. That may be true; he merely plucked their feathers one at a time until they flew the coop while they still had wings.
As a consequence, I necessarily started a side career negotiating
separation agreements for my colleagues.

One tough rooster who wouldn't let his feathers be plucked was
Charles Hetherington, whom I admired. His departure was a big
disappointment to me because I found him a bit starchy yet the
most intellectual and effective executive in the company. He
phoned me from Calgary to say he was resigning, explaining: "I
worked with this guy once before in Pacific and I don't intend to
work for him at Westcoast." He refused to let me negotiate a termi-
nation settlement, saying he didn't want anything other than to get
out fast and clean. Charles's leaving with ill will on both sides was
as costly as it was unavoidable. With him aboard, our recovery
would have been more rapid and our future development more impressive. But the chemistry between Charles and Kelly was too ex-
plosive.

I would not presume to judge how damaging the total impact of
that exodus of executive talent was to Westcoast. It was personally

distressing to me as the new boy who needed a lot of counsel and support in a new business. Searching for the positive aspects, I recall the improvement in the decision-making process that resulted. Under benevolent Frank McMahon, the executives felt personally secure but their responsibilities were frequently shuffled, overlapping and seldom definitive. The result was procrastination in current matters and lack of direction for the future. Frank achieved the seemingly impossible. He actually had too many ideas for growth, given his lack of skills for organization and execution. The new boss, with a clear mandate from Phillips Pete, changed all that.

Under Kelly Gibson, there were good decisions and a few poor decisions; but there was no indecision. I liked that. His one-man attack on Westcoast's decision backlog was a rejuvenating experience for the second-tier managers. To Kelly's credit, a great deal was accomplished and the first impression of the new regime was positive. It was unfortunate that the senior group could not be held together long enough to make the necessary personal adjustments to an admittedly marine-corps atmosphere. Together, we may have been able to take the edge off the bayonet and become an inspired team.

Another positive fallout from this experience was the way it prepared Westcoast for our first rate hearing. The National Energy Board had no fault to find with respect to our operating expenses. They had never examined such a lean executive group and they could not criticize extravagant corporate-jet costs or their other favourite targets.

Although the time I spent with my former colleagues was brief, I have respectful regard for all of them. Doug Owen was a good executive who departed in 1970 before there was any serious altercation of which I am aware. He had been demoted from president and chief executive officer to make room for Kelly as chairman and CEO. He sincerely felt he could not adjust to the personality who had replaced his revered chief. Some complained Doug was a bottleneck with his desk piled with unanswered recommendations. That was unfair, given his lack of autonomy and the indistinct terms of reference. Doug's main strength I observed was in the financial area. With Dave Hunter, his assistant treasurer, and John

Payne, his comptroller, he stickhandled the company through its most perilous days. That took a lot of skill and finesse. If Doug had any fault, it was his failure to assert himself with Frank McMahon and the board by demanding a job description and authority befitting an aggressive corporate president. He could have handled it.

Bob Stewart stuck it out quite a time, considering the humiliation he faced. Having been parachuted from Bartlesville to Vancouver to be president, he was perhaps doomed from the start. Frank McMahon administered the first demotion and Kelly followed with a series of downgradings. As the English say, he was sent to Coventry. The end came when I had to tell Bob that we needed his space at head office and accommodation would be found for him at one of the subsidiaries down the street. He moved but soon resigned, sold his Westcoast stock at one of its highs, and never regretted the separation. Selfishly, this was a loss to me. Bob was particularly cordial to my wife and me. His social graces were superb. He was active in community affairs, becoming the best-known Westcoast executive in Vancouver. Similarly, he enjoyed a good reputation in the industry and was the first director elected to the Pacific Coast Gas Association in the U.S. from a Canadian pipeline. A good team player, with a fine personal presence, he could have helped us under more sensitive direction.

Len Youell was a real veteran, having been corporate secretary dating back to the founding of Pacific Petroleums. Frank McMahon had unqualified trust in him and they developed a special personal relationship. Intensely loyal to the company above all, Len persevered for an impressive period. All his colleagues were disappointed, but understanding, when he finally left in 1974.

Lloyd Turner was a vice-president with the task of corporate communications and government relations. As a former newspaper editor, he excelled at both jobs. He, too, was very close to McMahon, performing a number of personal and confidential assignments on his behalf. His death in 1970 was sudden and very sad. He died of a heart attack while dining with his good friend Frank McMahon. As I began making myself known through the corridors of the Legislative Assembly in Victoria, I soon sensed how highly the MLAs regarded Lloyd. In fact, in their tributes to

Westcoast for starting the gas industry in B.C., they referred to Frank and Lloyd with almost equal admiration and gratitude. After Lloyd's death, and following a large addition to the Fort Nelson processing plant, the northern MLAs requested through me that the enlarged structure be named the Turner Plant. We declined with the explanation that this sort of tribute should retain its distinctiveness. We had decided not to use the names of any other executives after calling the Fort St. John installation the McMahon Plant honouring Westcoast's founder.

Peter Kutney's case was a bit different. Kelly preserved his claim of never firing anyone by demanding that John Anderson do it for him in this instance. But that final step came only after the questionable procedure of first reducing Peter's title from group vice-president to vice-president, gas supply and sales, then cutting his salary; the Coventry routine again. When that didn't work, the axe fell in 1971 for an undeserved fate. He was one of the most competent pipeline gas buyers in the business. He was both shrewd and aggressive in negotiating gas-purchase contracts with the producers, all to Westcoast's benefit. Pacific Pete, as the largest gas supplier to Westcoast, thought he was too shrewd and too aggressive.

Morris Kilik was Kutney's assistant working out of Westcoast's gas-buying office in Calgary. Because Morris was well trained in that specialist responsibility, Kelly agreed he should succeed Peter and move to Vancouver. However, Morris was very bitter about the injustice in his superior's removal. In two visits with him and his wife, I encouraged them to accept this promotion which would be good for Morris's future and the music career being pursued by his wife. Finally, they agreed; that is, until a phone call from him about a week later. Kelly had offered Morris a drive to the office that particular day. In those few minutes, he criticized Kutney and described what would be expected of Kilik in his role as a negotiator of contracts with the gas producers. Morris phoned me the minute he arrived at his office to say the promotion he had accepted was now refused and he was resigning from Westcoast altogether. My personal concern about this bizarre happening was heightened a few months later. I met Morris in the Palliser Hotel and he refused to speak to me. Another casualty, another scar on Phillips.

Don Duguid started in engineering. He designed and constructed the Saratoga processing plant, which has been a profitable enterprise from day one. He moved into promotional activities, where his marketing studies supported the founding of Pacific Northern Gas. Don's earlier experience with Imperial Oil equipped him well, but his tendency to let his natural enthusiasm interfere with his technical objectivity produced some unachievable projections, and trouble. Don's unique imagination generated more off-the-wall schemes than management could properly consider. The final scolding he received from Kelly in 1971 was absurd in retrospect. He was charged with wastefulness in converting one of the company's cars to use compressed natural gas, as a demonstration vehicle, when the written rules said that only standard equipment could be provided for any company car. That new use of gas is one of the most popular promotions in the business today. Don had been on the right track.

The exits of Hal O'Keefe and Gord Matheson can be explained together, the circumstances being so alike. Both were long-time and mature Westcoast people. Hal was head of the aviation division, which comprised a Falcon jet and five helicopters. Gord was the senior pilot. Due to the heavy use of the Falcon by Frank McMahon and his wife Betty, the two pilots, Hal and Gord, were something akin to an extension of the McMahon's personal household staff. I was put in charge of the aviation division and instructed to lock up the Falcon and cancel the insurance. Hal O'Keefe attempted to gain some revenue from a ski-lift operation with the company's helicopters. When that was not successful, the fleet was sold to Okanagan Helicopters in 1971 and Hal left for a better position. Gord Matheson was offered a pilot's position with Pacific in Calgary but resigned unhappily in protest. He returned to Westcoast some years later, as chief pilot until his retirement.

The circumstances surrounding Ray Mordan's resignation aroused more distress in me than any of the others, as uncomfortable as they all were. After a noteworthy professional career with various Imperial Oil companies, including service in South America, Ray joined Westcoast to run their new crude-oil pipeline in British Columbia under the name Western Pacific Products and

Crude Oil Pipeline Ltd. He soon was promoted to take charge of Westcoast's engineering and operation of all the pipelines and processing plants. Ray's competence was exceeded only by his personal and professional ethics. He had a sophisticated management style and a loyalty to his staff which his critics considered somewhat protective.

Ray Mordan and his wife Dougal were the first Westcoast people to welcome Betty and me into their home. We became fast, admiring friends, and still are. My first assignment involved working as Doug Owen's assistant in seeking cost reductions in the field operations. This obviously required close liaison with Ray, and his cooperation was total and effective. I agonized with him through his efforts to get Pacific Pete to comply fully with the terms of our gas-purchase contract with them. Ray rolled with the punches for a long time, aided by a measure of support from me. But the end resulted from an event still vivid in my memory. One of Ray's senior people telephoned me to say how offended he was by Kelly coming into his office to ask how many times he had taken ideas to Mordan that were either rejected or not even acknowledged. A few minutes later, the same objection came from another of Ray's men. I intercepted Kelly in the corridor and persuaded him to discontinue his mission, which was being interpreted as an investigation to justify firing their popular boss.

Those two particular interrogations led to Ray's resignation in 1971 without any request for a separation settlement. Despite the gravity of this event, in my opinion, Kelly and I had a calm and purposeful review of it all. He admitted that his approach was awkward but insisted his intentions had been misunderstood. He merely desired to encourage these men to flood the company with good suggestions and he would guarantee they were properly considered by their bosses. I wanted Ray back on the team so keenly, I took a message of reconciliation to him. He agreed to return after about a month which we described as vacation. Alas, the return engagement fell apart. The interferences with his operations continued, so Ray resigned a second and final time after a few months. "Please Ed, don't do me any favours," he said, "by conning me again." Fortunately, unlike the Kilik case, I didn't lose a friend.

Having devoted so much space to the executives who departed, I should also refer to two competent and courageous charter directors who stood up to Kelly during a dramatic board meeting. After he took over, Kelly held the first two board meetings in Calgary, with D.P. McDonald as provisional chairman. The first I attended was on 8 June 1970. Frank resigned; D.P. surrendered the chairmanship to Kelly; Doug Owen gave up the CEO title to Kelly, and Frank Ross and Norman Whittall were expected to drop off the board. I watched them as they read the agenda and noticed they exchanged a few words. When the time came, they both said they refused to resign, and it became a very confused scene. We learned that Kelly had asked D.P. McDonald to secure their resignations, but D.P. had decided to do nothing about it and had not informed Kelly. I suspect this was intentional. Wily D.P. sandbagged Kelly that day, a trick he was able to repeat when his favourite Peter Kutney was fired. D.P. had been Frank McMahon's agile lawyer from the start of their careers. He obviously had learned more than courtroom cunning.

Subsequently, director Frank Ross told us he would offer his resignation as soon as he was satisfied Westcoast had given Doug Owen an honourable separation settlement, which eventually was accomplished. However, charter director Norman Whittall stood his ground. He did not resign until 1975 at the age of 84 and became one of my solid supporters. Norman was an honourary director until his death at 93.

The Honourable Frank Ross, former lieutenant-governor of B.C., was a wealthy and influential industrialist from Vancouver. He was well connected in Liberal party circles, a convenient credential for a supporter of enterprising Frank McMahon. He was also one of the originals who bankrolled Frank's wildcatting. His personal involvement never faltered, but he did discontinue his financial participation when the stakes of Frank's unsuccessful wildcat ventures ran into many millions. That cautious decision cost him a fortune, literally.

Another generous sponsor in those early days was Col. Victor Spencer of chain-store fame. He also tired of the slot-machine game of putting so many bucks into McMahon's dry holes. He thereby lost the opportunity to add to his already substantial fortune.

Norman Whittall was different. He was the only one of McMahon's first sponsors who ponied-up every time the famous wildcatter demanded more money for what seemed an endless and decidedly expensive string of dry holes. The rest of the story is well known. Frank finally scored big; and Whittall's reckless gamble made him deservedly richer. Appropriately, he became president of the new Pacific Petroleums. Is it any wonder Ross and Whittall had an indestructible bond with McMahon, and it hurt to be asked to resign?

This loyalty tug of war was also a burden for me. I resolved it, in a sense, by working to this code: Frank was my idol, so I admired him; Kelly was my boss, so I obeyed him.

Putting together this particular portion of my story has required a determined pursuit of one of its objectives. Westcoast Transmission was a government-regulated monopoly. Thus its affairs are in the public domain; and an examination of the style and conduct of all of us in the company is both valid and constructive. I have never been so candid on this subject, except with my wife and my friend and colleague John Anderson. Some of these revelations would be new even to them.

Returning to the point of proper perspective and balance, I must emphasize that Kelly recommended and supported every promotion I received, including becoming chairman as his successor. In the same supportive way, he proposed every salary increase and stock option I received. One may ask, how can my assessment of Kelly be so critical? How can I be so ungrateful?

The answer is I am not ungrateful and any criticism merely surfaces with a close look at an inordinately complex personality. Evidence of his good side is our continuing personal relationship after his retirement. This is the same man with whom my wife Betty and I enjoyed a delightful dinner in Palm Springs only three hours before his near-fatal stroke. This is the same man for whom I shared an all-night hospital vigil with his wife Julie, feeling heartsick about the prognosis we both expected from the doctors. I was thrilled with the later assurance he would make it.

Another sterling quality of this complex man was his devotion to his mother and his attention to her every imaginable want. I am not referring merely to all those physical comforts he generously showered upon her, which he could readily afford; it was his unmatched dedication in spending personal time with his mother that stirred me most. It was almost a religion for Kelly to visit his mother every single day he was home in Calgary. When he returned from any trip, short or long, he went first to see his mother, even before going home or to the office. That his mother lived to her mid-nineties was possibly the result of her son's love and his sacrificial gift of time making her feel truly special.

As all of Kelly's friends know, he has long been a member of the United Church and is an active and dedicated member of one of their Calgary congregations.

It is not true to say that Kelly had a split personality. He had a prismatic personality with colours of every hue flashing in all directions. In social situations with his wife Julie, he was absolutely charming. To his fellow Rotarians, he was a pillar of the community. To his friends in the prayer breakfast movement, he was a role model. To his fellow directors of the Royal Bank, he was a corporate leader. However, to some of his peers in the oil industry, he was an overrated executive. And to certain of his executives and other employees, he was a bully. As a superintendent in the Stettler oilfields, he was called The Scorpion; but only behind his back, because he had a great pair of fists. To me, he was frequently lovable, more often pitiable as a character overplaying his role as the oil industry's James Cagney.

In a social sense, my wife Betty was one of his admirers. Kelly reciprocated that feeling toward her. On one occasion, she went into a fit of laughter when Julie Gibson addressed her husband by the pet name "Baby." Kelly asked Betty what was so amusing and she blurted: "That name is so delightfully inappropriate." He hugged her for that answer because it authenticated the tough image he fostered and enjoyed. They remained the best of pals and Kelly was always solicitous of her wellbeing. Anyone who adores my wife can't be all bad.

John Houchin, president of Phillips Petroleum, was active in the

President Eisenhower prayer breakfast movement. Into that fellow-
ship he introduced Kelly, who was later central in establishing a
similar prayer group in Vancouver. He came to Vancouver every
Wednesday and Thursday in the early years: on Wednesday, to attend the prayer breakfast before appearing at our office; and on
Thursday, for the weekly meeting of the B.C. region Royal Bank
directors. Kelly was something like the patron of the prayer sessions
both in Calgary and Vancouver.

On the occasion of a Royal Bank reception, Earle McLaughlin
told me what an effective bank director Kelly was. Another Royal
Bank director claimed that Kelly drew the highest amount of re-
tainer and meeting fees of any board member every year. He never
missed a full meeting of the bank board or any of the committees on
which he served. He faithfully attended the Royal Bank weekly
meetings in Calgary for the Alberta directors as well as the weekly
meetings in Vancouver for the B.C. directors. When colleagues
mentioned how well prepared Kelly was for every meeting, I did not
spill the beans. Kelly would sometimes distribute selected, non-
confidential bank agenda items to Merrill Rasmussen, John Anderson and me, instructing us to submit some briefing notes on any
subjects where we may have some background, opinions or expertise. More directors should make this practical use of resources.

My boss was a politician groupie. He liked to be in their presence
and he lusted for their personal acceptance and recognition. This
was an unusual trait, but not objectionable, because it did assist
Westcoast to some extent. To my definite knowledge, he was admired by many senators, MPs, MLAs and senior officials. Most noteworthy among his fans were Donald Macdonald, Peter Lougheed,
Don Getty, Dave Barrett and Marshall Crowe, all having some influence on the company's destiny. Kelly always seemed to have
ready access to Pierre Trudeau, though I have no idea whether that
represented beneficial recognition.

Kelly sought my advice on one political move when Premier Peter Lougheed of Alberta offered him the chairmanship of Pacific
Western Airlines. He asked me the double question: "Can I handle
it; should I take it?" Perhaps a bit eagerly, I answered: "Sure, go for
it!" He then told me he had already decided to decline.

Kelly suffered two keen disappointments as a groupie. He aspired to be a senator. At his bidding, I was a nuisance in lobbying Senator Ray Perrault, through his assistant Colin Watson, a former Westcoast employee, and other less visible people in Ottawa to sponsor my boss for this prestigious appointment. I persisted and they tried without any semblance of success. His Liberal friends in Alberta were worked to no avail. A pity! He would have jarred the slumber of that solemn chamber. Also, his attendance record would have put the others to shame.

Premier Don Getty's initiative to hold an election in 1989 to select Alberta's nominee to the federal Senate came too late. Had the province tried this same manoeuvre when Kelly Gibson had the hots for a seat in the red chamber, the election campaign would have seen some pyrotechnics, not the dim-bulb show it was, despite the final choice of popular and competent Stan Waters.

His other political miscue concerned Premier W.A.C. Bennett. On arrival in Vancouver, as head of one of the province's largest corporations, Kelly properly sought an interview with the premier to pay his respects. Despite courteous letters, phone calls and use of intermediaries, Mr. Bennett would not see him. The premier didn't realize that one did not get away with that high-handed behaviour with this particular oilman; and Bennett didn't.

A few months later, the top Socred fundraiser had an appointment to see Kelly. Kelly invited me to join the meeting, promising: "You'll enjoy this." The bagman was put at ease by "Mr. Cordial" describing Westcoast's willingness to facilitate the electoral process and asking how much his visitor had in mind as a donation. "Well, Mr. McMahon had given as much as $50,000," he replied. Kelly observed that was fair enough but asked for assurance the premier would be advised personally how much Westcoast contributed. Quite eagerly, the man said: "Of course, I'll tell him myself." The ambush fully in place, "Mr. Aggrieved" replied: "Bennett thinks he's too big to see me, so I'll be too small to help him. Tell him he won't get a nickel—ever!"

Our visitor meekly followed me to the elevator. Still in shock, he volunteered that he didn't think it would be a good idea to take that message to the premier. I agreed. I learned later that Mr. Bennet, being an admirer of Frank McMahon and grateful for what he had done for British Columbia, was displeased with the way his friend had been displaced by an oilman from Alberta.

Kelly did not claim any intellectual powers. Indeed, he was quite modest in seeking the assistance of his executives in Pacific and Westcoast and was generally grateful for anything we contributed in that sense. He undoubtedly knew everything that was essential about running oil-field operations, but a cerebral executive he was not. To appreciate this circumstance, it must be remembered that he was hired by Frank McMahon and moved overnight from the oil rigs to an executive office with absolutely no preparation. What he did possess were guts, determination and a punishing work ethic that damaged him physically and interfered with the relationship between him and his two adopted sons.

Referring to Frank McMahon again reminds me how baffled all of us were that there was some personal conflict between him and Kelly that was never reconciled. After the notable turnover of control at Westcoast, Frank arranged a big dinner party in Vancouver to honour Kelly and Julie and the former's ascendancy. Second only to his fame as a wildcatter, Frank's reputation as a party host was supreme. This was to be a lavish affair at the McMahons' palatial home, expensively catered by Trader Vic's restaurant.

About one week before the big event, the guest of honour phoned to say that he and Julie would not be coming to the dinner because the embossed invitation did not make it clear he was taking over at Westcoast Transmission as Frank's successor. All Frank said was: "Well, I tried anyway; cancel the dinner, forget the whole thing and relax." We had to point out this would cause a lot of consternation and would actually be an inconvenience to some of the guests who had accepted the invitation. Several Phillips Pete executives were in Russia and had made special plans for an early return to Bartlesville, coming by way of Vancouver in order to attend the dinner. Frank finally told us to go ahead if we wanted to and thought we could get the guest of honour to change his mind. "But don't beg," he laughed.

Kelly remained adamant when I telephoned him, explaining he had to assert himself because Frank was not accepting the reality of the takeover situation. I believe it was Doug Owen who suggested the solution that finally worked. We drafted a dignified card which would be printed and placed on every table at the dinner. The text went into some detail about the reason for the gala celebration, particularly honouring Kelly's willingness to assume command. He approved the suggested announcement as supplementary to the inadequate invitation and came to the party.

Frank and Betty McMahon's dinner party was a huge success. It taxed the capacity of their large Marine Drive home and garden and was generously reported in the social columns. None of the guests could have sensed the wobbly underpinning of the event. The superb food and drink were matched only by the poise of the hosts and the gracious demeanour of the two honoured guests. Julie Gibson was a delight, as usual. She obviously had programmed Kelly by pushing his southern-charm button because he was magnificent. Most of the guests were oil people from out of town so my wife Betty and I were the strangers in the crowd. We were comforted by Kelly's sensitivity to this and the trouble he took to introduce us to everyone there. It was a happy event we will never forget.

The invisible characteristic of Frank McMahon that impressed me most was his cooperative demeanour when bought out and shoved aside by Pacific Petroleums. He was totally above the way others might have reacted to his perceived humiliation. I was apprehensive about my assignment to monitor his expenses on his contract as a consultant who would never be consulted. Actually, it was a simple task. He and his efficient secretary Edna Resky, to whom I am deeply indebted, were more than cooperative. He said: "Don't worry Ed, I can pay all my expenses; I won't be claiming any from Westcoast." This embarrassed me because I realized how bush-league it must have appeared to Frank when the Falcon jet was grounded, with insurance cancelled, to make sure he would not use it.

One of my last official encounters with the man I admired so much was laced with classic McMahon humour. I showed him a board resolution appointing him Chairman Emeritus. He read it stoically, then frowned: "Migawd, Chairman Emmer-itis; it sounds like a disease."

As a consequence of the early departure from Westcoast of so many senior executives, I prematurely became Kelly's man in Vancouver. That inevitably led to a clash in business styles. Most of our disagreements were not crucial and I could yield honourably. However, after a dispute about a personnel matter, I was summoned to Calgary on a Saturday morning for a little talk. The little talk became a two-hour blast about his disappointment with my performance. I was not cutting operating costs fast enough; I was not tough enough; the operating people were walking all over me; and, I was not spending enough time in the field. When Kelly finally said that a good operating executive like Al McIntosh would have me for lunch, my fuse went. I realized I had a great deal to learn about pipeline and oilfield operations, but my vanity about my ability to handle people and inspire performance compelled me to blurt: "I need your help in understanding operations, but I don't need your advice on leadership qualities. I was president and the chief executive of a company with more employees than Pacific when you were still carrying a lunch bucket to work on a rig." That tore it! I was given the silent treatment for several weeks, which was more a respite for me than the intended punishment.

When the quiet spell eventually was broken, it was to bawl me out again. After another litany of my shortcomings, I replied that his dissatisfaction had become so serious he should recommend to the board that I be fired. He snapped: "Now I find you're a quitter too." I laughed outright. After a bit, so did he. It's a puzzle; I call his bluff and we end up in hysterics.

It was in 1970 that John Anderson received a lateral transfer from Pacific in Calgary to Westcoast in Vancouver as general counsel. John confided in me later that he was encouraged to make this move without much of a salary increase because Ed Phillips wasn't going to survive and he would likely become president. Unfortunately for John, he fell out of grace even before he was fully settled into his new assignment in Vancouver.

John left his wife Marie and their two sons in Calgary to finish the school term. He purchased a home in West Vancouver but was living temporarily in the Hotel Vancouver. Kelly was annoyed by this situation which, by his standards, represented executive weakness and a fault serious enough to report to the president of Phillips Petroleum. His solution was direct, if not brilliant. He instructed me to tell John that he had overstayed his time in the hotel and would have to make other living arrangements at his own expense. Simultaneously, he sent his wife Julie to visit Marie Anderson at her home in Calgary to advise her that she really belonged with her husband in Vancouver. Knowing Julie, I am sure she handled this mission with sensitivity but it still left Marie in tears. After telling Mrs. Gibson to follow her own advice and move to Vancouver herself, Marie telephoned John while in that state of mind.

John took my message calmly about moving out of the hotel. Understandably, he threw a fit about the admonition of his wife. He told me about greeting Kelly the next morning outside his office and angrily telling him he would punch his face to a pulp if he or Julie ever attempted to order his wife around again. According to him he challenged Kelly: "You draw a salary as president and CEO of this company, yet you spend only one or two nights a week in Vancouver, charging the company a hotel suite on a permanent basis. I am here every day and content with a single room. Don't give me that nonsense about the need for an executive to be on the job every day and have his wife and family living with him. Where's yours?"

That was a black day. Kelly returned to Calgary without seeing any more of either of us for the rest of that visit. We consoled each other and John realized he had blown his big chance. That ugly incident flashed into John's mind every month as we paid the invoices for that hotel suite for the next seven years.

But pity our disappointed boss. He now had two senior executives in Vancouver in whom he had no confidence. As usual, he had a quick-fix solution. Without any deception, he informed us later he could move someone from Calgary to take charge of Westcoast. Almost in one voice, we assured him that move would solve our indecision. The day that person moved in we would be out, as we were contemplating anyway. Nothing happened.

The foregoing experiences were followed by awkward episodes too numerous to mention. Consequently, the bond between John Anderson and me became stronger. Both of us, and our wives, agree neither of us would have remained at Westcoast without our mutual-support sessions. When I was in trouble, John said and did everything to temper my reaction. I tried to be just as helpful to him when it was his turn. As time went on, John became more and more the target and I certainly found occasion to sympathize with him a lot.

Reminiscing now, I am almost ashamed of the juvenile way we conspired to thwart our boss in Calgary. Because Kelly judged an executive by the number of hours he slogged away on the job, rather than by what he accomplished, he insisted that John and I should work every Saturday, as he did in Calgary. We were willing to work the full seven days a week if it were necessary, but we rebelled at the order to be at our desks every Saturday regardless. Kelly would telephone on Saturdays to check if we were on the job. On weekends, all telephone calls were routed to the gas-control department. We had these cooperative people fib to Kelly that we were elsewhere in the building, at the moment, but would call him back as soon as possible. We phoned in for messages. When tipped off by gas control, we promptly called Kelly to tell him what the gas sendout was for the day and anything else of interest.

Our chairman quickly got wise to this silliness, whereupon we suggested we would alternate on working Saturdays. That was not good enough for him. He installed direct phone lines into each of our offices so he could be sure we both were at our desks when he called. Fortunately, he couldn't see that John was in golfing clothes and I had on my riding outfit, both of us ready to cut and run as soon as the duty call was finished. Am I proud of that? No, it was shameful.

The reason our conflict with Kelly never subsided was his uncompromising style. He was a driver more than a leader. His method was to prod rather than to inspire, simply because it seemed quicker. He had been a quick success at Pacific and he reasoned his methods would do the same at Westcoast. The fact is, the tempo quickened and the results improved.

Although Westcoast Petroleum, one of Westcoast's major subsidiaries, was a small oil-and-gas company with a small oil pipeline, it was a gold mine of stories of pipelines, personalities and internal politics. In 1968, the management trio of Doug Owen, Charles Hetherington and D.P. McDonald had convinced Frank McMahon that Westcoast should become more aggressive in its oil-and-gas exploration effort. It was not difficult to gain the chairman's approval to take their operating division public, in order to raise exploration funds. As a result of the public financing, the Westcoast Production division became Westcoast Petroleum Ltd., with Westcoast Transmission maintaining a minority shareholding.

In 1971, the new Westpete chairman was D.P. McDonald. Outside directors included Jack Mayne, chairman of Alberta Gas Trunk Line and a former Royal Bank officer; Mel Fenichell, Eastman Dillon; Mike Scott, Wood Gundy; and Dick Whittall, Richardson Securities and a son of Norman Whittall. The company was headquartered in Calgary, with Westcoast's oil pipeline, Western Pacific Products and Crude Oil Pipeline Ltd., being amalgamated under its control.

The prominent president of Westcoast Pete was Bill Hamilton. A lawyer who spent his entire career in the oil business, Bill had been recruited from Total Petroleum where he had a solid reputation for building a good land inventory for that French company.

Kelly Gibson, when he became Westcoast's chairman, took an active interest in this oil and gas subsidiary, being more comfortable in that milieu than in pipelines under government regulation. Wearing his other hat as chairman of Pacific Petroleums, Kelly was thrust into inevitable conflict. He had unsuccessfully attempted to have John and me sell Westpete to Pacific, so his desire then appeared to be to maintain the status quo in the smaller Westpete operation and channel any family expansion in oil and gas to the much larger Pacific Petroleums. Considering the superior resources of Pacific, this could have been a sound move, but it posed a threat to Bill Hamilton. He was known as a nimble deal-maker in the oil patch and had been hired for an expansionist thrust at Westpete.

What might have been anticipated soon happened. After a few months of confidential negotiations, Bill reached general agreement on the acquisition of an American-owned oil company of a fair size. The price was set, and sorting out the senior executive positions had been more or less settled. The remaining condition was approval by the boards of both companies. Kelly exercised Westcoast's influence and declared the plan should not be considered. There was no motion, no seconder, no vote and no deal. The declared reason for that rejection was a $70,000 finder's fee to be paid to the U.S. investment firm, Eastman Dillon, through Mel Fenichell on Westpete's board. According to Kelly Gibson, this was prohibited by a formal procedural rule at Pacific.

In 1972, there was a shake-up on the Westpete board of directors that cannot safely be described as unrelated to the new control of Westcoast by Pacific Pete, nor to Bill Hamilton's acquisition plan being aborted. Directors Fenichell, Scott and Whittall, all securities executives, resigned. They were replaced by John Ballem, Q.C., of Calgary; Jim Byrn, prominent Vancouver businessman; and me. The next year, Kelly replaced D.P. McDonald as chairman.

Under Bill Hamilton, no further acquisitions were attempted. However, many deals short of takeovers permitted steady progress in land assembly, increased reserves and rising oil and gas production. Our chairman came to think we should be doing still better if we were so determined not to sell the company to Pacific. Fair comment, and Bill and Rob Laurence, the exploration vice-president, were making every effort for that growth. Despite that dedication, Kelly was not comfortable with our progress. Over time, that conviction led to a chill between him and the president. Never one to conceal his disappointment, Kelly finally told John and me that Bill Hamilton had to go. His charge was poor performance, which he felt he had to support with the heavy intelligence that some of his friends told him Bill was spending too much time playing cards at the Petroleum Club. It was no joke, but John could not resist kidding me that Bill's problem was that he did not learn how to fake slogging away every Saturday as Anderson and Phillips had done.

The Westpete president did not have to be fired; he sensed the deteriorating relationship and was thus content with a modest settlement, departing honourably. I have recorded executive departures that caused personal regret. This was another, but John Anderson felt it even more deeply. He and Bill had been lawyer friends for many years, both having graduated in law from the University of British Columbia.

Thus began the reign of Kelly the Enforcer. His powerful presence had great impact on my earliest years at Westcoast. Nothing was too trivial to escape his attention and criticism. He claimed that this kept us on our toes, but more often than not we assumed that posture looking over the fence for another job. Many talented middle and lower managers did leave Westcoast during those trying early years. In time, however, most non-management staff were sheltered from the weekly chill from Calgary. Good things began to happen and operations improved steadily.

····· **3** ·····

A REASONABLE
RETURN

When I arrived in 1968 the financial situation at Westcoast was desperate. The company had started its pipeline operations in 1957. It took ten years to pay the first dividend, and the price of its common stock had dropped considerably from its heady promotional days. The gas-marketing situation was most fragile. Raw natural gas was being purchased by Westcoast at the wellhead at a price which was very low but subject to either negotiated or arbitrated increases. On the other hand, the processed gas sold by Westcoast was fixed at low prices on long-term contracts. Because of some arbitrated price increases for purchased gas which could not be passed along to the distributor customers, the company was heading for bankruptcy. The return on rate base hovered between 3 to 5 percent, whereas 15 would have been normal.

Charles Hetherington and Peter Kutney, with D.P. McDonald's assistance, were working on a Fourth Service Agreement with El Paso Natural Gas, the sole U.S. buyer, but the potential benefits of increased selling prices were many months away. That contract represented more than two-thirds of Westcoast's total sales volume, about three-quarters of its total revenue.

At the same time, the new YoYo gathering pipeline in northeast

B.C. failed before it was put into full service. After costly, unsuccessful attempts to repair over fifty successive breaks in that pipeline during the saturated season in the muskeg, the line was abandoned. The cost had been tremendous, and Alberta Phoenix were sued for providing faulty pipe for this sour-gas application. Shortly after his arrival, Kelly intervened to settle the $13 million claim out of court for only $6,800,000.

Days later, my family and I were enjoying a weekend at Harrison Hot Springs. There was some congestion at the tennis courts which, the attendant explained, was caused by a small group of lawyers and spouses from Davis & Company in Vancouver. "They're celebrating some kind of victory in a pipeline lawsuit," he offered. My weekend was ruined.

The American gas distributors supplied by our sole export customer, El Paso, agreed to slightly higher gas prices to generate funds and permit a replacement pipeline to be constructed. The Canadian customers, B.C. Hydro and Inland Natural Gas, would contribute nothing in the way of an increased gas price. Their fixed-price contracts permitted that refusal, it must be recognized.

Big-inch, high-pressure gas pipelines provide an essential public service. They function as a type of franchise or utility, enjoying certain necessary monopolistic privileges. Accordingly, they are subject to government regulation in the public interest. The essential factors of their integrity are safety, continuous service and environmental sensitivity. Profitability is also necessary but is rigidly controlled.

There has been some deregulation in the pipeline industry, but price and profit control are still very much in the public domain. Regulators examine and approve all capital expenditures, just as they annually monitor all operating expenses. Pipelines are very capital intensive. Operating expenses are sensitive to load factor and distance, thus the close scrutiny.

Under the general scheme of regulation, pipelines are authorized to charge prices for their service that are estimated to yield a stated percentage return on rate base; that is, on the depreciated cost of all assets used in providing the service. That controlled revenue is the regulators' calculation of the total funds required to pay the pipeline's imbedded debt interest and its budgeted operating expenses, leaving enough profit to represent a reasonable percentage return on its shareholders' equity investment.

That regulatory process all sounds very precise, almost a sure thing for the pipeline. However, when he set out to found Westcoast, McMahon did not enjoy that sophistication and comfort. His was an entrepreneurial solution to a wildcatter's predicament. He had found a lot of gas in northern British Columbia and adjoining Alberta which had to be sold to pay his debts and satisfy his appetite for more exploration funds. The modern price-and-profit safety net was not in vogue in 1957. Even when this regulatory method became available, Frank declined to apply for a hearing. He took his own chances on dealing gas to a shaky export market some 800 difficult pipeline miles from his wells, with no economic outlet for natural gas along the way. At that time, even the Vancouver gas market was unprofitable.

Westcoast's underpinning was gutsy but unsound, the basis of the ridicule which McMahon suffered from the eastern financial community and the reason for the firm's incipient bankruptcy. Fortunately, management realized the seriousness of the situation and were struggling valiantly for a solution, directed primarily at negotiating higher export prices.

Gradually, the effect of the voluntary, new pricing agreement with El Paso started improving revenues from export sales. A severe cost-reduction program also helped the earnings situation. However, the mere appearance of Westcoast avoiding bankruptcy led the gas producers to institute the arbitration procedure for higher wellhead prices. The first arbitration was initiated by Petrofina in 1972. Their nominee was Gordon Pearce, a well-known energy economist in Alberta; Westcoast's was lawyer B.V. Massie. The chairman selected was Norman Hyland, former chairman of B.C. Packers and a director of many firms. The majority decision was to increase the current 13 cents per mcf wellhead price to 16 cents. This 23-percent rise was definitely all we could manage at the time without going bankrupt.

Imperial Oil requested the second arbitration in B.C. in 1973. The two nominees were again Pearce and Massie. Their chairman was Ralph Shaw, former president of MacMillan Bloedel. The majority decision for these particular gas contracts was to raise the price from 12 cents to 18 cents per mcf. With this 50-percent hike, we knew it was curtains unless our Canadian and U.S. customers would voluntarily accept an increase on their firm-price contracts for the gas purchased from Westcoast. The savaged margins made the desperate situation quite evident.

To buy raw gas at the wellhead for 18 cents per mcf and sell it for 28 cents to B.C. Hydro was patently impossible. Even the 32 cents charged for export gas left a margin of only 14 cents per mcf. That was a slim figure to pay Westcoast for all the costs of gathering gas from hundreds of wells, processing it to sales-quality and hauling it 800 miles to market. It is not an exact comparison, but it is interesting to note that the sales-ready gas B.C. Hydro was buying for 28 cents per mcf was sold for an average residential price of something over $2.00. We would have gladly swapped our margin of 10 cents for theirs of $1.72. Any reasonable examination would conclude that Westcoast was heading for big trouble.

The third arbitration award later in 1973, again instituted by Imperial Oil, is a story in itself. The desperate outcome of the second was nothing compared to the disaster brought on by number three. The same nominees, Pearce and Massie, sat with chairman Ross Alger, the mayor of Calgary.

The Alberta producers had received a voluntary price increase for their export gas sold into the San Francisco market and transported by another pipeline. They wanted the same increase for gas sold to Westcoast from Alberta, whether for export or domestic sales. They successfully lobbied the Alberta government for a change in the Arbitration Act so that only residents of Alberta could sit on a case involving the price of gas produced in that province. Even more damaging, the Act's amendments mandated that the arbitration award could not be less than the most recent wellhead price achieved by any other negotiation or arbitration. The latest price settled in Alberta had been the large increase Pacific Gas and Electric in San Francisco gratuitously tossed to Alberta and Southern through its subsidiary, Pacific Gas Transmission, all of which was a corporate-family transaction. As a protest to the discriminatory arbitration legislation, Westcoast refused to send its lawyers and executives to the official hearing in Calgary. Imperial Oil showed up, naturally, and the hearing proceeded without any defence by us. A ridiculous 167-percent increase from 12 cents to 32 cents per mcf was the outcome. The adjective ridiculous is not out of place considering that Westcoast would have to pay 32 cents for raw gas in northern Alberta, gather and process it for delivery all the way to Vancouver to be sold to B.C. Hydro for 28 cents, a loss of 4 cents before any costs were added.

Westcoast adamantly refused to pay the new charge, and this messy situation terrified the gas-utility distributors in the Pacific Northwest because Canadian gas represented about 70 percent of their total supply. In a remarkable display of cooperation, they unanimously applied to the United States Federal Power Commission for authority to pay increased prices to Westcoast and to establish a fund of $80 million to support accelerated gas exploration in Canada. Two conditions they sought were agreement of the two B.C. utilities also to increase their purchase price and for the Alberta producers to return to the pricing level before the bruising 32-cent award. The Alberta producers were willing, but the B.C. distributors resolutely refused. David Cass-Beggs, the chairman of B.C. Hydro, rudely dismissed Kelly and me from his office, suggesting the next time we appeared he would expect a price reduction for the benefit of his B.C. consumers rather than a suggested increase.

The encounter between Gibson and Cass-Beggs was not a meeting of the minds. It was a contest between opposites. The pipeliner was heated in his argument, using emotional emphasis frequently to make his point. His crafty country-boy approach, with fractured grammar, grated with the academic style and lofty language of the frigid but articulate Hydro chairman.

Our second largest Canadian customer was Inland Natural Gas. For their part, they reduced gas sales prices to all their consumers. This obviously made it awkward for the B.C. Energy Commission to agree to any increase in the wholesale price they paid Westcoast. Thus, the only other significant opportunity for increased revenue in domestic sales was cut off at the pass.

All of this was a new experience for Kelly, particularly the regulatory constraints under which we operated. At an executive-committee meeting, he vowed to get even with Cass-Beggs and wanted it recorded that Bob Kadlec, Inland's president, was never to be allowed on Westcoast property, a childish embargo which was only amusing to good-natured Bob.

Thus began a feud with our only Canadian customers. In total contrast, Westcoast's relationship with El Paso and the gas-utility distributors in the Pacific Northwest became progressively stronger. Hugh Steen and Travis Petty, El Paso's two top men, must be regarded as the staunchest friends Westcoast ever had in the United States.

Adding to the gnawing perception that Westcoast was destined not to survive, another disaster occurred in the summer of 1973. The Beaver River and Pointed Mountain gas fields, operated by Amoco near the 60th Parallel, went to water. The producing gas wells reduced the reservoir pressure, which is normal. The unexpected result was migration of underground water into the reservoir and a rapidly rising water table that reached the producing level of virtually every gas well in the fields. Overnight, a supply of 300 million cubic feet per day was lost for good. Amoco spent a small fortune in remedial drilling to solve the water intrusion, but the entire field was eventually abandoned. Westcoast lost about 30 percent of its total gas supply, a commercial embarrassment that would persist for six years.

This gas-field failure shocked the industry. The first call offering assistance came from Don Getty, then Alberta's energy minister. He said he would do everything possible to arrange supplementary gas supplies. Unfortunately, physical limitations and B.C. political interference prevented any significant inflow of new Alberta gas. Accordingly, Westcoast announced that all customers would be cut back on a pro-rata basis because the winter daily demand could not be met. The two Canadian customers, particularly Inland, launched an impassioned public-protest campaign that intimidated the provincial government into ordering Westcoast not to curtail any B.C. customers, thus putting the damage of the gas shortfall totally on our U.S. customers. Despite Westcoast's objection to the British Columbia New Democratic Party government's discriminatory ruling that resulted from Inland's protests, the exports to the United States were curtailed by about 300 million cubic feet per day that first winter. On the coldest days, our U.S. customers received not much more than half their contract entitlement. At one point, they claimed that 150,000 people were temporarily laid off because of shutdowns at cement plants, pulp mills and other industrial concerns lacking alternate fuel installations.

To say that the U.S. customers, who had been so supportive in our previous predicament, were displeased would be grossly understating their grievance. An official of Washington Water Power in Spokane dramatically, if not seriously, suggested that the Marines should be called in to open the gas valves at the Sumas border crossing. It is a frightful embarrassment to acknowledge that some curtailment persisted for six winters on peak-demand days. That failure represents the blackest service record of any big-inch pipeline in North America. The provincial politicians were informed forcefully of the damage their arbitrary export curtailment had caused, yet they seemed unconcerned about the welfare of American citizens. This episode could have been on the minds of the Americans during negotiations between Canada and the United States on the Free Trade Agreement. In the energy section, FTA provisions preclude precisely this type of natural gas curtailment by Canada in the future.

The U.S. was later to experience an energy crisis of its own that had nothing to do with the Westcoast curtailment. At its worst stage, we were able to help and thereby gain some good public relations. During a record cold spell in the winter of 1976–77, the New England states were desperately short of energy, with a breakdown of essential services threatened. President Jimmy Carter made a personal visit to that region to assess the situation. He appealed to Canada for immediate energy aid, on any basis. Canada's National Energy Board responded the same day by requesting Canadian pipelines to ship all the natural gas they possibly could to the United States. Remarkably, the NEB advised that all the regulatory paperwork would be sorted out after the emergency was over; just start the gas flowing today!

Simply by making telephone calls to pipelines in the U.S.,

Westcoast was able to put an extra half billion cubic feet into their country-wide pipeline network over those weeks. By cooperative displacement and energy swaps, the equivalent heating value arrived in New England. This energy-relief effort on an immediate basis, by an unfettered natural-gas industry, was rewarded by a personal letter of gratitude to the Canadian government from President Carter. The media were complimentary but had difficulty explaining how these large volumes of gas could move from Canada that fast, particularly the volumes from northern B.C. all the way to New Jersey.

The government in power in 1973 was Dave Barrett's NDP. As a prelude to the record of this era, a remarkable paradox must be explained. Quite emphatically, it was the switch from a Social Credit government to the NDP that later made the most positive alteration to Westcoast's future. For historical accuracy, it must be acknowledged that Westcoast accomplished under a socialist administration what we could not do under the free-enterprise government. Give me full marks for guts in making such a statement.

Our chairman, Kelly Gibson, must singularly be credited for setting the stage for this most beneficial turnaround in company fortunes. He and I were together in Jasper over the last weekend in August 1972, when Dave Barrett was elected. In his homespun fashion, Kelly simply said: "Dave Barrett may be a socialist but he is now your elected premier and you've got to work with him. Play with the hand you're dealt and never shoot the dealer. Don't let your shirttail hit your ass until you are in Victoria offering your support to Barrett."

After calmer reflection, we decided that our chairman should make the initial courtesy call, which proved to be perfect strategy. The mission was immensely successful. Kelly's account was hilarious. He explained: "I suckered him with my li'l ol' country-boy pitch and it was all downhill with a tailwind from there."

Apparently, Barrett was in shirtsleeves in the premier's office, which inspired his visitor to shed his suit coat. The premier put his feet on the desk, without his shoes. I asked Kelly if he matched that act and he said he didn't. I tried to be smart with: "How come, holes in your socks?" He nailed me with: "No, no desk."

Obviously, they got along famously, with the new premier saying that he would welcome helpful suggestions from Westcoast. After which, according to Kelly: "The place got busier than a cow's tail at fly time, with staff people being ushered in and out to see the strange sight of the first capitalist visitor making peace with a socialist premier." They became, and still are, fast friends.

I made the follow-up visit, a dull event by comparison. I had known of Dave Barrett in the personnel department at Belkin Packaging. No play-acting was in order, even when Dave told me how much he admired Kelly Gibson. He informed me that Jim Rhodes, his principal confidant, would soon be prominent in the province's energy affairs and I should get to know him. This was encouraging because the NDP energy minister, Leo Nimsick, was not an impressive person in that role.

Just before I left, Dave talked about advertisements the mining industry were going to publish castigating the NDP. "Their approach is not like yours; if they want a fight, they'll get it," he threatened. Unfortunately, he unwisely introduced a punitive tax regime which almost killed the mining industry and the province's economy with it. This destructive policy contributed largely to Barrett's defeat in December 1975.

As Dave Barrett hinted, Jim Rhodes soon appeared as chairman of the B.C. Energy Commission. He called a full-scale hearing for a general examination of the gas industry. It was an unintended bitter experience because the gas producers, utility distributors, industrial gas users and all other intervenors took turns accusing Westcoast of every transgression imaginable. Al McIntosh had two shots at us: first, as a representative of the Canadian Petroleum Association; and, next, as vice-president, operations, of Pacific Petroleums, as a gas supplier.

On the opening day, 12 June 1973, D.P. McDonald created a humorous interlude. The commission's articulate counsel, Martin Taylor, took more than an hour setting the scene. He vilified Westcoast with scorching eloquence. D.P. couldn't take it. He stood up in the audience and shouted: "This is disgraceful; nothing like this has happened since Charles the First!" The audience roared with laughter. Counsel continued undaunted. Some days later, when I was on the stand, D.P. thought of an argument I should make, so he came out of the audience right to the witness desk. In his frenzy to make his point, he knocked a pile of books and documents onto the floor with a great clatter. He was still giving me instructions while our heads were below the table as we gathered up the spilled records. It was amusing to everyone but not to me. Jim Rhodes, the hearing chairman, had difficulty maintaining his customary dignified composure.

During this same hearing, Kelly accused eminent counsel Mike Goldie of Russell and DuMoulin of being the true CEO of Inland Natural Gas rather than that utility's president, Bob Kadlec. Goldie gave Kelly a lecture on the role of counsel.

In the closing days of the hearing, I returned to the stand as a policy witness. Ross McKimmie, our counsel, finished leading me through some rebuttal statements and the chairman took over. Jim Rhodes was obviously fishing for something or signalling some personal opinions by asking almost leading questions. At the break period, I told Kelly and Ross that we may have lucked into a chance to drop a bombshell by agreeing to discontinue our unprofitable marketing activity and become a gas transporter only. Kelly agreed and Ross McKimmie was quite enthusiastic, only cautioning me to avoid specifics which may compromise us in the future.

When I returned to the stand, Ross explained that I wished to make a closing statement. I recall saying something like: "Mr. Chairman, throughout these days of testimony, you have heard the unanimous and vigorous protests of the gas producers that Westcoast is exhibiting all the evils of being the exclusive purchaser for their product. At the other end of the pipeline, the utility distributors complain passionately that we are the exclusive wholesaler of the gas they need. You could logically conclude, therefore, that no one is satisfied with our marketing operation.

"Specifically, the producers claim we do not pay enough for gas at their wellheads; and the distributors allege we charge too much at their intakes. You could logically conclude, therefore, that Westcoast can't possibly solve both problems and make both groups content.

"Westcoast respectfully suggests that this hearing should declare it beneficial for us to discontinue the marketing role and become strictly a contract carrier. This restructuring would permit the producers of gas and the distributors of gas to settle their pricing complaints in direct, buy-sell negotiations with each other. We would agree to consider such a scheme."

Faced with the possibility of dealing directly with each other without the comfort of Westcoast as a punching bag, both the producers and distributors, particularly the latter, did not like the idea at all. Nevertheless, the seed had been planted. Jim Rhodes phoned me some weeks later to say he had been giving some thought to my testimony. We had some private discussions which he used to determine if we were truly serious, or merely deflecting some of the criticism.

The time seemed right to move. The basic strategy we could suggest to the NDP government, through Jim Rhodes, was not new. It was generally what we had recommended unsuccessfully to the National Energy Board and to the W.A.C. Bennett government a year earlier, through Frank Richter, the respected energy minister.

Our strategy involved well-known but never-applied provisions of the National Energy Board Act. Although the export contracts with El Paso were at a fixed price for twenty years, the NEB Act permitted the Board to recommend to Cabinet an arbitrary increase in the border price of natural gas which the U.S. buyer would have to accept. U.S. regulators would normally authorize their pipelines to flow-through such statutory price increases, if not excessive, to their American customers. Thus our scheme of increased export prices was no threat to our friends at El Paso. Our need was great and our pleading intense, but the NEB chairman, Dr. Robert D. Howland, wouldn't take the political risk. In my judgement, he was too close to retirement to be that progressive and helpful.

The next-best, and only other, alternative depended on the will of the provincial government. Our NEB export authorization required the export price to be at least 5 percent above the domestic price in the contiguous Canadian market area. The sales prices were then 28 cents per mcf to B.C. Hydro and 32 cents for El Paso sales to the Pacific Northwest. We had asked the previous government simply to ratchet the export price to 42 cents by ordering

B.C. Hydro to raise the contract price it paid to Westcoast to 40 cents per mcf. The suggested increase of 12 cents to the B.C. consumers was only a 6 percent addition to the marked-up price of about $2.00 that the residential gas users were paying Hydro. On behalf of the Canadian Petroleum Association, Al McIntosh had also recommended that same ratcheting possibility.

B.C. Hydro was the sacred utility cow resulting from the takeover of private B.C. Electric by the W.A.C. Bennett government. This probably accounted for the Socreds' reluctance to impose government will on Hydro. Furthermore, an abiding distrust of big business prevented them from believing that Westcoast would devise a plan to divert all of the windfall profits from this deal to the provincial treasury and to the gas producers, after the pipeline's 15 percent return. Whatever their thinking, the Social Credit government had turned us down. So much for free enterprise; back to the socialists who were now in power.

We had become well acquainted with Jim Rhodes. To discuss this particular subject, Kelly and I met him at the Hotel Vancouver in early October 1973. I outlined the pricing plan we had recommended to the previous administration. Rhodes seemed impressed, obviously recalling the commission's hearing and his own research of the problem. He asked us to draft our concept of an agreement outlining the arrangement that would secure the windfall profits from the increased prices for the provincial treasury and the gas producers. In what has to be a record achievement, we actually signed an interim agreement for that purpose on 13 November 1973, merely six weeks after our preliminary conversation. The B.C. Petroleum Corporation, with Rhodes as its first chairman, thus came into being, on his birthday by coincidence. Nearly two decades later, that agreement remains in effect, a triumph for the NDP government originally, and a continuing happy challenge for the Socreds to reap its economic benefits without acknowledging its socialist genesis.

The authors of the draft document that significantly established Westcoast's most prosperous years were Jack Smith, our chief financial officer, and Ron Rutherford, a brilliant engineer, economist and pipeline strategist who had joined Westcoast from Inland Natural Gas. Its success is their lasting legacy. Jack became vice-president and chief financial officer of Westcoast, and Ron was appointed vice-president, corporate development.

Introduction of the BCPC scheme was complicated because of the large number of parties involved in Canada and the U.S. Its basic elements, however, were simple. The NDP provincial government agreed to order B.C. Hydro to pay a higher price to Westcoast which would automatically elevate the export price at the U.S. border. Westcoast agreed to assign all its 170 gas-purchase contracts with the producers to the BCPC. The government thus became the sole buyer of gas in B.C. and for any former Westcoast contracts in Alberta.

Exemplary courage is not an exaggerated label for Premier Barrett's willingness to impose a gas price increase on every gas consumer in the province, in order to extract more from U.S. gas users. Guts, a coarser term, is more accurate. We had become inured to governments always taking the soft option. For his political fortitude, the treasury of Barrett's administration was later rewarded handsomely.

Westcoast would initially charge for and receive all of the revenue the ratcheted export price produced. Export sales were three-quarters of total income, so the boosted annual revenue was massive. Westcoast withheld from that revenue its cost of service and the agreed 15-percent rate of return. The remainder was remitted to the BCPC to be distributed on a negotiated formula to the provincial treasury and to the gas producers. The effective Westcoast guaranteed rate of return would be negotiated each year with the BCPC and submitted to the NEB for approval.

Discussing the all-important B.C. Hydro price which would trigger this grand scheme, we referred to the 12-cent increase from 28 cents to 40 cents per mcf, originally proposed to W.A.C. Bennett's government. Dave Barrett, on Jim Rhodes's advice, said that was not enough. It should go from 28 cents to 58 cents to escalate the U.S. border price to about 61 cents per mcf, due to the clause requiring the export price to be at least 5 percent above the domestic price. We all agreed, and planning the intricate installation of the BCPC program began in earnest.

First of all, it was more difficult to switch our 170 gas-purchase contracts to the government than we expected. As much as they criticized us at the public hearing, the producers instinctively trusted the new socialist administration even less than they believed Westcoast. Eventually, all the majors were persuaded except Dome Petroleum. Their president, Bill Richards, was unyielding and belligerent in refusing to sign up with the BCPC. I spent a lot of time with him, somewhat sarcastically complimenting his company on its willingness to be a free-enterprise martyr at such huge expense. I emphasized that his only alternative was to shut in his gas because we had surrendered our marketing position and the BCPC was now the province's only gas buyer. Bill stubbornly held out for a while after the new program commenced, until he tired of selling no gas while others were reaping record prices.

Imperial Oil was smarter; they signed up promptly. Ironically, and to our great enjoyment, Imperial never collected from us the 32-cent price which the phantom arbitration case had ordered us to pay a few months earlier.

Recounting the immensely profitable change in B.C. energy policy without highlighting the contribution of its chief architect would be a serious chronicling deficiency. Jim Rhodes was that person. A former NDP MLA, he also operated a profitable business with non-union employees, a firm he sold the day the NDP government was elected. Friends described him as a professing socialist and practising capitalist and teased him about being the first free-enterpriser to sell out when the socialists arrived. As a freak coincidence, the sale of his printing business was finalized on election day. Premier Barrett appointed Rhodes, in rapid succession, chairman of the B.C. Energy Commission, then chairman of the B.C. Petroleum Corporation and, finally, chairman of B.C. Hydro.

Considering the unprecedented personal power conferred upon Jim Rhodes, it is fortunate he was as enlightened a public servant as the oil-and-gas industry could wish. We found him to be a quick learner with a highly developed sense of fairness, a combination that equipped him well for his extensive responsibility.

Transferring the gas-purchase contracts from Westcoast to the

BCPC was a hard sell. Jim's courage in facing industry leaders in large, open meetings helped neutralize their early resistance. His forthright manner in answering their searching questions and providing unequivocal assurances swayed them to "give the guy a chance to prove his drastic policy changes will work," as they expressed it.

After the producer hesitation was resolved, the next troublesome snag developed in the United States. After more than a decade of litigation, El Paso had been ordered to divest its northwest pipeline system to a new company, Northwest Pipeline Corporation, headed by John McMillian, whom we did not know. The transition was in progress when Travis Petty of El Paso accurately warned us that McMillian would likely fight the BCPC export-pricing pressure play, which it truly was. Accordingly, we decided not to provide him the full details before announcing the dramatic new plan to all concerned at one session.

Marshall Crowe, the new NEB chairman, well briefed and in accord with what we were doing, was a real statesman in his cooperation in this very important matter of international trade. He invited all parties to his office for a weighty announcement in gas-export policy. We were hard pressed to have all final contracts and agreements in place to meet the deadline of Crowe's meeting. In fact, a blow-up on the evening of our departure for Ottawa almost sidetracked us.

We were scheduled to leave Vancouver at 5 P.M. Westcoast's plane would take Kelly, Jim Rhodes, his lawyer Joe Pelrine, John Anderson and me. Just as I was leaving the office for the plane, I received a panic call from Ron Rutherford. He was in the lobby of David Cass-Beggs's office. The chairman of B.C. Hydro had been instructed by the government to sign the contract with Westcoast for a price increase from 28 cents to 58 cents per mcf. However, Ron had been waiting an hour and Cass-Beggs wouldn't see him.

I telephoned Jim Rhodes about this serious last-minute hitch. He immediately called Dave Barrett and received this response: "Tell your man to hold tight, I'll tell him to sign that contract." Ron arrived at the plane about thirty minutes late, still laughing. He said the secretary ushered him into Cass-Beggs's office. The chairman said not a word and didn't even look up or read the contract. He angrily signed the last page and shoved it back at Ron.

On the plane, with the crucial contract in hand, Kelly enthused: "I told you I'd get my revenge on that guy." Years later, in one of my visits with Dave Barrett, I asked what was the worst mistake he made in his thirty-nine months as premier. Without an instant's hesitation, he declared: "Hiring Cass-Beggs."

The meeting with the National Energy Board the next day lacked nothing in drama, colourful debate or tough business. It was entirely successful and put together all the intricate pieces of the new plan for marketing B.C. gas for both domestic and export sales. But it was a shambles with respect to decorum.

The session, with chairman Marshall Crowe presiding, featured the attendance of Donald Macdonald, the federal minister of energy, and Alex Macdonald, the attorney-general of B.C. The principals attending included Jim Rhodes and Joe Pelrine; John McMillian and his lawyer; Travis Petty, president of El Paso Natural Gas, and his lawyer; Kelly Gibson, John Anderson and me from Westcoast; another NEB member and several senior staff, including their counsel.

Despite the obvious deduction that John McMillian would be opposed to the arrangement, we underestimated the extent of his fury. He flew into a histrionic rage, focusing his attack on Kelly Gibson, who escalated the dispute with appropriately vigorous rebuttal. In shouting confrontation, the Texan with his colourful drawl and colloquial expressions was matched by the Oklahoman's accent and humorous rejoinders. Had there been flags flying with the sound of fife and drum and cannon shot in the background, the scene would have resembled the War between the States.

Clearly, the Texan and his company would be the loser. Marshall Crowe explained that the NEB could make no other decision, having regard for the provisions of the National Energy Board Act. Mr. McMillian would have to agree to the new price increase from 32 cents to 61 cents per mcf which was the statutory percentage above the price in B.C.; otherwise, the export contract would be terminated as required under the Act. This dispute became more direct and less formal when the argument did not abate. Several times, John McMillian was interrupted to be reminded that his choice was simply 61 cents or no gas. He threatened to make the no-gas choice, then start litigation for damages with the support of the U.S. state department.

The NEB chairman and the energy minister could not have been accustomed to this type of conduct in their formal sessions. However, the occasional relaxed expression on their faces indicated they saw some entertainment value in the scrap's intensity, if not its intellectual level.

McMillian scored some good points. He said that Westcoast was trying to double his price of gas at the same time they were curtailing him by as much as 300 million cubic feet on peak days. He observed, accurately, that the curtailment was discriminatory because all Westcoast's Canadian utility customers were receiving their full requirements. Thus, his twenty-year contract for firm supplies was arbitrarily being reduced to an inferior, interruptible status. "With the connivance of the Canadian government, you are giving me the double whammy!" he persisted. He accused Kelly Gibson of lacking the courage to resist the B.C. socialist government which technically had no authority to order selective curtailment.

At this point, McMillian's lawyer, Dave Watkiss, must have sensed that his client could be burning some bridges. He quietly asked me to leave the meeting with him for a brief conference in the corridor. He merely said: "I'm the outsider in this forum and don't want to break up the meeting, but would you ask for a caucus adjournment so that I can confer with my client on this threat of 61 cents or no gas?"

After a brief caucus, the mood changed to the extent that McMillian attempted to gain some accommodations for agreeing to the increased price. He wanted all Westcoast customers placed on pro-rata curtailment and he demanded that Alberta gas be brought into the B.C. system to make up for the loss of production from the Beaver River and Pointed Mountain fields. Both of these requests, which Westcoast considered reasonable, were not acceptable to the NDP government in Victoria. Their representatives at the meeting affirmed that determined position. After about three hours of argument, Northwest Pipeline Corporation signed the agreement as originally proposed.

The plane ride home was enjoyed by a jubilant group, fully aware of the momentous import of the new export-pricing policy. The theatrics of the day were succinctly summarized by Kelly's observation: "Ol' Johnny-Tex shore got his tail in a knot today." As future events unfolded, the wounds from this altercation took longer to heal than the time to untangle his tail.

The new B.C. Petroleum Corporation marketing plan was the culmination of a strategy adopted by Westcoast more than a year before its attainment. Simply stated, Westcoast accepted a regulated ceiling on its profits in a swap for a guaranteed return on its capital rate base, which return would not vary regardless of gas volumes or sales prices. With respect to the former tight financial squeeze on Westcoast, being caught between rising wellhead prices and firm sales prices, combined with a gas-supply shortfall of 30 percent, the new status as a contract carrier without marketing vulnerability was like being a born-again pipeline. Hallelujah!

The agreement was new to the industry. Soon after it was announced, TransCanada's president, George Woods, visited Vancouver with some of his staff for a full study of the details. He left very impressed with the prospect for much improved returns for the gas producers, the pipeline and the provincial treasury. He was envious but could not see how TransCanada could make the same deal, export volumes being a smaller proportion of their total gas deliveries.

The NDP government in British Columbia had successfully broken the earlier reluctance of the National Energy Board to exercise its statutory authority on export pricing. However, not all the credit can be attributed to the NDP. Another factor was the retirement of the NEB chairman, Dr. Howland, succeeded by Marshall Crowe. It is possible the former was at a stage in his career when ploughing a new furrow was not particularly attractive. His successor, fortunately, was noted for his progressive thinking, fairness and courage.

In the months following this gas-pricing breakthrough, world oil prices went on a rampage. As oil prices soared, the NEB ordered a

sequence of price increases for gas sold by Westcoast to the Pacific
Northwest. As permitted by the Act, export gas prices were ad-
justed merely to keep pace with the prices and equivalent heating
value of other fuels sold in the same U.S. marketing area. Progressively, the border price escalated from 32 cents to an unbelievable
$4.94 US per mcf. While the export pricing was increasing to a
multiple of fifteen times, the selective curtailment against U.S.
shipments continued on peak days through each winter, albeit with
less severity. Westcoast's American customers no longer called us
Canucks; we were blue-eyed Arabs. But they had no trouble selling
all the gas we could ship, despite those wild prices.

The optimistic forecasts of increased benefits flowing from the
BCPC were accurate. As provincial coffers were being swelled with
revenues from the oil-and-gas industry, Premier Dave Barrett
boasted in almost every public speech about this singular achievement of his government. He always attributed this to the cooperation he had received from Westcoast Transmission. This apparent
love affair did not endear the company to the Social Credit party in
opposition. Nor did his frequent reference to Ed Phillips in this
connection contribute to what had been a good relationship with
the Socreds. Barrett's claim was accurate and, although it will
never be admitted, the succeeding Socred government, under Bill
Bennett, was the greater beneficiary after they took over in 1975.
At the peak year, the Socreds received about half a billion dollars
from gas and oil revenues and sale of crown lands to the industry,
compared with a scant $13 million in 1972, the year before the
BCPC was formed. This exceeded all other sources of government
revenue except personal income tax. It was the first time our industry produced more revenue for the administration than liquor taxes.

While in power, Dave Barrett played this situation like a violin,
and the melody was money. Westcoast's common-stock price had
been about $30 when the NDP government was elected. Because of
the premier's public threats to take over Westcoast and B.C. Telephone, among other companies, our stock price collapsed to $18. It
was languishing a bit above that level when the gas export price
started moving above the $1.00 level, beginning to provide very
high returns for the treasury. Jim Rhodes telephoned me to say the

premier wondered if the Province could purchase the 13 percent of Westcoast stock owned by El Paso Natural Gas. I explained that I was sure they could because El Paso had divested the northwest system and were not particularly interested in continuing a Canadian pipeline investment. I offered to arrange a meeting with El Paso to negotiate a direct purchase. To that, Barrett later replied: "No, I don't want to play any games. I want to buy this stock through a broker just like you capitalist bandits do." He did just that, and a Toronto broker did well on this purchase. I learned later that this broker had recommended the transaction to Jim Rhodes, suggesting that BCPC buy El Paso's 1,157,125 Westcoast shares. Rhodes advised the broker to approach the premier and just happened to be in Dave Barrett's office when the enterprising stock salesman made his call. Apparently, Rhodes convinced his boss that the block of stock would be a good buy at $22. Barrett respected the cold call of the broker and gave him the order.

Effectively, our enterprising socialist premier had callously knocked down Westcoast common-share price from $30 to $18 with his takeover talk, then jumped in to buy as it was rising to $22. No one successfully complained, even during the legislature's question period, because he took every opportunity to boast how he had increased the gas price to the Americans and then used their own money to buy back the only U.S. ownership in the B.C. big-inch pipeline monopoly. This was a bit of stage acting, but not far from the truth.

After the stock purchase was completed, I telephoned Dave Barrett to explain delicately that his holding did not automatically qualify a government representative for a seat on the board of directors and that the shareholders would not likely elect one. My timidity was unnecessary. He replied with a laugh: "We wouldn't go on the board if you asked us. Just don't let the stock go down and make me look bad."

The Social Credit party, under new leader Bill Bennett, returned to power in B.C. in December 1975. After an appropriate interval of time to disguise my eagerness, I offered to repurchase the government's shareholding in Westcoast at $25 per share. This would equate to $8.33 on the basis of a three-for-one split a few months

later. The response was firmly negative. Gerry Bryson, the deputy
finance minister, gave me the news by saying: "Bill Bennett said if
Phillips feels $25 would be a good deal for him to buy, that's suffi-
cient reason for me to say it would be a good deal for the government to hold."

That was not to be the end of my connection with that block,
which became 3,471,375 shares after the split. They were put into
the basket to sugar-coat the assets the government fed the British
Columbia Resources Investment Corporation to launch their bold
experiment in privatization. There was no particular magnetism in
that valuable asset of Westcoast's shares pulling me toward them,
but I did later become chairman of BCRIC and enjoyed seeing that
investment being exploited in a very profitable way—another en-
trancing twist of fate that enriched my total experience as a businessman dealing in the fickle domain of politics.

When the Social Credit government returned to power,
Westcoast was in a period of improving fortunes in all aspects but
one. Gas demand was rising, capacity was being increased by capital rate-base additions and profits were better. Sadly, however, the
huge loss of gas supplies from northern B.C. and the Yukon in 1973
still had not been replaced. This necessitated continuation of the
plaguing curtailment problem with the U.S. customers. Northwest
Pipeline learned that Westcoast, under aggressive persuasion from
the B.C. government, had declined to contract for new gas supplies
offered from Alberta. They alleged that this arbitrary refusal of a
remedy for the shortfall nullified our legal claim of force majeure
and they engaged the U.S. state department in a vigorous protest.
Protracted negotiations between Ottawa and Washington eventually led to a high-level meeting with B.C. government officials in
March 1977. It was attended by several executives from both of the
companies directly involved and there were representatives from
Washington, D.C., from the National Energy Board in Ottawa,
and from the Alberta government, including Dr. George Govier, a
respected expert in natural-gas marketing.

The opposition by the B.C. government had been inspired by
the president of the B.C. Petroleum Corporation, George Lechner.
He was personally convinced that the introduction of more Alberta

gas into the B.C. system would ultimately displace gas to be sold in the future by his B.C. producers. His political bosses agreed with him. Westcoast argued that the Alberta contracts offered were relatively short-term in nature, with very low take-or-pay levels which meant they could be cut back substantially before the shipments from any B.C. producers were endangered. Dr. Govier's learned presentation supporting Westcoast's case was not successful. The meeting ended with no solution.

Properly concerned that the force-majeure defence was becoming weak, Westcoast determined it had to defy the wishes of the Socred government and contract for Alberta gas with the approval of the National Energy Board, which was the regulatory authority controlling Westcoast, not the B.C. government.

The National Energy Board had earlier approved Westcoast's purchase of additional gas supplies in Alberta. This should have been the end of the matter, but the disappointing conflict was becoming more severe between Westcoast, B.C.'s only big-inch pipeline, and the Socred government. As a last minute effort to settle this dispute amicably, I telephoned James Chabot, B.C.'s energy minister, and explained that I was calling from the NEB offices in Ottawa. I repeated our concerns, shared by the NEB, that our force-majeure claim was in jeopardy and we could be sued for breach of an international sales contract, with huge damages assessed.

The minister was polite, even cordial, but very firm. He said it was the responsibility of his government to preserve the future of the gas industry in B.C. using every device they could. I reminded him of the protective provisions the proposed Alberta gas-purchase contracts now contained as a result of his intervention and resulting amendments. Then I suggested we issue a joint press release emphasizing that his efforts had properly and effectively modified our original plans. I offered to wait for two hours, before issuing our own press release, to see if more time would permit him to agree. His reply was to go ahead, there would be no change in their attitude. We had no choice, fully aware of the irritation our decision would create.

On 4 April 1977, Chabot finally announced that the government of B.C. would agree to the export of additional gas supplies purchased in Alberta.

Westcoast's resistance to B.C. pressure was necessary but not a comfortable posture. We bought the emergency Alberta gas as planned, feeling it was a sad family fight that should never have started but became a disagreement that would take a long time to heal. Some comfort was gained from unanimous support in the industry for our resolute action. Understandably, most of the plaudits came from the United States. As with all disputes with elected politicians and appointed government officials, this victory was pyrrhic at best.

4

THE QUEST FOR
AN ARCTIC GAS
PIPELINE

The official starting gun for the arctic pipeline rush was fired formally in March 1974, when Canadian Arctic Gas Study Limited, familiarly known as CAGSL or Arctic Gas, filed applications with the National Energy Board in Ottawa and with the Federal Power Commission in Washington, D.C. A winner of the great race would not be declared until 4 July 1977. What happened in the intervening forty months can only be described with superlatives. Almost every pipeline, major oil company and large distribution utility in North America joined in the battle. The substantial prize was the permit to build the largest private engineering undertaking in the world, estimated to cost $26 billion at least. As an international venture, it would dwarf the Panama Canal and the St. Lawrence Seaway and exceed the cost of the future 'Chunnel' between England and France. It would require an estimated $180 million merely for all the applicants and intervenors to participate in federal, provincial and state regulatory hearings in both countries.

The lure of arctic energy reserves started a frenzy that lacked the personal drama of earlier gold rushes. But it was considerably more massive in capital expenditures, technological challenges, unbelievable equipment requirements, calling for the ultimate in environmental safeguards, altogether making an unprecedented logistical assault on the hostile north.

A small oil pipeline had been built in the arctic during World War II as a security measure. Completed in 1944 by the United States, it was a companion project to the Alaska Highway. Called the Canol Pipeline, it ran 930 kilometres from Whitehorse to Norman Wells where oil had been discovered as early as 1920. Its cost was five times the original estimate. Canol was an operating disaster due to permafrost damage, and it was soon abandoned.

In the later years leading up to March 1974, there had been intensive jockeying for position. First at the gate in 1969 was the Northwest Project Study Group, comprised of TransCanada Pipe-Lines Limited and several major American petroleum companies. They envisioned a gas pipeline from Prudhoe Bay via the Mackenzie River Valley to markets in the midwestern United States and eastern Canada.

Next, in the same year, was the Gas Arctic Systems Study Group, formed by the Alberta Gas Trunk Line Company Limited to consider a pipeline from Prudhoe Bay, through the Yukon, the Northwest Territories and Alberta to the midwestern United States.

In early 1969, Westcoast announced a pipeline that was the product of Charles Hetherington's fertile mind. It was to move only Canadian gas from the Mackenzie delta along the Mackenzie River to a bifurcation point north of the 60th Parallel and then split into two separate lines, one going through B.C. and the other through Alberta. This idea was ahead of its time and it didn't last much longer than the initial press release. It had even less influence on Westcoast's stock price, an intended by-product.

Also, late in 1969, Westcoast formed Mountain Pacific Pipeline Ltd., proposing a pipeline from Alaska to mid-continent through the southern Yukon and British Columbia.

Perhaps the best all-round but lowest profile strategist of all the companies involved in this great contest was Ron Rutherford. He was an engineer and B.Comm. whose first employment was with Shawinigan Power in Quebec. Later he served in a number of energy posts for the government of British Columbia before joining

Bechtel Corporation, the worldwide energy consultants and builders. Ron was pivotal in building the Inland Natural Gas system for John McMahon, Frank's youngest brother, and became a vice-president of that firm. Westcoast attracted him from Inland in 1969 to serve in the gas-supply division, reporting to Peter Kutney. He was soon moved to Pacific Northern Gas where he succeeded quickly in converting that new and struggling distribution utility into a fine subsidiary contributing nicely to Westcoast's profits.

Concurrently, Ron was Westcoast's strategist in the monumental pipeline battle to come. His education and experience in both engineering and economics equipped him well for this responsibility. But it was his instinctive ability to devise rapid adjustments or alternatives, to meet changing circumstances, that distinguished him from most other competent pipeline experts.

In 1969, Westcoast was poorly equipped to engage in any contest. It was understaffed at all levels and the operations had been cut to the bone in a desperate cost-reduction campaign. There were scant profits and the largest major pipeline addition to the gas-gathering system was being abandoned because of faulty pipe. Nevertheless, the determination of Frank McMahon sustained our interest in the arctic.

Rutherford's first advice to Westcoast was that the two existing pipelines in B.C. and Alberta (Westcoast Transmission and Alberta Gas Trunk) should be exploited to move Alaska gas to the lower forty-eight states. Specifically, he advocated joining both of them at their northern extremities to tie in with a larger mainline from that point to the north slope via the Alaska Highway. In a broader sense, he drafted, and management accepted, a basic two-point policy objective. First, the Alaska Highway was the most logical pipeline route for arctic gas and offered the least-sensitive environmental problems. Second, a pipeline definitely should not be built across the north slope of the Yukon and Alaska because the cost would be prohibitive and the environmental damage severe beyond calculation. These guiding principles, almost prophetically resembling the later edict by Justice Berger, were never abandoned by Westcoast. They did, however, put Westcoast in conflict with the other major proposals.

In 1970, a new consideration had to be added to all the plans. Imperial Oil made a significant gas discovery in Canada's Mackenzie delta, increasing proven reserves to about 5.3 trillion cubic feet.

In the meantime, Westcoast did little with Mountain Pacific Pipeline, largely due to lack of partners and its own limited resources. And in 1972, the Northwest Project Study Group and the Gas Arctic Systems Study Group merged to form the Canadian Arctic Gas Study Limited. This huge consortium, including more than a score of members at one time, filed regulatory applications in 1974.

Arctic Gas, whose members included the heaviest hitters in the industry, spent huge sums on impressive route searches and engineering studies on pipeline installations and operations in permafrost. Compared to Westcoast's unavoidable poor-boy approach to its own project, Arctic Gas was a first-class effort in every way. But one flaw occurred which created the most stunning development in the whole story.

A relatively small and upstart pipeline company called Alberta Gas Trunk Lines (now NOVA) was becoming restive as a member of the Arctic Gas consortium. Its president, Bob Blair, was a product of the Bechtel consulting organization, as were Ron Rutherford and Al Green, Westcoast's chief engineer. Blair had almost unmatched pipeline design, installation and operating experience. He was also a passionate nationalist, more than willing to expound on that subject. Bob Blair became concerned that control of this important international project was not being shared equitably between Americans and Canadians. Most CAGSL decisions were being made by a small, powerful committee in New York. Further, emerging financial arrangements appeared to indicate that Canadians would not have majority control even over the portion of the pipeline going through Canada.

The evidence is clear that Bob Blair and his principal colleague, Bob Pierce, made every effort to change this course of events, as members of the consortium. They were unsuccessful and, to the utter amazement of the entire industry, they resigned from Arctic Gas and committed Alberta Gas Trunk Lines to going it alone in direct competition. There were other disagreements having to do with routing and technical matters, but it must be acknowledged that the defection of one small, regional company to challenge what seemed like most of the industry was the gutsiest business decision of the time. Bob Blair's critics, and there were many, described the move as foolhardy, often using more uncomplimentary terms than that. They were yet to feel his greater sting.

If Westcoast was financially incapable of sponsoring an arctic pipeline, AGTL was not a great deal stronger. They did have the advantage of almost unlimited gas reserves in their province and economic stability as a quasi-government company, being the exclusive gatherer and transporter of gas in Alberta. Bob Blair was not particularly well known outside the province at that time. Westcoast's relationship with AGTL was similar to that of the other shippers using their system. We were concerned that some of the big expenditures they would have to make for arctic pipeline research might migrate into the cost-of-service all other shippers paid to Alberta Gas Trunk Lines for their normal transmission service. In any case, under the name Maple Leaf, AGTL launched an expensive and thorough project, all on their own. The unimaginative name Maple Leaf was clearly the banner for Bob Blair's passionate nationalism.

It is important to register that Alberta Gas Trunk Lines did not solicit a single partner for their huge undertaking, and that includes Westcoast. On the other hand, we were invited on a number of occasions to align Westcoast with the Arctic Gas consortium. On one occasion, Vern Horte, the president of Arctic Gas, made a special trip to Vancouver to extend an invitation to us. We had great respect for the membership of their group. We declined their generous financial terms of admittance simply because that move did not point toward achieving our ultimate but unpublished determination to build the arctic pipeline along the Alaska Highway and through British Columbia. Furthermore, their route across the sensitive north slope of the Yukon and Alaska was a policy prohibition with Westcoast. Our strategist, Ron Rutherford, advised us that we should be flattered by the approach but it would be a mistake to join Arctic Gas, whose pipeline was designed to bypass all the existing systems. Therefore, Westcoast remained on the sidelines of this great event; but not for long.

Finally, one memorable day in September 1974, Ron advised the executive committee that we should attempt to join the AGTL Maple Leaf project, which had been given the corporate name of Foothills Pipelines. His reason was the possibility of linking the existing systems of Westcoast and AGTL to reach into the arctic with a single pipeline for either Canadian or Alaskan gas, or both. Contrary to Rutherford's preference, the Arctic Gas project had listed the Alaska Highway route as the least desirable of their five studied alternatives for the transmission of gas from Alaska. No wonder we could not join Arctic Gas; their last choice was Westcoast's first and only selection of a route.

The executive committee agreed with Ron's recommendation to join AGTL, although our chairman's support was more in a spirit of cooperation than conviction. Kelly cautiously observed that we really didn't have enough money to get into a contest we were certain to lose. That judgement was rational, but those of us working full time at Westcoast still were inclined to march to the tune of Frank McMahon's jig: if the idea was good enough, money didn't matter.

Because AGTL were not seeking partners, to our knowledge, we were uncertain as to the welcome we would receive. Nevertheless, Kelly arranged a meeting in Calgary with Bob Blair, Bob Pierce and Reg Gibbs. Reg, a lawyer, was president of their Pan-Alberta Gas subsidiary and we knew him as one of the forces behind the iniquitous changes to the Alberta Arbitration Act. Not a good start.

We quickly stated our desire to join forces, acknowledging that we had limited financial resources. On the plus side, we stoutly claimed that no pipeline in North America could equal Westcoast's operating experience in the hostile muskeg country and discontinuous permafrost in northern B.C. and the Yukon. We became a partner in the time it took Bob Blair to rise and shake Kelly's hand, stating rather dramatically: "This is the biggest day for our project so far!"

We discussed some specifics, but very few. Bob said we would be welcomed without any entry fee and we could pick our own share of participation up to 50/50. We chose 30 percent initially. Later events pushed that share to 40 and finally to 50 percent. This cordial reception boosted Kelly's personal interest somewhat, but he warned Ron and me again about playing such a longshot.

At our first formal Foothills meeting, it was agreed that Westcoast's ranks were too thin to permit the transfer of many people to the Maple Leaf project permanently. Fortunately, AGTL were well staffed and their executives and engineers took most of the positions in the partnership. Ron Rutherford, of course, was welcomed as a strategist and senior executive in the Foothills structure.

AGTL brought to the partnership many fine people who fought this contest to the end. Among the more prominent were Bill Deyell in engineering, along with Don Olafson, Ed Mirosh and Walter Hennion; Dianne Hall in administration; Bruce Simpson in finance; Kent Jesperson who is now president of Foothills; and John Burrell in charge of the Whitehorse office.

In due time, Ron Rutherford advised our partner AGTL that we should explore the possibility of combining Westcoast's pet Alaska Highway route from Prudhoe Bay with the Maple Leaf pipeline from the Mackenzie delta. Concerns about a route along the Mackenzie River and the perils of crossing the north slope of Alaska and the Yukon were growing. Some feared that this resistance would lock in the Canadian reserves in the delta. This problem was relieved by Rutherford's idea for a pipeline along the Dempster Highway to access Canadian delta gas. These concerns convinced Bob Blair to look at the Alaska Highway route to Prudhoe Bay. It was accordingly agreed that Westcoast should probe into this possibility with the State of Alaska and the federal authorities in Washington, D.C. Also, we were to look for a pipeline associate from the United States, who would be needed if this important change were to be instituted. Bob Blair felt he should not be too visible in the new strategy because he had recently been promoting the movement of only Canadian gas along any pipeline he would build.

This significant change in strategy was checked out in early 1976 with pollster Martin Goldfarb. He emphatically affirmed that the Canadian public would not accept a pipeline in the Mackenzie

River valley because of environmental concerns and the opposition of the native peoples. Goldfarb further held that the Dempster Highway would be considered by the public to be a better route for Canadian gas. This development proved to be pivotal. As a measure of the man, Bob Blair pragmatically accepted the inexorable drift to Westcoast's original concept, and he became the revised project's most visible and vocal advocate.

Westcoast's first formal meeting about the Alaska Highway route was arranged by consultant Arlon Tussing with the U.S. Senate energy committee, chaired by Senator Warren Magnussen of Washington state. In two days of hearings, we seemed to make a favourable impression. Realistically, our assessment had to include the sobering reminder from some of the senators that they already had two competing proposals in Alaska. One was for a pipeline by the Arctic Gas consortium, and the other for shipping the gas in the form of LNG by formidable El Paso on a tanker route to southern California. In a private session, our best encouragement came from Senator Ted Stephens from Alaska, when he kindly entertained us for dinner.

Later, we had a number of meetings in Alaska with their senators and with many of the state's energy officials, again with the assistance of the influential Arlon Tussing. We found the mood to be definitely anti-Arctic Gas and pro-El Paso. We seemed to be welcomed especially by the energy department people. Although AGTL was not a part of these meetings, for strategic reasons, Ron had explained the unique arrangement AGTL had in the province of Alberta. The Alaskan officials were most intrigued, believing AGTL could be the model for an intra-state pipeline in Alaska and thus boost revenues from this new-found energy resource.

Such an ambitious undertaking required political support, and Premier Bill Bennett was our most consistent and open advocate. He held productive sessions with the governors of the Pacific Northwest states to secure their influence in the FPC hearings in the U.S.A.

The arctic pipeline twice appeared on the official agenda of conferences of all the fifty U.S. governors. Governor Jerry Brown of California was one I was assigned to lobby. That state was the larg-

est gas consumer in the United States. The Los Angeles area alone
had more gas meters than all of Canada. Obviously, the governor
was very influential on natural-gas matters at both the federal and
state levels. Governor Brown knew little about Foothills and was
sympathetic to Arctic Gas, as the made-in-America project. However, he finally accommodated me by agreeing to take the formal
position that the choice between Foothills and Arctic Gas, as the
pipeline to cross Canada, should in the final analysis be made by
Canadian authorities. That was all I had requested and could have
been expected.

On one occasion, Bennett invited Governor Jay Hammond from
Alaska to a dinner in Victoria so that I could spend a couple of
hours with him privately explaining the advantages of the route
down the Alaska Highway. He became a supporter of the Foothills
concept but clearly preferred El Paso as a company to handle the
project.

The premier also provided an official letter of support, on short
notice, for filing with our FPC application. It was delivered by mes-
senger just in time for me to take it on the plane. The energy minister of B.C. at the time, Jack Davis, pleaded our case at every meeting of the energy ministers of all the provinces. Throughout the
contest, every media comment by B.C. politicians was supportive,
including the B.C. caucuses of both the federal Liberals and Tories.

There is an explanation for this unusual level of support from
British Columbia, contrasted with the relative silence from Premier
Peter Lougheed in Alberta. If the pipeline route were to follow the
Alaska Highway down through British Columbia, the economic
benefits would be much greater for that province. For example, Canadian Pacific Airlines, then based in Vancouver, would garner almost all of the increased air freight and passenger traffic because of
their prominence in B.C. and the Yukon. Similarly, the Caterpillar
agency in British Columbia (Finning) would automatically be the
supplier of immense amounts of heavy equipment. On the other
hand, if the Mackenzie River valley route were chosen, Pacific
Western Airlines, owned in Alberta and covering the Northwest
Territories, would be the beneficiary as would the Caterpillar agent
(Angus) holding the Alberta and NWT franchise.

Westcoast attempted to reciprocate the assistance of the B.C. government, although the opportunities were not great. During a provincial election, Don Phillips, a prominent Socred cabinet member, asked if I would make a speech on his behalf at the opening of the airport expansion at Chetwynd. I agreed and he emphasized that I should arrive in the company jet. This airport was a tiny facility with one hangar and a single strip which had merely been lengthened. Using any excuse for a political speech, Don had erected a stand with bunting and ribbons. After the short, forgettable speeches the crowd was served hot dogs and beer and invited by the minister to inspect our plane. Apart from a single-engine two-seater, it was the only airplane on the field. The minister wanted that display more than my speech. All he said later was "Thanks Ed, how could I have opened an airport without a real aircraft in sight?"

About the same time, the premier's staff wanted a television publicity opportunity and the CBC had agreed to cover the opening of Westcoast's new $100 million gas processing plant near Chetwynd. I explained that it was not ready and was not processing any gas, but they insisted we stage a symbolic opening anyway with lots of photogenic gas flames. We built a big stand with a bulky hand-control valve on it. Again we had lots of speeches and then came the big moment.

The premier and I together turned the valve wheel and a huge flame roared forty feet into the air. The crowd applauded the pyrotechnics with delight and the premier beamed. I was more subdued because I knew that flame was not from the unfinished gas plant. It came from tanks of propane we brought in for the event and concealed under the stand with red, white and blue bunting. The premier was never told of the deception. Nor was the CBC, and a short clip of the event made the evening news.

The *Vancouver Sun* ran a full-page feature story by Howard Mitchell, a veteran newspaper publisher and printer, who gratuitously opposed the Alaska pipeline. Mitchell's focus was faulty, but his skill as a writer was fleetingly damaging. I requested equal space for a rebuttal, which was not granted by the *Sun*. They reasoned that my authorship would appear too self-serving and suggested that an independent supporter would be more persuasive. They were correct. I put them in touch with Gordon Gibson, who submitted a full page of eloquent logic that helped our cause immensely. I doubt if the *Sun* ever had copies of one of their stories distributed more widely in North America.

Gibson, who had been on Prime Minister Trudeau's staff, was a frequent visitor to our office, personally studying our project so that he could articulate his well-informed preference for the Alaska Highway route. He even monitored some of the hearings in Washington, D.C. Liberal Senator George Van Roggen was a definite friend in the way he familiarized himself with the details and vigorously attempted to persuade his colleagues in the upper house. Senator Bud Olson, from Calgary, was another who spoke out on our behalf.

Iona Campagnola, then minister of Indian affairs and northern development, was convinced our project was superior. On different occasions she gathered fellow MP's and cabinet ministers in her Ottawa office to hear a personal presentation from us. She didn't waste her time on the believers and was quite effective in corralling the Members of Parliament who needed to be briefed and converted.

Once we had gained the agreement of Alberta Gas Trunk Lines to link together the Alaska Highway and Maple Leaf routes, the search for a U.S. pipeline associate for Foothills commenced, that firm to be responsible for the portion of the international pipeline going through Alaska.

The Alaska Highway part of the enlarged Foothills proposal became popularly described as the Alcan Project (much to the displeasure of the Aluminum Company of Canada). Our first choice for an Alcan associate in the state of Alaska was El Paso because of our previous close and rewarding association. However, El Paso were wedded to their LNG project and were not interested. Next, we approached Tenneco because of their magnificent reputation in the United States, particularly in the corridors of Congress. They also were committed to another Canadian proposal called Polar Gas, with an impressive membership including TransCanada Pipe-Lines and, later, Petro-Canada. Ron Rutherford had done consulting work for Tenneco so he was able to approach their engineers personally. I was acquainted with one of their prominent directors, but neither solicitation altered that pipeline's loyalty to Polar Gas.

Finally, in some desperation, we invited Northwest Pipeline Corporation, our new export customer headed by John McMillian. He had just wrested the northwest division from El Paso after lengthy divestiture proceedings. John accepted without too much hesitation because we agreed to do all of the work for him in the initial stages. While he was getting to know the business and recruiting some expertise, Westcoast actually prepared the first intervention to the Federal Power Commission in Washington on behalf of Northwest. That was only the start of the way the American associate was virtually wheel-barrowed into our group.

The mating scene at the introduction of the proposed new associate John McMillian to Bob Blair will only be appreciated with some description of this interesting person. John was a handsome, well-groomed man, just a bit short and chubby. He was a likeable and personable companion in a social setting (actually, a raconteur deluxe).

Our associate-to-be was a jet setter who had just married a beautiful woman younger than his son. He was well known in Hollywood and enjoyed hosting entertainment people at his splendid home overlooking Salt Lake City or in the ski resorts nearby. His favourite toy was a custom-fitted airliner, complete with an ensuite bedroom and a lounge called the Throne Room for his wife, Anna Marie. His previous leased aircraft had been a Jetstar owned originally by the Shah of Iran and outfitted with regal trappings that titillated the colourful McMillians.

McMillian's senior executives referred to him as my-way-or-the-highway John, indicative of his management style. His frequent references to his social activities shaped that side of his reputation in a direction that appeared not to trouble him at all. We didn't give him that high a rating as a pipeliner, but the fact was, he had been immensely more successful, financially, than all of our group put together. And, in the meantime, I was learning a new language in the association with so many Oklahomans and Texans.

John was reputed to have made his first fortune in the oilfields of

Australia and New Guinea. He told me about making a lot of money in Australia and then moving to Alberta, "Where I lost it all to them Calgarians," he complained.

His acquisition of the northwest system from El Paso was a real coup over many substantial competitors. His stature in Texas was formidable as a bagman for the Democrats. The popular television show, 60 Minutes, featured McMillian's political influence with people such as political heavyweight Robert Strauss in one of its uncomplimentary segments. This caused our project some embarrassment, but not as much as a critical column by Canadian syndicated correspondent Marjorie Nichols, then based in Washington. When McMillian threatened to sue her, Marjorie told me that she had more damaging material on tape if I wanted to hear it. McMillian accepted my advice to cool it. When my friend Marjorie and I appeared together on another television show, she taunted me with the charge that Foothills had the best project in the pipeline battle but the worst American partner. Other negative characterizations led the host, Jack Webster, to refer to her target as Mr. McBillion.

That is the man whom Ron and I took to Calgary to meet Bob Blair and Bob Pierce for the first time. John unfortunately came on as having an ego bigger than the White House. He failed to impress our partners and it was a meeting to be forgotten. Bob Blair clearly was not ready for a name-dropping American partner who knew very little about pipelining. Kelly, of course, had not forgotten their Ottawa confrontation. The meeting was brief and chilly. Most of the talk came from the side of the table occupied by McMillian, Rutherford and me. From the other side came little but the impassive stares of Blair, Pierce and Gibson. Bob Blair ended the meeting with: "Thanks for your suggestion, Ed, we'll think it over." This untypical indecision was a message in itself.

Ron and I returned to Vancouver in a very disappointed state. We needed an American pipeline associate and Northwest was our last chance. We were determined to try again but agreed we had to effect a reconciliation between Kelly Gibson and John McMillian before there was any point in raising the Northwest Pipeline name again with Bob Blair and Bob Pierce. This strategy took a bit of time. Meanwhile, Foothills made its official application to the National Energy Board for the Maple Leaf project on 20 March 1975.

With better preparation and the support of Kelly Gibson, the next meeting with John McMillian, Bob Blair and Bob Pierce was successful. Strange to relate, our Calgary partners became and remain fast friends with McMillian.

Northwest Pipeline Corporation officially became the extension of Foothills for the U.S. portion of the Alcan Project in May 1976, and their first application was filed with the Federal Power Commission in Washington in July. The package of regulatory applications was wrapped up neatly the next month when Foothills applied to the NEB for the Canadian portion of Alcan. We were now proposing one pipeline from Prudhoe Bay down the Alaska Highway to tie in with another from the Mackenzie delta, along the valley of the Mackenzie River. The original idea of tying our two existing systems together at the top was not achieved.

Complete regulatory applications were now in place in both countries. The final three combatants were Arctic Gas, Foothills and El Paso. The last mentioned project was for the LNG tanker route for Alaska gas only. The essential comparison to be made is thus between Arctic Gas and Foothills, being competing pipeline proposals for both Alaska and Canadian gas.

As to total resources that could be mustered, even a David and Goliath analogy would be an understatement. Foothills was a modest corporate partnership of two, relatively-small, regional pipelines. Arctic Gas, on the other hand, was a collection of the mightiest petroleum companies, pipelines and gas utilities in North America. Their roster included several of the Seven Sisters and a *Fortune* magazine list of the major pipelines and utilities. We were chided on one occasion that our entire group was smaller than the public-relations crew of Arctic Gas.

There was a flip side to this mismatch in size. Arctic Gas was huge, ponderous, expensive, inflexible, slow to react, totally predictable and influenced by too many partners with conflicting agendas. That is, their vertical organization of all sectors of the industry could not be harmonized. Foothills had the advantage of being a manageable size, inexpensive, flexible, quick to respond, unpredictable and having only two masters with identical agendas, along with an American pipeline associate that was an obliging one-man show.

In the give-and-take of the spirited hearings, it was most noticeable that Arctic Gas took weeks to respond to any important issue because of their unwieldy corporate structure. They had a step-ladder organization of committees, all of them sequentially being required to develop a policy position for consideration in New York by the executive group of a handful of major members. With Foothills, the response would be available later in the day or by the next morning because our major decisions were made, often by telephone, by an executive committee consisting of only four people—Bob Blair, Bob Pierce, Kelly Gibson and me. Fortunately, that committee was endowed with technical and operating experience in pipelines superior to that of the non-pipeliner senior executives of Arctic Gas meeting in New York.

The senior Arctic Gas counsel for the Canadian NEB hearings was Michael Goldie, whose vast experience in regulatory affairs was held in high regard. He paid an unintended compliment to the adroitness of Foothills when he made an opening statement one morning. He said: "Mr. Chairman and members, I have difficulty planning the case I wish to present today because I have not read the morning's *Globe and Mail* and have no idea what changes Foothills are going to make to their project today." He was to learn, to his dismay, that there would be constant nimble footwork by Foothills almost to the day of decision, mostly orchestrated by Ron Rutherford and the executive committee.

Comparing individual leadership, it was no contest in Canada. Bob Blair, with an outstanding career of pipeline experience, clearly surpassed Bill Wilder who was chairman of Arctic Gas. Wilder possessed impeccable connections with the Liberal party, which was perceived to be supporting that particular project. Similarly, he was an acknowledged expert in financial underwritings. However, he was out of his element in this sort of contest where the policy witnesses had to possess a high degree of technical expertise and knowledge of the project. On the other hand, the top leadership of Arctic Gas in the United States featured more experienced people, Bill Brackett of the Northwest Project Study Group especially, but the important decisions on route approval eventually were going to be determined by the National Energy Board in Canada.

Both contestants engaged qualified consultants for every discipline imaginable. With budget constraints, Foothills depended on just one or two experts in each field, whereas Arctic Gas were able to throw full teams into the debate. In the matter of numbers, the battery of lawyers employed by Arctic Gas was legion. More than their numbers, their individual reputations were intimidating. Possibly the best-known counsel in the U.S. on regulatory matters for pipelines and utilities, R. Clyde Hargrove, led the Arctic Gas legal contingent in Washington. He possessed a vast knowledge and an ego to match. In his pompous way, he seemed to forget that this case involved a cross-Canada pipeline. In possessive terms, he carelessly emphasized U.S. control when before the U.S. tribunal. We made sure that his arrogant posture did not wash in Canada before the NEB.

The Foothills lawyers were virtually unknown before the hearings, but they served us exceedingly well. Those of us who had to give months of testimony always were confident in the preparation they made, their leading of our evidence on the stand and their cross-examination of our competitors' submissions. Reg Gibbs from Calgary was our leading counsel in Canada. Jack Lutes from Vancouver, a lawyer formerly with Westcoast, was a specialist on technical questions of cost-of-service and rate structure. Both Reg and Jack represented us with distinction and greatly enhanced their professional reputations.

Securing legal counsel to represent us in the FPC hearings in Washington was a problem. So many applicants and intervenors were involved that all the skilled regulatory lawyers were directly engaged or had some other conflict. We finally selected a young lawyer, George McHenry, who had recently hung out his shingle, with his partner John Staffier, after serving in the legal department of the Federal Power Commission. He had to be the surprise of the entire contest. George blossomed like a desert rose with this opportunity of a lifetime. He worked at a relentless pace and his effectiveness became openly admired by counsel on the other side of the room.

Discussion of legal counsel is most relevant in any account of regulatory hearings. The quality of any proposal and the excellence of its witnesses can only win a case with skilful handling of the intricate process by the lawyers. As an indication of the amount of that talent required, John Anderson and I counted ninety-two men in the room we could identify as lawyers the day the hearings commenced in Ottawa. There were even more present on opening day in Washington.

Engineering talent should have been a persuasive factor in any assessment of the two groups. The engineers of Arctic Gas were numerous and very professional. However, they clearly were deficient in actual operating experience compared to the Foothills technical people. This is understandable because only AGTL and Westcoast had operated big-inch pipelines in the forbidding northern terrain. Westcoast, in particular, had built and operated pipelines through both muskeg and permafrost. When Administrative Law Judge Nahum Litt of the U.S. Federal Power Commission issued his decision, he commented that the engineering testimony by the Foothills and Westcoast experts was superior to any other he had heard.

Another telling difference between the two consortiums lay in the compensation arrangements for Foothills and Arctic Gas. The latter built a large corporate group of executives who had left their previous employment with the confident expectation of enjoying a lengthy and lucrative career with the new Arctic Gas pipeline as the winner. Bill Wilder, as chairman, had the capable assistance of Vern Horte as president. Vern was a knowledgeable pipeliner. He made a career gamble by resigning as president of TransCanada PipeLines to take the same position with Arctic Gas. The team of Wilder and Horte had no difficulty recruiting competent people in the industry, because the odds quoted for their success were very high.

Foothills wanted to demonstrate a different approach, hoping to indicate a combination of frugality and unselfish dedication. The four members of the executive committee all agreed not to take any salary, considering this particular task was covered in their regular compensation from their respective companies. To be totally factual, this account must indicate how this idealistic policy was later fractured. Kelly Gibson, like most observers in the industry, had difficulty seeing how the Foothills project had any hope of success. He told us early in the contest that he could not continue working for this unpromising cause without compensation. John Anderson and I agreed that a modest figure could be justified, if only to retain his condescending support.

Bob Blair was not keen about the recommendation in this respect but was typically accommodating. He agreed with my suggestion that he also take a modest salary, so that Kelly could be paid as vice-chairman. Bob explained that he would merely remit whatever he received from Foothills to Alberta Gas Trunk, his employer.

A banking dispute erupted during the NEB hearings. It had its beginnings in April 1973. After closing a routine public financing of $50 million for Westcoast's general purposes, Jack Smith, our young and exceedingly capable vice-president and chief financial officer, was planning to put the proceeds out on ninety-day loans. He invited six institutions to bid, the customary arrangement being that all would bid for the loan at the same specified time and the high bidder would be notified within minutes. When the bids arrived by telephone, they were reported to John Anderson who relayed them to Kelly. When he learned that the Royal Bank was in fifth spot, he ordered that nothing was to be decided that day. Early the next morning, Jack was summoned to Kelly's hotel suite to be presented with a new bid he had just received from the Royal Bank, quoted as of that hour for immediate response. That new bid was fractionally higher than the best one quoted the day before and Jack was instructed to place the $50 million proceeds with the Royal Bank.

Jack objected to this process, explaining that all bids of the previous day would likely be higher, because of the volatility of the money market. Kelly ordered him to place the business with the Royal Bank, regardless. Jack returned to the office to relate this experience to me. When I attempted to describe how this shifty manoeuvring of bids could damage our relations with the other financial institutions, Kelly seemed nonplussed. All he said was: "I don't understand why you're complaining that I used my connections to make a lot of money for the company."

A few years later, without reference to any of us, including the chief financial officer, Kelly arranged a substantial standby loan for Westcoast with the head office of the Royal Bank. He explained that he wanted to have this money available in case some good deal came along requiring action. When I commented that we could readily gain access to capital if needed without the additional interest expense of a standby loan, he countered: "The way you're spending money on that Foothills project, we'll need the loan sooner than you think." This loan did not fit the money-management program devised by Jack Smith. Jack explained that the standby loan was unnecessary and the standby charge was a budget burden. If Smith's professional sensitivity compelled him to take that position, it was nothing compared to the chairman's sensitivity to his rank as chairman. Kelly's displeasure with Westcoast's financial expert was soon manifested in an incident of far greater significance.

By this time, the NEB pipeline hearing had reached the stage where the senior financial witness for each applicant, together with the company's banker, was presenting evidence to affirm that bank financing would be available for the obligations to be undertaken. This presented a problem for Westcoast which troubled our partners and our legal counsel. The Royal Bank was Westcoast's only banker. They basically disqualified themselves in this particular case by being the principal supporter of Arctic Gas, giving evidence on their behalf on all financial considerations, not just loan accommodation. Foothills counsel refused to expose Jack Smith to cross-examination by Arctic Gas lawyers until Westcoast had support from a major bank. Our people claimed that our case would be severely damaged if one of the two Canadian partners had to admit that they did not have a formal arrangement with a banking institution for their share of the large Foothills project.

The Canadian Imperial Bank of Commerce had provided a battery of witnesses to buttress the Foothills case. Additionally, both the Bank of Nova Scotia and the Bank of Montreal were supporting AGTL as a partner in Foothills. Westcoast was an orphan, in this sense, without a bank. At our request, the Bank of Commerce were prepared to provide a witness to appear with Jack Smith. This banking accommodation was confined to the new pipeline project and had nothing to do with the regular banking business of Westcoast Transmission.

Jack reported to the Westcoast executive committee that the minor crisis had been solved by the cooperation of the Bank of Commerce. They had provided a letter of support to be entered as evidence. Kelly, a director of the Royal Bank, couldn't conceal his disapproval. He declared that Westcoast had only one banker and Jack was to destroy the Commerce letter. When the predicament of not having a banker to go on the witness stand was explained to Kelly, he said he would call Royal Bank chairman Earle McLaughlin, and the Royal Bank would do whatever we wanted. After lunch that day, he told me everything had been arranged with the Royal Bank chairman. We would receive a comfort letter in time for Jack's scheduled appearance on the stand. We were all relieved, particularly Jack Smith and our lawyers.

The next day the Vancouver branch of the Royal Bank telephoned to say that they had a letter they wanted to deliver personally. When I suggested they take it directly to Jack, they said it was necessary to see me because they had instructions from head office to charge a $50,000 fee for the comfort letter. I told them not to deliver the letter as I would prefer to have no formal knowledge of such an unacceptable demand. The reaction of the Vancouver representatives gave me some clue they were embarrassed about the fee for this modest accommodation by the bank that enjoyed 100 percent of our business. They explained that the amount had been negotiated between Mr. McLaughlin and Mr. Gibson. "In that case," I told them, "collect the $50,000 from Mr. Gibson. You won't get it from Westcoast Transmission."

There is a mysterious element in this happening which may never be explained. With great trepidation Jack was put on the stand to give evidence that Westcoast could indeed finance its portion of the project. He was the only financial witness standing naked without a banker. When cross-examination was invited, opposing counsel asked not a single question about the notable absence of support testimony from a bank. Our counsel could scarcely believe it when Jack was dismissed. We have a suspicion that the Royal

Bank, which had such powerful influence within Arctic Gas, had demanded of their counsel that Westcoast must not be embarrassed on this issue.

Later, the Vancouver executives of the Royal Bank were sincerely apologetic. Not long after that event, they voluntarily approached Jack Smith to suggest that the standby loan, arranged by Kelly some months earlier, be cancelled because they would have funds for us when needed, even on short notice.

Kelly Gibson's loyalty to the Royal Bank went beyond anything that institution would have expected from one of its directors. Nevertheless, he persisted and Jack Smith suffered some difficult times.

From the start of the partnership between Alberta Gas Trunk and Westcoast, it was agreed that Bob Blair would be the official spokesman to the media for Foothills. As I was on the stand on a regular basis, my public exposure increased. With the actual encouragement of our partners, on one occasion, I was advertised as the principal speaker in Toronto on the subject of the Alaska pipeline contest. Kelly claimed that was a breach of our agreement and ordered me to cancel my appearance. This embarrassed everybody concerned, particularly our hosts in Toronto. Bob Pierce covered for me by sending another speaker who read my prepared material.

At about the same time, Kelly received a telegram from David Waldon, the chairman of Interprovincial Pipeline, complaining about another of my speeches. Although Interprovincial was an important member of our competitor, Arctic Gas, Kelly did quite a job on me and declared again that I was to be muzzled except for formal appearances as a witness. I had to accept my boss's rigid command, but I did let him know that I thought he seemed to be forgetting who the enemy was in our struggle. To me, the problem was his difficulty in accepting my increasing prominence in this international affair.

When called upon to be policy witnesses, Bob Blair and Bob Pierce were superb anytime they took the stand. Bob Blair showed the best side of his showmanship when he appeared at a hearing in Washington, midway through the contest, dressed in an Indian buckskin jacket. This was quite appropriate because the thrust of the day's session had to do with native rights in the Yukon which posed much less of a problem than the same question in the Northwest Territories, where our competitor's interests were concentrated. Bob's costume seemed to give extra credibility to our presentation. The Yukon Indians who were present to hear one of their own representatives give evidence were most impressed with Bob in his colourful regalia.

Bob Blair outfitted himself for special effect on other occasions, but it did not always work as planned. For a pipeline speech in one of the remote northern communities, he looked like he was the groom at a frontier wedding. Fortunately, there was no television and the event was covered by only one small newspaper. Its account starting with: "Mr. Blair was elegant in a brilliant velvet suit and cowboy boots," continued with a favourable description of our dynamic leader, but reported very little about the pitch he made to impress the local people.

Because the media attention was understandably focused on our leader and spokesman, Bob Blair, his vice-president Bob Pierce constantly dwelt in his shadow. This may have been uncomfortable for him, yet there was no lack of loyalty, dedication or effectiveness. Pierce skilfully prepared most of the policy evidence. It was helpful that he had an uncanny ability to predict the peregrinations of the typical politician's or regulator's mind. He spent more time on the stand giving policy evidence than any of us, travelled the most and spent the most time in hearings or meetings. After any particular strategy had been determined, it was Bob Pierce, along with Ron Rutherford, who diligently coordinated most of the evidence to be provided by the experts in their various disciplines.

On one occasion in Washington, Bob Pierce was sitting with me in the audience when Judge Litt was presiding. On a question of international law, the judge observed that a Canadian lawyer was in the audience and he would like to have his advice. Judge Litt then asked Bob Pierce a fairly difficult question. Bob bluffed his way through that first question, commenting to me as he sat down that he was only guessing because he hadn't practised law for many years. The chairman seemed to appreciate the first answer so he asked Bob another which was even more difficult. Bob was clearly stumped and got out of it by remarking: "Your honour, if I am to continue giving legal advice, I would prefer to be put on the stand and be paid for my professional services." The whole room laughed and Judge Litt declined his offer.

John McMillian was quite different. He was not effective as a policy witness, but he took part on a regular basis, much to the poorly concealed chagrin of his supporting team. At the request of Bob Pierce, I spent a lot of time attending the FPC hearings in Washington. I saw John on the stand many times and I shuddered whenever he stepped up to the witness table. Opposing counsel had no difficulty with him. And his defence generally was a display of belligerence. One time, I heard him say: "This ain't no 'Onward Christian Soldiers' show; I'm going to build me a pipeline through Alaska no matter what all you smart lawyers think."

We all witnessed a similar episode before the NEB in Ottawa. Mike Goldie professionally but clearly exposed John's lack of knowledge about anything except generalities. I was sitting at the witness table near John and became concerned about how flushed he was, giving every indication of a blow-up. Then it happened. He partly rose from his seat, pressed against the edge of the table and stretched out his hand toward Goldie. He didn't advance beyond that mildly threatening pose but he did shout: "I didn't come all the way up here to Canada to listen to all your kind of lawyer talk. I've had all I want to hear from you."

This flare-up was the after-hours talk of the day because these proceedings generally are formal, tedious and boring. John's histrionics became more and more exaggerated as the tale was passed along. I was visiting Marshall Crowe in his office later that day and by that time the story was that John had actually scrambled over the desk and tried to grab Mike Goldie by the neck. Marshall was highly amused by the incident and was obviously disappointed when I toned it down to merely a gesture.

Time and time again, evidence given by John McMillian had to be repaired by our subsequent witnesses. I will recite one example that never was effectively neutralized. Without our concurrence, he emphatically declared on the stand that the U.S. portion of the Alcan Project could be financed without any government assistance. This startled us simply because we didn't believe it. When we challenged John privately, he quoted the advice of the head of a New York investment firm. We weren't impressed by that particular individual, nor were First Boston, our financial advisors, who had earlier refused to give evidence that the U.S. project definitely would not need public assistance.

As far as the Foothills project in Canada was concerned, our supporting bankers and financial institutions had demonstrated that we could finance our part of the pipeline, and we so testified. Our difficulty now became to avoid public disclosure that we and our U.S. associate were split on this very important issue. We were constantly stickhandling our way through tough cross-examination on this aspect both in Ottawa and Washington. In the end, we were more than correct. John McMillian eventually persuaded the three producers in Alaska to provide financing for 30 percent of the project. He admitted he needed 40 percent from them to justify going for a government aid package, but that question was not resolved before the entire project went on hold.

John McMillian was not our greatest witness, but he was unsurpassed as a host for late-night parties after our strategy and testimony had been planned for the next day's session. He had a permanent suite in the Watergate Hotel and was generous in using it to entertain us. He also knew the finest restaurants in town and the maître d's all seemed to know him and his wife, who was making good use of her time in Washington by attending a school for artists.

Twice, Foothills had jolts of downright good luck. The first occurred as soon as the hearings opened in Ottawa on 12 April 1976 with Marshall Crowe as chairman of the hearing panel. As the former chairman of Canada Development Corporation, a member of Arctic Gas, Crowe had participated in many decisions of the applicant now appearing before him. Also, and much less importantly, there had been some idle gossip about Crowe having gone on a fishing trip with a group that included an official from Arctic Gas. This all seemed very innocent to us but Arctic Gas were obviously disturbed enough to question the propriety of Crowe being chairman.

Foothills could not believe what was being suggested and most of the intervenors were dumbfounded by Arctic Gas challenging the acceptability of a chairman with the outstanding reputation as a public servant enjoyed by Marshall Crowe. As I recall, the legal expression was that he should step down for "reasonable apprehension of bias." I suppose that meant he was not being charged with actual bias but merely a certain concern about bias being alleged later. To me, it sounded like legal lingo for the strategy of preventing the other guy from crying foul after he loses the fight.

Mike Goldie, as lead counsel for Arctic Gas in Canada, stated his client's request for Crowe's withdrawal in very measured terms. Admiring Goldie as we did, it was difficult for us to comprehend him making a strategy move of this extreme importance and potential damage. I have no direct knowledge, naturally, of the deliberations that led to this tactical decision. The rumour throughout the hearing was that Goldie was quite opposed to this strategy but was overruled by the Arctic Gas executive committee in New York together with their U.S. counsel. Supposedly, they were confident they were going to win the case and they wanted to be sure that Foothills would have no avenue of appeal, such as charging the chairman with bias. Foothills and most of the intervening companies and public interest groups argued against his removal. The Canadian Arctic Resources Committee thought he should step down on the basis of his being interested in some of the important early decisions of Arctic Gas.

A long legal battle ensued, right up to the Supreme Court of Canada, where three justices ordered Crowe's removal. After he stepped down, Geoffrey Edge assumed the chair. At that time, Edge was associate vice-chairman of the NEB. The other panel members were J. G. Stabback, associate vice-chairman, and R. F. Brooks, a board member.

Something we will never know is the degree of humiliation suffered by this distinguished person. In Marshall Crowe's shoes, I would have been disillusioned and bitter; but I do not have that gentleman's poise.

Just as Fortune smiled on us at the opening, she gave us a most bountiful blessing near the end of the hearings. Justice Thomas

Berger published an elaborate report on his environmental investigation and findings. The bottom line was recommendation of a ten-
year moratorium on pipeline construction in the Mackenzie valley
and a permanent ban on crossing the delicate north slope of the Yukon and Alaska, through a national wildlife range. This meant the
end of the Maple Leaf portion of the Foothills project which was to
pick up gas reserves from the Mackenzie delta. But it virtually
anointed our Alcan or Alaska Highway route to move Alaska gas
from Prudhoe Bay to the lower forty-eight states.

To look behind the scenes of the Berger Report, I will have to re-
sort more to opinion than to factual knowledge. Foothills laboured
throughout the contest under the impression that the Liberal government and its department of energy strongly favoured the Arctic
Gas proposal. If that assessment were true, we have to ask what odd
stroke of genius led the government to appoint Justice Berger for
this task. He was known to have keenly developed sensitivities to
the environment and native rights. Others subsidized by the government in this fashion at the same time, such as NDP strategist
Mel Watkins, had similar environmental inclinations. Why would
they be commissioned when a negative report on the Mackenzie
River valley was almost sure to evolve? Foothills is confident that
the NEB would have reached the same final decision as to the pipeline route, with or without the Berger report, but realistically we
have to feel that Fate in some way favoured our success. Activist
groups sponsored by the Roman Catholic, Anglican and United
churches also contributed to the embargo on the Mackenzie River
valley as an energy corridor.

The redoubtable Stuart Hodgson, Commissioner of the Northwest Territories, was an advocate of strategic development in the
arctic that would be beneficial to his territory and its native citizens. A properly regulated petroleum industry met his publicized
personal criteria, including a pipeline in the Mackenzie River
valley.

A mutual friend told me that the energetic commissioner was agitated by the story that Justice Berger was appointed by Prime Minister Trudeau on the advice of Jack Austin, deputy minister of energy. He could foresee Berger's recommendations and didn't like

the picture at all. When the final report confirmed Hodgson's fore-
boding, his agitation turned to outrage, I was told. He was not concerned about the permanent ban on a pipeline across the environmentally tender north slope, but he thought that the ten-year moratorium for the Mackenzie River valley was preposterous.

Soon after the colourful Berger report was circulated, another
publication started appearing in politicians' offices all over North
America. It was a blistering and knowledgeable rebuttal of Justice
Berger's conclusions. I do not know who financed it, but there was
a certain Hodgson imprint on its punch. When the Alaska Highway pipeline project is revived, with a connection to the gas reserves in the Northwest Territories, I hope that Stuart Hodgson is
standing beside me to hear that announcement.

For the benefit of our preferred Alaska Highway route, Foothills
had great support from Art Pearson, commissioner of the Yukon.
We met with him frequently and he took the trouble to travel to
Vancouver several times to be brought up to date. Pearson also fa-
cilitated our successful negotiations with the powerful Council for
Yukon Indians.

Busy as I was with strategy issues, monitoring the hearings and my
own testimony and lobbying efforts, in mid-1976 I became the pro-
tagonist in a hazardous, but in retrospect humorous, diversion.
Early one morning before breakfast, I received a telephone call in
my hotel room in Montreal, where I was visiting on routine pipeline business, from a man with a slightly nervous and agitated
voice. He ordered me to return to Vancouver immediately to receive a message recorded on tape explaining how I could save my
own life and avoid the Westcoast pipeline or one of its compressor
stations being blown up. Just like in the movies, he warned that his
plan would be put into immediate action if I went to the police, and
demanded that Westcoast pay him $1 million. I tried to keep him
on the telephone long enough for Jack Smith to appear at my door,
so that at least two of us would hear the voice and double our
chances of recognition. He was too smart for that and hung up.

I waited until eight o'clock Vancouver time to phone John Anderson, asking him to notify the police and check my mail for the

tape. Sure enough, the tape had arrived and John telephoned to outline the instructions. I was ordered to deliver $1 million to an identified go-between in Prince George within three days or there would be an explosion somewhere on the pipeline and I would also be a victim. The tape had arrived wrapped in a $100 bill. The bizarre accompanying explanation was that this would pay for the long distance calls that had been charged to a Westcoast number in some fashion. That was an odd twist, according to the police, but I did not think $100 was a very big investment for a million-dollar pay-off.

The RCMP assigned two senior officers from their serious-crimes squad. They were annoyed that John had opened the tape, exposing himself to the risk of an explosion. Their first reaction was that this was an inside job by someone having access to a Westcoast telephone in Prince George. I hustled home to be met by the Mounties and taken to the office to be told my part their investigation. This was shaping up to be a stimulating relief from the pressures of life in the executive suite until they said they wanted to wire me for sound and have me meet the designated intermediary. Rather than witnessing a television drama, I was going to be real live bait in a trap.

The tape recording was a long diatribe about big business not doing enough to combat drugs. Specifically, the voice said that his son had died of drugs at the age of twenty-one and he was going to use the $1 million from Westcoast in a personal campaign against drug abuse. He had some knowledge of pipeline operations because he described how vulnerable we were in so many locations.

The RCMP voice experts analyzed the tape thoroughly. They determined the voice was of a man about fifty-five years of age, medium build, Anglo-Saxon heritage, likely born in Canada, with a grade-ten education, and had likely progressed from a labouring job to the rank of supervisor or foreman. Of most significance to me, they were certain this was no hoax and he was deadly serious. We responded immediately with some discreet security measures, but full protection of 2,700 miles of pipeline would be impossible even if we called out every soldier and boy scout in Canada. As to the caller, the best we could do was refer to him as the "Voice."

With the two police present, I reached the intermediary by telephone and arranged to meet him in the lobby of a Prince George hotel the next day. He was expecting my call but his voice was extremely nervous. Clearly, he was agreeing to deal with me under extreme duress.

With one policeman beside me, one in front of me and one in the row behind on the plane ride to Prince George the next morning, I felt more secure than the time I had sat across the aisle from Margaret Trudeau and her security people on a trip from Ottawa to Vancouver. My escorts described the security arrangements at the Prince George airport, assuring me that the crowd was under surveillance by several more plain-clothes Mounties. After arrival, I was taken to some unidentified spot and stripped to the waist to be strapped with batteries and transmitting equipment. A switch was on my belt under my vest and a trial signal was sent to an unmarked car out on the street manned by local officers. They signalled that all was okay, so I called a cab for the hotel.

As I had been instructed, I tried out the equipment as soon as I entered the lobby so that the unmarked police car down the street could tune for the best reception. For some reason or other, likely nervousness and concentrating on Mounties, I whistled a few bars of "Rose Marie." I was told later that the local Mountie in the radio car who had not met me said, "What's with this character, he deserves to be shot."

Within a minute or so my designated contact came down the stairs to the lobby. He looked the part of a real thug and I sensed he was my man immediately. In my three-piece dark suit, I stood out like a priest at an Orangemens' parade, so he was just as quick to recognize me. When I acknowledged my name was Phillips, he invited me to the bar for a drink. Being mid-afternoon, we were the only people in a dark and dingy bar, except one waiter and a bartender. My repulsive companion ordered a double rye on the rocks; I asked if I might have a Dubonnet. Again, I was told later that when that came over the radio, the local cop exclaimed: "That Vancouver guy can't be for real, they don't have any Dubonnet in that bar."

Our taped conversation lasted about twenty-five minutes. I attempted to get the name of the Voice, which was futile. I asked the Thug to go with me to the police because we were both in trouble and needed protection from the Voice. The Mounties had suggested to me that this man was likely under heavy blackmail pressure, possibly in a murder case, from the person who sent the tape and had no choice but to perform this dangerous mission. Actually, he was more nervous than I. Dressed in a denim jacket and jeans, without a shirt or undershirt, he was sweating buckets. I was perspiring enough to be relieved I had applied twenty-four protection that morning.

Eventually he revealed his concern. He was certain I was a hitman from the mob in Vancouver. He offered me $5,000 in cash on the spot if I would give him a day's head start to drive for the hills in his pick-up. I tried to convince him that I was not involved in crime, and I realize how ridiculous it must have seemed when I handed him my business card as assurance. He slapped the card on the table as if he had just drawn a ten to a deuce and another ten in his hand. When I persisted that we both should to go the police, he growled: "One word to the police and I'll be tits up." Asked what that meant, he elaborated: "You know, man, flat out on a marble slab with my tits up."

When I repeated that we were both in serious trouble with the Voice and should get out of that man's control, he became almost angry, claiming I did not understand what we were dealing with. With that, he opened his jacket and showed me a wound in the fatty flesh just above his right hip. He said he had an argument with the Voice three days before and had been shot. Whether he had or not, I cannot judge, but the ugly looking wound penetrated from the front to the back, indicating passage of a bullet just as he explained. I asked why the wound was not dressed, to which he replied he could never go to the hospital with a bullet wound; he took a room in the hotel and treated himself for three days.

All I got from him was an indication that he had met the Voice years ago on a construction job. Other bits and pieces of the conversation led the police to believe the Voice may have been a shop steward or a union organizer. Finally, I told the man I could not take his money and certainly couldn't promise him any protection.

We parted with my advice that he go to the police and with his final request that I take his $5,000 and let him hit the hills.

Stepping out to the street, I flagged a cab with a woman driver. The door had hardly closed when she asked if I was busy that night, emphasizing that she looked pretty good when she was dolled up. I had forgotten to switch off the microphone which meant the police car was still recording the conversation. Next, she said older men seemed to think she was pretty nice. I didn't care to have it recorded for the world to hear that this over-the-hill bimbo had sized me up as an old man. In any case, the hilarious solicitation continued until she dropped me off at the rendezvous spot with the police.

When I finally met the local cop, he was still laughing about "Rose Marie," the Dubonnet, the business card and the cabby hooker. He said he was still not sure his police buddies from Vancouver were not putting him on with the whole episode and suggested that the Prince George detachment could not use me for any more investigative work unless I changed my drinking habits. He didn't know that Frank McMahon had hired me over a Dubonnet, and if my career was coming to an abrupt end it might as well be celebrated with the same drink.

The police then explained that they knew the Thug very well. He was a crook who ran the serious gambling in that area and his joint was a focal point of drugs. They were not anxious to put him in jail because surveillance of his moves gave them a lot of information about the arrival of narcotics and other local criminal activities. The wild part of the story is that he had gone to the local Mounties for protection from me. He told them he was meeting a hit-man from the Vancouver mob, so the police assured him they would protect him in the bar by having one Mountie act as a waiter and another as the bartender. I still do not know how to react to the knowledge that two policemen were required to protect a menacing, overweight thug from a little guy like me in a three-piece suit.

The next strategy was for the police to tail the Thug to see if he would come back for another meeting. Sure enough, he had headed for the hills. I was put up in a hotel for the night and offered a gun to put under my pillow. I refused the armament with the explanation I would likely do more damage to myself if I were disturbed in the night and tried to use it. As a compromise, I stayed wired for sound that night and the Mounties slept in rooms on either side, both with radio receivers. They complained I snored.

The Thug never reappeared, so the police had me put an advertisement in the personal column explaining the rendezvous did not work and I required further instructions from the Voice. Nothing resulted.

A security guard was posted at my home around the clock for about two months. During that same period, all telephone calls were taped and the police required me to record all my hotel telephone calls when I was travelling. Nothing happened. After about a year, the RCMP sergeant told me the case had not been dropped but the investigation had produced no solid clues and was not very active. The $100 bill is still locked in the file.

As the seriousness of this episode passed, my nickname around the office became Inspector Clouseau. Admittedly, I have never whistled "Rose Marie" since that time, but I still enjoy a Dubonnet now and again. And I learned a lot about Prince George. A three-piece blue suit in that town will get you $5,000 cash and a date for the night. I solemnly declare that I have never returned to claim either. But if I retrieve that $100 bill, it goes for a case of Dubonnet.

····5····

FOOTHILLS
VICTORY

Prior to this writing, only a handful of people have had any
knowledge of a secret pact proposed during the pipeline hearings
that could have resulted in a unified project and a cease-fire in the
heated competitive shoot-out. That it was not successful does not
take away from the significance of the fact that some of the parties
were willing to cooperate sensibly in order to bring an end to the
immensely expensive regulatory battle in both countries, which ultimately cost scores of millions of dollars and years of senior executives' time.

In mid-1975, Ron Rutherford and I developed the plan that
eventually gained the personal approval of Bob Blair, Kelly Gibson,
John McMillian and even our opponent Travis Petty from El Paso.
To bring it all together, we then only required an understanding
with a key member of Arctic Gas. We selected TransCanada Pipe-
Lines as the target simply because of their perfect fit in the visual-
ized merger. To judge the boldness of this move, it is important to
remember that Bob Blair had angrily withdrawn from the original
Arctic Gas consortium. He was now willing to rejoin them, with an
olive branch, confident the proper amount of Canadian control
could now be achieved.

We reasoned that whatever pipeline project gained approval to bring arctic gas to market would be so huge that all of the contestants would ultimately have a part of it, and the resources of all would be required to finance it. After all, this was not a dispute about which gas producers would be winners and which would be losers. Nor did it concern any conflicting interest among the gas-utility distributors. Hence, why the big fight if the ownership of the pipeline connecting the wellheads with the city gates could be carved up equitably? It was essentially a pipeline-transmission battle.

We judged that Travis Petty would be a key pipeline executive who could safely be approached without prejudice. He personally felt more inclined to pipeline transmission, even though his company, El Paso, had proposed to move the Alaskan reserves by LNG tanker. We discussed with him the equity share he could have in the pipeline through Alaska with our U.S. associate, Northwest Pipeline Corporation. After much consideration, he informed us confidentially that he would be willing to make a deal and settle for that share to compensate for giving up El Paso's LNG proposal. We sensed that El Paso was tiring of the great expense of the adversarial FPC hearings and could recognize that their chances of success were diminishing.

The El Paso tentative accommodation having been put in place, the next piece of the puzzle for a solid truce would be TransCanada. They would be offered an equitable share of the Canadian segment of the pipeline with the Foothills partners, AGTL and Westcoast.

Other than being asked to deal with Bob Blair, the unpopular dissident of their original group, the gas-producer members of Arctic Gas would not be affected one way or the other by the eventual ownership of the pipeline. Similarly, the distribution-utility members of Arctic Gas would receive their gas requirements at the same price and quantity, regardless of the pipeline ownership. For the undeniable benefit of all, there obviously would be a shorter hearing, earlier decision and accelerated commencement of cash flow.

Ron Rutherford travelled to Connecticut, Detroit, Chicago and other cities where he had personal friends in the lower echelons of Arctic Gas participants. His discreet enquiries about a truce were abruptly turned aside. In addition to that negative response, the rivalry between Foothills and TransCanada PipeLines was so intense that we realized a direct approach about joining forces would be treated only with suspicion, if not disdain. We decided that some trustworthy and totally neutral intermediary would be essential to convey our secret message to TransCanada about a possible ceasefire. The definite risk would be TransCanada revealing this approach as a way of embarrassing Foothills in the hearings; an admission of weakness, so to speak. We concluded that the proper person for this delicate mission would be Norman Chappell, energy expert at the Canadian Embassy in Washington, D.C.

During the FPC hearings we had regularly visited Norman Chappell to keep him fully informed of all developments as we analyzed them. The other parties involved in the hearings similarly confided in this popular Canadian official. We trusted him totally because he never gave the slightest hint of what he was hearing from the others, giving us confidence that our intelligence was not being disclosed either. Chappell understood the aspirations of all the players intimately. Further, he had mentioned his concern that the decision process was taking too long and the desired economic benefit to Canada was being delayed.

We spent many sessions with Chappell and his staff members, Bob Blackburn, Bruce Watson and Trish Lorte. We gave them a thorough understanding of what we were attempting to accomplish with this mid-hearing truce. Chappell was very cautious and made it his business to determine whether El Paso was truly ready to make a deal which did seem somewhat incredible to him, given the aggressive way they were still fighting their own case for LNG transport. He found out, as we had known, that there was a philosophical conflict within the El Paso organization about the decision to use ocean tankers as opposed to their core business of overland pipelining.

Eventually, Chappell informed us that his staff's intelligence on this question had been submitted to Ottawa. He naturally declined to give any indication about the report's contents or conclusion, but it was obvious he was not expecting to play any personal role beyond that stage. After a few weeks, Ron and I were called to the embassy to be informed that we could safely go to Ottawa and outline our proposition to an official in the energy department named Bill Hopper. In August 1975, I presented myself to Bill, whom I had come to know when I served on the energy minister's National Advisory Committee on Petroleum. He was most cordial and receptive, but somewhat incredulous about our idealistic scheme of putting five fighting tomcats into the same bag, TransCanada, AGTL, Westcoast, El Paso and Northwest.

I enjoyed my visit with Bill Hopper on that mission, although I instinctively felt it was inconclusive. Similar to many Ottawa officials, he likely felt that TransCanada as part of Arctic Gas was a sure winner and didn't need to cut any deal with Foothills. On the basis of his frequent references to Kelly Gibson and how much Kelly was respected by energy minister Donald Macdonald, I told Ron Rutherford later that our mistake was in not having Kelly take our unusual plan to Hopper. Ron did not agree. He felt that the mission was so delicate it was necessary the message be carried by the person who had talked directly to the other parties involved and was intimately associated with the complex variety of corporate interests that would have to be satisfied. Whatever the reason, the idea died in Ottawa and we continued the expensive and exhaustive regulatory battle.

It is quite possible that the embassy in Washington advised Ottawa that this proposition was too hot to handle. I have never enquired and do not intend to use the freedom-of-information procedure for a pointless investigation. Why would I take the risk of discovering that Norm Chappell, Bob Blackburn or Bill Hopper thought I was a crackpot? Emotionally, I feel a profound opportunity for enlightened corporate cooperation was missed. But, selfishly, I am glad the hearings continued to the end because Foothills ended up better off than if the secret merger plan had worked.

Gradually, some observers began to concede that we might have a chance of winning. To my knowledge, the first financial institution to form that opinion was Quebec's Caisse de Dépôt. After spending considerable time with us in Vancouver, on one occasion, the Caisse's next stop was the office of Norcen in Toronto. That company had a major investment in this venture as an important member of the Arctic Gas consortium. Shortly after that meeting, Norcen's chairman, Ed Bovey, telephoned me to say he was stunned to be told by this important financial institution that Foothills looked like the winner. He wanted to know, in a friendly way, what we had told them that produced that conclusion. Although he was a good friend, I didn't help him much, replying, "We didn't knock your project, we merely described Foothills, and the conclusion was obvious."

Throughout the representations to the FPC, the American Gas Association in the United Sates maintained a cautious, neutral position. However, just before the Washington hearings concluded, Bud Lawrence, the president of the AGA, dropped just the slightest hint to me that he thought this contest would be settled by essentially a Canadian decision and Foothills had an advantage in its pedigree. Bud had to be diplomatic in this observation because the principals in Arctic Gas were members of his association, while Foothills was not.

We came to feel that the Canadian Gas Association was indirectly supportive of Arctic Gas, though it did not take any formal position. The president of Pacific Petroleums, Merrill Rasmussen, and I were both on the board of the Canadian Gas Association during the pipeline duel. We had a number of unpleasant sessions attempting to keep the association neutral. The CGA membership roster was dominated by the members of the Arctic Gas consortium and its leaning to that project seemed to surface in a number of ways. Most offensive to us was their inaccurate projection that gas reserves from the Mackenzie delta were urgently required in central Canada and that Ontario's users had to be served by accelerating the approval of the pipeline along the Mackenzie River valley. Their subjective picture of depleting Alberta gas reserves and their faulty market forecast were distributed widely while the NEB hearing was in progress. John Anderson and I had an opportunity to give evidence to a House of Commons committee that the CGA study had widely missed the mark on their low estimate of available Alberta natural-gas supply. The fact that Mackenzie delta gas is still not required for the Canadian market more than a decade later confirms the inaccuracy of the CGA's low estimate of reserves in the traditional producing areas of Alberta and British Columbia.

In February 1977, Judge Litt released his recommendation to the Federal Power Commission. He rated Arctic Gas the best proposal and gave El Paso second place. Foothills was ranked third, but his comments were so derogatory he certainly would have placed us lower had there been any others in the race. We were initially discouraged but soon recognized the report's unreasonably negative tone toward the only Canadian-controlled project was a decisive miscue that we could exploit on our home ground. The NEB hearings were still in progress in Ottawa, so we had time to devise a new strategy; actually, more time than required by an instant strategist like Ron Rutherford.

Judge Litt hammered us for the system design of lower pressure and smaller pipe diameter than advocated by Arctic Gas. He highlighted a number of other Arctic Gas advantages in his reasons for decisions. We were confident that these so-called advantages were unduly expensive and their costs had been underestimated—lowballed, in other words. We simply reasoned that if that is the type of pricey pipeline the U.S. is willing to pay for, that's the type of pipeline we can build.

Accordingly, within a mere twenty-five calendar days Foothills filed a redesigned project. Because Judge Litt liked the Arctic Gas higher-pressure pipeline of forty-eight inches diameter, we designed a new one of fifty-six inches. Try topping that! Our amended application was complete with the required changes in pipeline location and design, and a new configuration of compressor-station power selection and location. Also provided were new cost estimates. This required a herculean effort by all the Foothills staff, but they had become accustomed to this type of work demand and were quite able to perform. So, with the expenditure of a great deal of effort and not very much money, we gave our project the classy new name of the "fifty-six-inch express system." These were times when multi-talented engineers like Bill Deyell, Ron Rutherford, Don Olafson, John Burrell, Al Green, Jack Kavanagh, Harvey Permack, Ed Mirosh, Wally Kosten and others showed their mettle.

The redesign would have a beneficial economic impact for Canadian suppliers, principally in the increased tonnage of steel pipe required and all the necessary ancillary equipment and hardware that would be manufactured domestically. It was calculated that the Canadian steel mills could produce 1.55 million tons of fifty-six-inch diameter pipe. That production was valued at $2 billion for the mills. The rated capacity of the new express system was 3.3 billion cubic feet per day. This represented a mammoth movement of energy, roughly equivalent to 550,000 barrels of oil per day.

That agile footwork promptly paid off. Judge Litt's damaging recommendation had been submitted to the Federal Power Commission in Washington on 1 February. Our fifty-six-inch express system was put on display on 25 February. On 1 May, the chairman and vice-chairman of the U.S. FPC recommended acceptance of the new Foothills express system. The other two commissioners stayed with Judge Litt's original preference for Arctic Gas. All four of them agreed that a pipeline system was superior to El Paso's LNG ocean-tanker project. With that even-split position in the controlling regulatory body in the United States, it was clear that our full attention could be given to the NEB hearings. Our destiny would now be settled in Canada, just where we wanted it.

The Westcoast annual meeting in the spring of 1977 was an important occasion for me because of the crucial timing with respect to the Alaska Highway pipeline. Judge Litt of the U.S. Federal Power Commission had just recommended acceptance of the American-controlled Arctic Gas project and scathingly denounced our Foothills plan. Justice Berger's environmental report was expected the next month; and the NEB hearings in Canada were drawing to a close.

Judge Litt's report revealed his singular concern for U.S. interests, which was to be expected. However, our Foothills executive committee decided that a stronger message on Canada's national interest had to be delivered before the hearings terminated in Ottawa. I agreed to make a hard-hitting speech at our annual meeting. My material was reviewed in detail by our partners and by John Anderson, Jack Smith and Art Willms, Westcoast's division manager of gas supply and sales. With a number of additions and modifications it was approved as just the type of information the Canadian public must receive at this juncture. I did not submit this speech to Kelly, knowing he would object on the basis that Foothills business was not an acceptable subject for a Westcoast annual meeting. Also, he would have warned me that my audience would include at least three oil-company executives from the U.S.A.

My half-hour presentation was titled "Canada's Energy Sovereignty." I began:

"Today I am compelled to be unhappily negative in order to expose a threat we see to Canada's national interest—the spectre of our country losing control of its own energy destiny in the north. If you think this is unduly alarmist, consider this testimony by R. Clyde Hargrove, counsel for the Arctic Gas Project, given before a U.S. Congressional House Committee hearing on February 17, 1977":

> Mr. Hargrove: Now the upshot of this is that regardless of which route is selected, that project is going to be owned on an equity basis and controlled by the majority of the shippers who are shipping gas through it. It is not going to be an El Paso Project; it is not going to be a Northwest Pipeline Project; it is not necessarily even going to be an Arctic Gas Project. It is going to be a project managed by the shippers who buy the gas. Now, if that pattern obtains which has been indicated in earlier contracts which were dismissed because of certain advance payments restrictions, and you include the recently announced tentative sales of Alaska royalty gas, the eight U.S. companies comprising the Arctic Gas Consortium will have . . . voting control of any project that is put through.

> Mr. Roncalio: Of any of the three projects that may be put through?

> Mr. Hargrove: Yes sir. Because we the shippers have to finance it.

I continued: "The transcript . . . leaves no doubt as to the totality of the United States control envisaged by Arctic Gas. Quite obviously, that is not how Arctic Gas describes the control of their project when giving evidence this side of the border. The public of Canada will have to decide whether or not that exceedingly candid

Arctic Gas statement about United States control sounds like the voice of a neighbour who will be truly grateful for the privilege of a 2,200 mile short cut across Canada for a United States pipeline.

"As to a grand design for a future international energy-sharing policy, Mr. Hargrove's lofty language discloses that ambition of their international but U.S.-controlled pipeline in Canada. He testified before the Federal Power Commission on April 8, 1977 as follows":

> But, far more important was the total theory that this project, whatever it may be, when it is completed, when it is in operation, this is the path to the north, this is the Arctic, and this is it, probably for good, for the transmission of energy to the entire North American continent north of the Rio Grande.

Warming to my subject, I declared: "Linking together those two statements, Canadians in all provinces may consider it presumptuous for a U.S. spokesman to assert that the only pipeline to be permitted into the Canadian Mackenzie delta gas fields 'probably for good' should be an international pipeline controlled by eight United States companies."

Later in my speech, when explaining that it would be preferable to have a Canadian-controlled pipeline going into our arctic region rather than one owned by eight U.S. companies having the privilege of dipping into the Mackenzie delta gas fields to share that valuable Canadian energy resource, I said: "I would sooner share a milkshake with King Kong."

Because of the personal respect I had for our Canadian competitors, I included this statement: "Let me emphasize, I do not attribute any sinister or disloyal intent to the Canadian members of the Arctic Gas consortium. Their pipeline concept had some apparent practicality when originally proposed about ten years ago; but the passage of time and dramatically changed circumstances (mainly disappointing delta discoveries, improved Alberta gas supply and the native land claims) created the serious international conflict of interest they could not have anticipated."

The thrust of my speech was not to oppose the proper sale of Canadian gas to the United States. After all, that was Westcoast's livelihood. It was to warn against the threat of a U.S. continental energy-sharing policy that would manifestly interfere with Canada's own energy destiny in the North. I concluded with the following statement of our company's posture:

"Consistent with Westcoast Transmission's special sensitivity to the gas-supply crisis of our best trading partner, we will maintain an aggressive posture in urging Canadian authorities to adopt two basic concepts:

1. Canada should respond with all neighbourliness and diligence to the U.S. gas crisis by accommodating their Alaska gas with a practical, NEB-regulated, treaty-protected, transportation system across Canada, following established corridors wherever possible, with the Canadian segments being owned and operated by Canadian companies.
2. Canada should encourage accelerated exploration in the delta and press on, without any avoidable delay, to determine the best way to move delta gas to Canadian markets. The pipeline must be planned along the right route, at the right size and for the right time, as determined solely for Canada's national interest."

The few Americans in the audience did not praise my reference to King Kong. However, they agreed that it was a forceful presentation which had to be made, acknowledging that they had no idea that the pipeline competing with us in Canada would be controlled entirely by eight U.S. companies. On the other hand, the Canadians enjoyed the speech and the media coverage was extensive, and there were media reruns after Foothills distributed about 2,000 copies of the talk across the country. Some portions found their way into our counsel's closing argument and rebuttal at the National Energy Board hearing. In the judgement of our partners, particularly Bob Blair and Bob Pierce, the speech they had helped to prepare was a strategic success. Westcoast's directors reappointed me president and CEO that afternoon.

On 9 May 1977, Justice Thomas Berger's report was issued. The NEB hearing concluded on 12 May.

During July, two strong expressions of support arose in the United States that were both unexpected and most welcome. The U.S. President's Council on Environmental Quality advised President Carter that our Alaska Highway pipeline project was the environmentally preferable route, largely because it would not cross the fragile north slope of Alaska as would Arctic Gas. Key U.S. federal agencies, including the department of the interior and the department of transport, also reported to President Carter that the Alaska Highway project was environmentally superior and the most economical and reliable.

Nothing can describe the deep emotional satisfaction and personal reward that engulfed all of us on 4 July 1977. Whether that date, with its historical significance of the independence of the United States, was selected on purpose or by accident does not matter. It was a day to mark a Canadian victory over a U.S.-led consortium that was the underdog upset of the decade. On that great day, the National Energy Board recommended government acceptance of the Alaska Highway pipeline project of Foothills, with route changes and other conditions. The board rejected the Arctic Gas application, calling it "totally unacceptable" environmentally. The reference to "route changes and other conditions" underlined the ability of Foothills to outmanoeuvre its giant competitor.

The scene in the NEB hearing room when the final decision was announced would have done credit to a Hollywood production. Reading of the comments leading to the decision took a long time, the suspense building without any early indication of who the winner would be. After about twenty minutes, there were two successive comments about the environment that gave me a clue that was sufficient enough for me to reach over and shake hands with both Bob Blair and Ron Rutherford to congratulate them. A few minutes later the punchline was delivered and a small proportion of the room erupted as though the Stanley Cup had just been won by an underdog hockey team from the West. The majority in attendance were dejected and slowly filed out of the room, understandably very disappointed. I endeavoured to reach some of my friends from the other side but only succeeded in shaking hands with a couple before they all disappeared. We were told later that they had prepared an elaborate victory party which would now be the most expensive wake of the year.

Slipping into a room to shake hands with some celebrating intervenors, I overheard the funniest remark of the day. It concerned two key personalities: Michael Goldie and Bill Wilder.

As evidence of our grudging admiration for these two fine men, we used our idle time gossiping about them, as I am sure they discussed our idiosyncrasies. In particular, we envied tall and handsome Mike Goldie and his extensive wardrobe. But his Saville Row suit jackets always seemed too tight and the pants too short. With debonair Bill Wilder, it was his haircuts that intrigued us. The top was as short as a Marine's and it appeared that the barber gave him a side scalping above the ears every Friday.

A Calgary lawyer, Jack Smith, had silently attended every hearing session without uttering a single word in twenty months. He was merely monitoring the proceedings on behalf of an intervenor. When asked if he had learned anything from this agonizing vigil, he replied: "All of the time was worth the tiresome effort even though I learned only two very valuable things: at all costs, to avoid Mike Goldie's tailor and Bill Wilder's barber."

Our victory celebrations had commenced in an Ottawa hotel before I found time to phone my long-time friend Dic Doyle, then editor of the Toronto *Globe and Mail*. Dic was incredulous and I distinctly recall him saying: "This is the most remarkable regulatory decision I have ever heard. It has recommended granting a permit to a company with a different name than the applicant, for a route it did not propose, and for a system design it did not include in its application. I can't believe it." *The Globe and Mail* had tried to beat the pack by forecasting the winner in their 3 July edition, the day before the NEB decision. Under bold headlines, a feature story by Jeff Carruthers speculated that Arctic Gas would be victorious. The reporter must have received contradictory intelligence later that day because the next morning's paper hedged their bet.

The dramatic arctic pipeline contest had been won by Foothills after several years of hard work by people who managed their regular jobs at the same time, so consideration of bonuses was clearly necessary. Northwest Pipeline Corp. in Salt Lake City reportedly paid their chairman, John McMillian, a $1 million victory bonus, with lesser amounts to the other executives. Bob Blair and his colleagues felt it was too early to pay any bonuses. I agreed.

After months of discussion, it was decided that some modest bonuses would be paid to non-executive junior people in both Westcoast and AGTL. However, bonuses for senior executives would not be paid until the total project was fully financed and ready to be built. The bonuses authorized, on this deferred basis, were considerably less than the pattern established by Northwest Pipeline. The project still being on hold, to this date they have not been paid.

With Foothill's triumph, Bob Blair was finally recognized for his courage in breaking away from the seemingly unbeatable Arctic Gas consortium. For this and his later expansion of NOVA, he has collected a trophy room full of honourary university degrees and man-of-the-year awards and has been profiled in the most distinguished financial publications in Canada. This adulation was all exceeded by his subsequent enrolment in the Order of Canada.

The period before the Foothills victory had been stressful times at Westcoast. Our success did cause our chairman to be less critical of all the executive time and other resources being expended on the Foothills project. However, he still imposed his unique brand of management philosophy on Westcoast Transmission. When I attempted to engage him in a serious discussion on this subject, Kelly merely expressed amazement I was not celebrating the company's increasing profits and my rapid promotions instead of fussing about his personal management style. I could not dispute his contention that the company was progressing and he was setting the tone.

It is true that I was promoted rapidly. It is also a fact that Kelly recommended every move. Even before the Foothills victory, I was made president and CEO in 1976. This was exciting progress but it would have been made so much more enjoyable if my generous sponsor had been able to discard the tough-guy image he seemed determined to flaunt.

Shortly after I was appointed president, I took a scheduled week's vacation to attend a wedding in Ohio. My boss was quite annoyed, claiming this indiscretion gave our people the impression that "lollygagging is more important than working." He knew of my planned trip but thought I should have cancelled it in order to travel the pipeline and let everyone know I was now in charge as their new president. He claimed that he had not taken a vacation in years. I guess he didn't attend any weddings, either.

Despite this conflict, we developed a type of détente, hoping to avoid any obvious public disclosure of the differences between us. But it wasn't easy. Kelly thought I was too soft; I thought he was too tough. He complained that our executives, especially John Anderson and Jack Smith, were too complacent because I did not apply enough pressure. I countered that in my opinion our managers seemed to have been intimidated and offended by his direction, especially his unacceptable practice of questioning them directly about some imagined failure of their superiors. I pleaded for a style of leadership that would establish attainable targets through which an incentive compensation plan would be effective, but the chairman would not permit an incentive bonus plan of any semblance at Westcoast.

The fallout for the unsuccessful contenders in the arctic pipeline contest was massive and enduring. TransCanada PipeLines later did join Foothills, but as a loser and on the winner's tougher terms. El Paso wrote off many millions in a losing cause which resulted in casualties among their senior executives. The picture that seemed to emerge was the El Paso pipeliners were wearing the white cowboy hats while the LNG types were capped in black.

The months following the NEB decision in favour of Foothills were marked by individual announcements that Arctic Gas consortium members were writing off their respective expenses over as long as eight years. Although there were enormous financial losses, the earnings impact on the multinational oil companies was scarcely noticeable, compared to the severe hit taken by the smaller distribution utilities, especially the Canadian members.

· · · · ·6· · · ·

A NEW
REGIME

Foothills' victory was such a momentous event, a great deal of Westcoast's history seems to be measured from that point. With the chairman's approval, John Anderson assumed more of the day-to-day responsibility for operations, and I concentrated on attempting to extend the enterprise in some profitable manner, either by diversification or expansion.

Whatever pressure was removed from me after the pipeline victory, that much and a bit more seemed to be heaped onto John Anderson. On a number of occasions, John was informed that Phillips Petroleum were not impressed with his progress and there would have to be some immediate improvement. Two Phillips Pete executives were on our board. I have no idea what, if anything, they may have said to Kelly about John's performance, or mine. However, I cannot conceive of undermining tactics like that being used by those seasoned executives. Unavoidably, the allegations took a toll on John Anderson, who was incapable of becoming a puppet. In all of my conversations with Phillips Pete executives, there was not even a hint of dissatisfaction with John. To the contrary, they were complimentary in their references to the job we in Vancouver were doing as a trio—Kelly, John and me.

Suffering a certain loss of confidence, John's personality altered enough to be noticed by the executives reporting to him. He seemed comfortable in discussing this circumstance with me, explaining that he was trying to find an appropriate middle ground between Kelly and me, as to the managerial style he would emulate. He candidly said that the real John was somewhere between Gibson and Phillips and it would be a mistake to try to be anything else.

John Anderson did find that midway, compromise position, but in the wrong fashion. He was a Kelly Gibson when dealing with about half the executives reporting to him; an Ed Phillips with the other half. He did not understand why loyalty was not immediately forthcoming. His executives, for their part, did not understand the personal turmoil he was undergoing. Some personnel dissatisfaction was inevitable.

John was a sensitive person. After two senior people expressed their disappointment with him during their resignation interviews, he was noticeably upset. He discussed their complaints with me and expressed his sincere concern, claiming he was totally misunderstood. We were the best of friends and there was no lack of candour either way. We worked on the problem together with my urging that he be his own man, not a hybrid Gibson and Phillips, nor a clone of either.

Later, in the year before his appointment as president, I saw a big improvement in John's attitude and approach. Nevertheless, there were some who complained that he was too intense and unapproachable. I acknowledged that he was intense but I knew better than anyone the powerful root cause. There was also the additional influence of his burning ambition for the company to succeed that was manifested in his work ethic and his impatience with others less inspired. John was an intelligent person who continued to strive for a people orientation after he became president and chief executive officer.

Although Kelly had some good gambling instincts in the oil business, he was hesitant about diversifying our pipeline interests. Nevertheless, he instructed John and me to make a full-scale presentation to the board of directors concerning the long-range plan. At the subsequent meeting, our diversification and expansion philosophy was approved, with Kelly neither approving nor opposing anything we said. It was with that authorization, absent any real enthusiasm from the chairman, that we proceeded.

One director, Merrill Rasmussen, president and CEO of Pacific Petroleums, was not keen about our program. His company, as the largest gas producer in British Columbia, had lost confidence in the energy administration of the province. He contrasted the enlightened bureaucracy in Alberta with the political interference in B.C. His preference would have been for Westcoast Petroleum to be transferred to Pacific in Calgary, contributing to our group's expansion in the more receptive jurisdiction of Alberta. Not being able to persuade John Anderson and me to sell Westpete to Pacific, Merrill suggested placing our subsidiary under Pacific on a management contract, as they had with Bailey Selburn before they took it over entirely. We did not agree. Merrill frequently reminded us of his low regard for the B.C. government as we continued to suffer political obstruction, but his disaffection with Victoria did not become much of an issue internally and we proceeded on the course approved by the board.

Although Kelly retained his permanent suite at the Hotel Vancouver, he was gradually reducing his time in this city. He usually stayed at the hotel Wednesday night, attended a Royal Bank meeting Thursday morning and came to the office that afternoon. That schedule eventually slipped to a trip every other week. He seemed to realize that his actual presence was not essential because I regularly sent him minutes of our weekly operating-committee meetings. These adequately served as the substance of our frequent telephone communications.

The year 1977 was a pivotal year in my life, opening as the worst of times and closing as the best of times. That period unquestionably featured the impact of one particular personality and one particular pipeline. The personality drove me to my lowest point of self-confidence; the pipeline helped to restore my self-esteem. The influential personality was Kelly Gibson and the way his apparent inability to adjust to his scheduled retirement in March 1977 affected our relationship.

It was about mid-1976 when I realized I was losing the exhausting contest of wills between Kelly Gibson and me. He was as relentless as ever, and his passion for a heavy drive factor in his image was beginning to wear me down. I felt it even before my wife remarked one evening: "You are not the confident executive you were twenty years ago; why don't you resign so we can return to Toronto?" I apologized for burdening her by talking about my problems. She countered that it was not what she was hearing but what she was seeing. She explained: "You're working harder than you ever did before, yet I can sense you are anything but happy." Aided by that bit of philosophy, I perceived what was happening. For six and a half years, I had been drained, doing the bidding of one man. On reflection, it is astounding how many of my personal and business activities I was testing with: What will Kelly think? What will Kelly say? What will Kelly do? This was preposterous. A role model can provide excellent training, and I benefited from serving under three superb mentors: George Huffman of Loblaws; A.W. McIntyre of Canada & Dominion Sugar; and Edward J. Tucker at Consumers' Gas. But at this time, I was fifty-nine years of age and Kelly was not necessarily a paragon of the virtues I wanted to emulate.

I suffered a mild heart attack which I believe I was able to conceal from him, but I cannot be sure of even that secret. Fortunately, it occurred early on a Friday morning in my office, and I was discharged from hospital in time for work the next Tuesday morning. The angiogram showed an artery blockage that did not require surgery, indicating the angina pains likely could be alleviated with medication. The cardiologist instructed me to log the circumstances at each angina attack. The pattern became clear; exertion was no problem, but stress was the villain. At this juncture, I decided, while making notes about chest pains, that I would also diarize some of the more upsetting allegations, criticisms or instructions from Kelly. What follows is based on extracts from those notes.

In my opinion, while I was having angina pains, Kelly was having withdrawal pains about his retirement. It was almost a year in advance, in April 1976, that he gave me a handwritten note I still possess outlining the first of the financial concessions he wanted me to recommend on his departure eleven months hence. From that point on, he was inclined to caution me about trouble I was in, and from which he would rescue me by personal intercession with either Phillips Petroleum or the Westcoast board. It was degrading to be told that my superiors were not pleased and my security depended on Kelly's pleadings. I felt sorry for my boss and friend, believing he did not realize how oddly he was acting and how he was getting under my skin. Kelly's handwritten note complained that his pension from Westcoast would only be $60,000 a year plus another $45,000 from Pacific. Accordingly, he suggested a salary for the first five years of retirement at $120,000 per annum plus an office and a secretary for that period.

In August 1976, my notes reveal that Kelly and I had another of our acrimonious sessions generally based on the tiresome accusation that I was spending too much time on the Alaska Highway pipeline, a losing cause. I attempted to explain the importance of the opportunity to expand our enterprise by the additional rate base of $1.6 billion. He interrupted my explanation with the following statement: "I know what you say in public about our chances on these pipelines but you will have to admit right in this room, between the two of us, that those fellows down East are not going to let us build our pipeline and the people in the States certainly are not going to let McMillian build it. We haven't even the slightest hope of getting either line and if you will say to me privately that we have, I have to say to you that you are carried away with the whole thing."

I admitted that we were in a tough battle but there was evidence of progress. I believe I can recall Kelly's actual words: "You are wrong. We don't have a chance on either and the reason I pushed you into upping our share of both Mackenzie Valley and Alcan was so that we would have more control and be able to stop some of the things that are going on that you and I know are wrong. There have only been two big things happen to Westcoast. The first was building the line itself, and the second was our deal with the Petroleum Corporation. The biggest thing we have to do now is run the business properly as a going concern and that means you have to stay on the job."

Kelly said one of his big concerns about Westcoast was that the top two men running the company, Anderson and Phillips, had no operating experience.

Kelly told me that he was very worried about the impression the directors were gaining during the year while I was on trial as CEO. He emphasized that they were all watching very carefully to see how I performed and that he was afraid something might happen next April if I wasn't more careful.

Kelly acknowledged that he had noticed that I had been travelling many weekends and even engaged in weekend meetings. However, he said our Foothills activity could hardly be described as business and he felt that was where I had been wasting my time. In his typical fashion, he warned me that next April might be unpleasant if I didn't understand that he was trying to be helpful with his advice.

Kelly was upset about Ed Molnar's resignation from Pacific. He said that Molnar was the third important man who had quit Pacific and he had told Merrill Rasmussen that Merrill's absence from the office was one of the major causes. He said he did not expect Merrill or me to operate just like he did. But a change in our ways was necessary.

I wanted to review all my absences from the office. Kelly objected but I persisted in going over the trips and having him acknowledge that I had worked most of the Saturdays and Sundays, and that there was only one full day that I took for personal business (actually, a stopover in Chicago about a job offer).

Kelly objected to my last letter to the directors concerning the choice of expansion of rate base or diversification. His greatest criticism, however, was reserved for the last page in which he said I was doing nothing but selling instead of giving facts. He reiterated his feeling that we hadn't a hope in Foothills and he couldn't understand why I had to write in such an enthusiastic and promoting tone.

In the preceding six years I had become accustomed to these illogical and unreasonable explosions so I maintained my composure without any particular difficulty. I was resolved not to have a confrontation with Kelly. In fact, Kelly may even have been disappointed that he could not generate a scrap.

Unless this important difference of opinion between us were resolved one way or another, it would be considered material and would have to be settled by the directors. That is why I wanted to avoid any confrontation in private. Some of the things I noted that Kelly said were so incredible in my view, I can imagine it would have been difficult for a third party to believe they were ever expressed. I felt I must continue to avoid a confrontation until either John Anderson or one of our directors was present. Kelly had at least supported my promotions and salary increases. I should be able to take a lot of flack on that basis alone.

This whole mystifying episode posed some serious questions: How long could I, as CEO, permit the company to pursue aggressively the Maple Leaf and Alcan projects without determining whether other directors agreed with Kelly? It would seem more disclosure was called for, permitting the directors to query management's actions if they had any doubts. Had I the responsibility to tell the directors about Kelly's misgivings? The confidentiality of our talks was an obstacle if I did have an obligation. But surely that burden fell primarily on him. Was he simply upset that I had been too visible and had received too much publicity as a spokesman and witness on these projects, prominence he felt should be his?

The inconsistency of Kelly's entire position was so inescapable that I had to put it down to a combination of withdrawal pains and an attempt to smarten me up by his usual device of using a sledge hammer where a tack hammer would have done.

In September 1976, my memo to myself records that Kelly requested my personal support for the following: a continuing salary for him from Westpete, post-retirement; $1 million after tax from Foothills; $1 million after tax from Northwest Pipeline; office and secretary for five years with $120,000 salary, and a continuing effort for a senatorship.

On 17 March 1977, about a week before Kelly's retirement at age sixty-five, my special diary noted another lengthy discussion with him, including his claim that it was going to be difficult for him to have the board accept me as his successor, but he was going to make a valiant effort to support me. One of his big favours would be preventing Merrill Rasmussen from succeeding in an alleged plot to become chairman of Westcoast, a plan I believe existed only in

Kelly's apprehension. Unless he changed his mind, he said that he intended to challenge Merrill about the latter's alleged motives.

Kelly said: "Well, this looks like the last time I will be able to tell you something you need to know. This is going to be unpleasant but I don't want you to get mad because it is for your own good. You and I had a very rough time in the beginning but we finally came to understand each other. Right now I regard you as a personal friend whether you have any feeling for me or not. You have worked hard to have your chance at the top job in this company and I have sup-ported you all the way. I had difficulty convincing the people that you were ready but I'm going to support you now that you have the job.

"Frankly, Ed, you have disappointed me in this past year. I in-sisted that the directors let you be chief executive officer for a year while I was still on the job. They didn't like the idea but they went along with it. Unfortunately, you still don't act like a CEO. You never have been one before and maybe I expected too much." At this point, I was going to counter that I was likely the chief execu-tive at Trane Company before he reached that position at Pacific. He cut me off with: "You be still until I am finished. This is for your own good and it will pay you to listen. You believe you can run a business by pacifying the people below you and pacifying the people above you. I watch you and it is a mistake.

"I am now beginning to think you are not able to stand up to Merrill and I know John will not, so I am telling you something has got to be done before the annual meeting to find out whether you are going to run this company or you are going to let Merrill take it over. You really are not tough enough for the oil and gas business anyway. Your style is more suited to the big manufacturing compa-nies back East.

"This whole plan is pretty clear to me and it means Merrill will be challenging my judgement when I sponsor you. If he gets away with it, I will resign from the boards of all the companies and be fin-ished with the group entirely. And don't think I'm kidding. I will do that the first move he makes. Ed, you seem rather naïve about the ambitions Merrill has."

The conversation moved to my dissatisfaction with being forced to purchase a share of Pacific's plane and a share of their house in Palm Springs. I declared to Kelly that I was not able to stretch that incident into a confrontation with Merrill about the control of Westcoast. Kelly replied: "Ed, you have always been stubborn about that plane and your refusal to use it. You gave me figures a year ago trying to prove that we should get out of the deal and I told you then we were never going to sell our interest. You should tell Merrill that you want to be billed every month for 29 percent of all the hours flown whether you use the plane or not. That way you will force yourself to use it like you should. You should use up all of your time every month even if you do nothing but run you and Betty to Los Angeles for weekends. Even go and pick up your kids and take them with you because that's what Merrill does. He does most of his flying in that plane for personal reasons and he's not bashful about using it to run his kids around.

"You and John have got to get smart. When I leave you will save $100,000 in salary and $40,000 in expenses. That's $140,000 you can spend on yourselves without showing any change in the profit. We have operated in a very cheap way around here. Sure, I got two salaries but you and John aren't earning that much, you get very little time off and you get very few perks other than the house. Hold on to the house, use it more and think of some other ways to use up money you save on me. But above all, Ed, you've got to stop your stupid resistance to using that plane. You are the chief executive officer and you have every right to use it for personal business just like Merrill does." I had to tell him to his face that I absolutely couldn't see myself changing my professional style sufficiently to allow me to use the plane in the way he suggested.

He replied: "I think I've got to talk with Merrill. I've always talked things out with Merrill and I'm going to ask him straight what he's trying to do. I'm going to tell him that if he thinks he's going to run you he'd better get another man because you will quit."

My response was quite important, so I will try to recall the actual way I stated my feelings, although the comment was obviously spontaneous: "Kelly, you, of course, can tell Merrill anything you want and I know you will do what you decide to do in any case. My problem with your suggestion is that it appears to be picking a fight where no fight exists. It is alright for you to tell Merrill that I will quit if he takes over as chairman and chief executive officer because I most certainly will. However, I wouldn't want you to tell Merrill that I have any evidence that that is his intention other than the fears you have expressed in the last hour." In summary, I could only conclude that Kelly was going through the most severe case of withdrawal pains I have ever known. For that reason, I think I was entirely right in being patient during his discussions.

Kelly remained in Vancouver overnight and started on me again the next morning, saying: "Well, you had a night's sleep on what I told you yesterday, what are you going to do about it? Now I want you to understand what my whole talk was about yesterday. I want you and Betty to be happy and to have an opportunity to enjoy the job you have worked so hard to get. I want Merrill to be successful in his job just like I want you to be successful here. You both can do excellent jobs for your respective companies as long as you get along and don't try to interfere in each other's business. How soon Merrill will make his move to become chairman of both companies, I don't know, but I expect him to push for Mac to be President of Pacific fairly soon. When he does that, I'm going to resign from the company and I hope you will let me remain at Westcoast in that event."

He continued: "What I am trying to tell you is that you need to be tougher and you soon will have to stand up to Merrill. Don't think he can fire you. If he makes one move in that direction, I will resign from his board and get on a plane for Bartlesville. I won't stand in the way of anything Merrill wants to do at Pacific because he has got a big and important company to run. But I will go straight to Bill Martin and tell him what's going to happen in B.C. if Merrill makes any move in the direction of Westcoast. As a matter of fact, your outside directors would also support you in any kind of fight like that."

I tried to calm Kelly a bit by suggesting that he was worrying unduly about this taking place, that all we needed to do was remain alert and run our business properly and the things he was talking about would never occur. With a bit of a laugh, Kelly replied: "That's just the trouble, Ed, you are not suspicious enough. I may be too suspicious but I still say you are being naïve about certain other people's ambitions."

Fortunately, departure time was approaching, so Kelly wound up the conversation this way: "And one last thing. I was really impressed by the way you handled yourself at Premier Bennett's dinner last night. The number of important people in this city you have come to know in a fairly short time is amazing. I always knew you could handle yourself that way and that's why your local directors will never let anyone else throw you out as long as you keep doing your job and just get a little tougher without being so trusting." Then Kelly grasped my hand and became quite emotional in saying that this was our last meeting and our last visit of this type and that he only expected to come over here four times a year from now on.

Such was the bizarre atmosphere as I approached the next month's 1977 annual meeting, the most important of my career. I was smothered by this man and his ability to keep me off balance. He persisted with the claim that Phillips Petroleum were unhappy with my performance and I only held my job by reason of his influence in Bartlesville and his assurance to them that he would continue working with me to make me a better man. He sincerely wanted me eventually to be a success. While I appreciated his noble intentions, his methods were tearing me apart. More punishing than anything else was the terrifying insinuation that I should be his clone in toughness.

Looking back, I believe that perseverance and patience prevented me from quitting in order to accept one of several jobs that had been offered to me. Also, there were two specific lifebelts thrown my way. First, the exhilaration of the dramatic regulatory fight for the Alaska Highway pipeline diverted my sensitivities in a propitious way. In that effort, I was working with partners and colleagues whom I admired. They appreciated my contribution and gave a helpful balance to my morale. We all agreed that we were making headway, with a most remarkable upset victory in prospect. Second, John Anderson revealed the difficulty he had had with Kelly Gibson for a greater number of years and convinced me that I had not been singled out as such an abysmal failure. John insisted that our chairman was not thinking straight, and not many escaped

Kelly's peculiarities. Consequently, John and I persevered, from day to day, knowing time would solve this problem if we both managed to hold our tempers and remain patient above all.

Kelly's moods were nothing if not mercurial, and he was capable of great generosity of spirit. A scant week after his tirade that March day in 1977, I received the following letter from him:

> A person, when he leaves something he has enjoyed and the people he has appreciated being with a lot, can just keep saying things over and over. I am most sincere in saying to you how much I appreciate our being together for almost seven years. We were a good team, a good balance. Without you Westcoast could not have gone from the low of July 1970 to the excellent results you had in 1976, your first year as Chief Executive Officer of the Company. I congratulate you and thank you for all your many efforts during these years.
>
> On the more personal side, I speak for Julie also in saying that we both have enjoyed knowing you and Betty. We consider you more than just business friends and we hope we will see you from time to time and not just in a business way.
>
> Our last meeting will not be forgotten. If you need anything from me or you think I can help in any way, you have my support.
>
> My best wishes go out to you for the future. I know you will continue to do a great job.

What can I say about a beautiful letter like that? Did I believe it was a ceasefire that would last? Yes I did, but sadly, I honestly believe that Kelly has no comprehension of the destructive effect of his personality foibles. He confided in me more than once that he was raised by an unreasonable father, but I am sure he does not recognize why others could resent his treatment as he did his father's.

Kelly Gibson moved into retirement following the Westcoast annual meeting held on 19 April 1977. He received a good financial arrangement from the board of directors for the next five years. I supported the plan but I cannot claim any credit for its provisions. Each time Kelly asked for my assistance in this matter, I told him I thought Phillips Petroleum would have to make the recommendations and they would likely be generous, having themselves put

Kelly in charge of both Pacific and Westcoast. Happily, the recipient was content with the way he was treated. He was proud of the U.B.C. scholarship permanently established in his name.

The peace he postulated between us in his warm, final letter did not last very long while he remained on the Westcoast board. Without going into the petty details, Kelly kept trying to split Merrill Rasmussen and me. It did not work. Merrill and I developed a good understanding when he forthrightly declared that we both had been working for a devious boss. I was not as candid with Merrill and never told him, or any person other than John Anderson, about the warnings I had received about his ambitions concerning Westcoast. For some reason I will never understand, Kelly similarly attempted to drive a wedge between Rob Laurence, the president of Westpete, and me. That mischief made Rob somewhat uncertain about me, but it was not harmful to our operations in any way. Rob soon took early retirement, for health reasons. I hope I was not the cause of his malady.

For the spring 1978 board of directors meeting, management prepared a recommendation for the agenda that a small part of our banking business be given to the Canadian Imperial Bank of Commerce. This was no reflection on the Royal Bank, which had served Westcoast admirably from the beginning. There were two specific reasons for the proposal. First, it was considered that Westcoast had grown to the size where two major banks would be justified, particularly in anticipation of the huge expenditures that would be required for our 50-percent ownership of the new Foothills pipeline. Second, this small bit of business proposed for the CIBC was to reward the institution for the superb way they had assisted the Foothills case during almost two years of regulatory hearings. It was emphasized that the portion of business going to this second banker would involve Foothills-related transactions, not any of Westcoast's regular trade.

On the Westcoast board there were two Royal Bank directors, Charles "Chunky" Woodward and Kelly Gibson. Another, Merrill Rasmussen, was a Royal Bank director-in-waiting, having been informed he was on Earle McLaughlin's list for the next vacancy. As I recall, Chunky was the first to speak, expressing some regret that we were thinking of enlisting another bank when we acknowledged that there was no dissatisfaction with Royal's performance. Merrill expressed the same sentiment but in slightly different, unprovocative terms. These were appropriate and reasonable contributions to the boardroom discussion.

Jack Smith, our chief financial officer, had made the formal presentation, with some supporting comments by John Anderson. As chairman of the meeting, I did not participate. All three of us expected Kelly to be in opposition to this prominent item on the circulated agenda. Our judgement was correct, but we were not prepared for the intemperate tirade Kelly mustered. He attacked neither Jack nor John, directing his protest at me, his successor to whom he had sent such a sweet letter on his retirement. Although he recited several of my sins, he emphasized three in particular. He charged this whole banking recommendation was the result of my ego trip with Foothills, during which I neglected the company, an ego now virtually beyond control because of the unexpected victory. Next, he accused me of trying to punish the Royal Bank for supporting Arctic Gas in the pipeline battle. Finally, he said I had been bad-mouthing the Royal Bank and I was now trying to get rid of them. To say that our board members were astonished by this assault would be considerably short of objectivity; they were stunned into silence. With the exception of John Anderson, not one of them knew of the constant friction between the former chairman and me, thus they were unable to comprehend the viciousness of our exchange.

This was all too much for me. If the directors didn't understand Kelly's display, they undoubtedly had more difficulty appreciating my uncharacteristic explosion, because explode I did.

For the enlightenment of all the directors present, I told Kelly that he was as incorrect in all his indictments against me as he had been guilty in his constant lack of loyalty to Foothills, even when he was drawing a salary as chairman of that pipeline project. I told him my first introduction to Frank McMahon came through Art Mayne, the number-two man of the Royal Bank, and I had been grateful to that institution ever since. Art had been a director of Westcoast and the first Canadian to be on the Phillips Pete board in Oklahoma. I reminded Kelly that I acted with the timidity of a lap dog when he learned in 1970 that my personal account was with the Bank of Montreal and insisted I switch to Royal, which I did.

Realizing that this was the crucial confrontation I had been expecting to happen sometime during my years at Westcoast, when there finally were witnesses present, I gave it the full shot. I recited some examples of the improper interferences by Kelly in our banking matters to the unfair advantage of the Royal. I exonerated Royal Bank officials at every level saying they would be embarrassed, if not ashamed, about what had transpired. I particularly detailed Kelly's personal and unnecessary agreement to pay the Royal Bank $50,000 for a modest comfort letter. I closed by inviting the directors to ask any questions they wished about all my allegations and to feel free to interrogate John Anderson or Jack Smith, who had remained in the meeting although he was not a director.

Kelly was sitting immediately to my right, so I was able to see him grab Merrill's arm and to hear him say: "You've got to say more; we talked about this before the meeting and you have to take a stand." Merrill appeared embarrassed, and said no more. The general, awkward silence lasted for a while so I said that management would withdraw its recommendation, there being no urgency as to timing, stating that we would renew the request at the next board meeting, possibly with some amendments.

As a tradition, the directors generally met a Trader Vic's for lunch after each board meeting. That day only four appeared. Taylor Kennedy left early to catch a plane, saying he would telephone me at home that night. Kelly, Merrill and Bob Roberts of Phillips Petroleum simply disappeared. Ernie Richardson had not been able to attend that particular board meeting.

At the luncheon were Chunky Woodward, Bill Tye, Pacific's vice-president, finance, John Anderson and me. The obvious tension in the air was broken by Chunky. Addressing himself to Bill Tye, he said the two of them had to work out a compromise to this serious difference of opinion. For his part, he said it was unrealistic to think the Royal Bank could retain all of Westcoast's business forever. He was willing to see some share go to the CIBC if Bill Tye could influence Kelly to move from his adamant opposition. To assist Bill Tye a bit in his mission, I said that we would be content to start with a mere 10-percent share for the CIBC. Bill agreed immediately and said he would report to us as soon as he had discussed the compromise with Kelly. From that point, we enjoyed our lunch. John and I were very grateful for Chunky's role and Bill's willingness to approach Kelly.

That night, Taylor Kennedy phoned from Montreal to apologize for not speaking up at the meeting. He said he was so shocked by the bitterness of the debate that he hardly knew how to react. However, he said he would take a definite position at the next meeting in support of management's recommendation. When I described the dispute at the meeting to the absentee director, Ernie Richardson, he was most upset. He was a vice-president and director of the Canadian Imperial Bank of Commerce and had never attempted to use his influence in any way. He said he was disgusted to learn that there seemed to have been such a breach of the accepted conflict-of-interest rules by his colleagues on behalf of the Royal Bank of Canada and that he would demand a full discussion on that subject at the next meeting. He also opined that Chunky Woodward would be as embarrassed as anyone by Kelly's lack of propriety.

My next contact was with Bob Roberts. Now, it was my turn to be dazed with his reaction. The Phillips Pete executive vice-president explained that he and Kelly had discussed the confrontation and Bob ultimately told Kelly that it might be best for all concerned if Kelly henceforth avoided becoming intricately involved with the management of Westcoast, because he was such a natural "take-charge guy." Kelly's reaction was so calm and indicative of agreement that Bob went further by suggesting that Kelly would likely be happier if he resigned from the Westcoast Board and all of its subsidiaries. According to Bob, Kelly accepted this as though it had been his intention in any case.

Very promptly, Kelly informed me unemotionally that he was resigning immediately from Westcoast and all its subsidiaries. He actually wished me well in the future and commented favourably on the team of Anderson and Phillips.

That was not the end of our association. I have already mentioned the later experience of being with him the evening of his

major stroke and spending that night at the hospital with his wife
Julie. My wife and I visited the Gibsons in Calgary several times.
While we were vacationing in Palm Springs, I frequently went to
their home to visit with Kelly while he was taking his therapy in the
swimming pool. It was a shock to us when Julie later died from a
heart attack. Naturally, we and the Andersons attended Julie's funeral, doing and saying everything we could to ease that serious
blow to her devoted husband. We all knew this sad event presented
Kelly with the most damaging blow he had ever suffered. We were
truly sympathetic and concerned, as were so many who knew of
Kelly's dependence on his wife.

I wouldn't claim that my attention to Kelly was driven only by affection. There was also the sense of obligation for the career opportunity he gave me. Also, I had a measure of sympathy for a human
being having difficulty with the true meaning of personal relationships. Although we have not seen each other for some time, I still
correspond with my former boss at Christmas, fully understanding
he cannot easily reciprocate as a result of his crippling stroke.

As far as I know, Kelly's pugnacious genes erupted only once after his total retirement. For an unknown reason, he was stimulated
by a news article to write a two-page, testy letter to Bob Blair in
1979, giving him a stern lecture about an incident that had occurred more than a year before. He sent me a copy of the letter with
no embargo on its use. The thrust was to object to being embarrassed before the other directors by Bob Blair's unfair criticism of a
statement Kelly had given to the press. He said Blair was a pretty
lucky fellow to have Westcoast and Gibson make him a darling of
the media and western Canada's number one businessman by media
standards. This hard-hitting letter continued in that tone but
ended with some pleasantries and a pledge of continued support.
Within a couple of weeks the following reply was received from Bob
Blair, an almost scriptural example about how one should "turneth
aside wrath":

Dear Kelly:
I acknowledge your letter of June 28 and will never do other than
agree wholeheartedly that your personal support and Westcoast

Transmission's good corporate behaviour as a partner in respect of Foothills have been and are great for my company and so for me personally.

Among the strong-willed personalities of you and I and our top colleagues, we have all said what we thought in particular situations at different times and I think it sort of evened out. I just look backward with high personal regard and admiration of people who undertook an extraordinarily and difficult [task], demanding need for leadership and managed to win thoroughly in spite of what the establishment and power elsewhere in the country was anxious to say about us at the time. I think therefore that we were all winners overall and will remember the years from 1974 to the present as among the best we have ever known.

The foregoing exchange exemplifies the unique character of Foothills Pipe Lines Limited. This was an amazing partnership that was successful only because it never forgot for more than a moment that the enemy was the other guy and not one of the partners. Other than very infrequent, chippy episodes like the one just mentioned, we spent all our time fighting our opponents in the pipeline contest and were never provoked into a family scrap of any lasting consequence. Of all the partnerships or joint ventures in which I have played a role in the last fifty years, I know of none better than that alliance. This affirmation over the years has led to arguments with some of Bob Blair's critics, but I remain firm in that conviction.

In 1978, a momentous development took place that affected the destiny of Westcoast. On 10 November, Petro-Canada acquired control of Pacific Petroleums from Phillips Petroleum in the U.S. Thirty-two percent of Westcoast was owned by Pacific Petroleums, thus effective control of Westcoast Transmission was now in the hands of Petro-Canada. Our first personal reaction was that we had been sold out by Phillips Pete. Their explanation was that the price offered by Petro-Canada could not be refused in the interests of their shareholders. Our second reaction was concern about our professional careers, feeling we could not adjust to the restrictive mode of being a crown-corporation satellite. Our fears were unfounded with the early discovery that Petro-Canada did not conform to this stereotype.

The distinguishing difference in Petro-Canada was its second chairman, Bill Hopper, who was anything but the quintessential head of a crown corporation. Although he was a public servant at the time of his appointment, Bill's academic preparation and working experience had been in the private sector of the petroleum business. His rookie years were spent in the Alberta oil fields. Later, he became a consultant, gaining exposure in a host of assignments in oil capitals around the world. At Westcoast, Bill Hopper gave management unrestrained room to move. In fact, he pressed the concept of expansion. Our organization eagerly responded to that support from its major shareholder. With Bill as chairman, they never lacked for ideas, which meant the management could concentrate on execution of all the plans.

Petro-Canada itself is not very profitable for its size. Its profits are less than those earned earlier by some of the smaller companies it has taken over. The reason is the handicap of having to pursue unprofitable exploration ventures in the national interest, rather than being totally oriented to the bottom line. In 1989, Petro-Canada's profit was $31 million, of which $22.7 million was earned through their equity position in Westcoast Energy. Additionally, they received a Westcoast dividend of $14.4 million which was wisely reinvested in that company's common stock. Nonetheless, in my opinion, there is not another oilman in Canada more suited to the unique requirements of Petro-Canada than Bill Hopper.

Bill and I made a sacred personal pact that contributed to our enjoyable and profitable relationship; he thoughtfully promised not to call me Edwin, if I would not call him Wilbert.

····7····

PREBUILD, ALASKA AND ARCTIC OIL

A number of significant events quickly followed the July 1977 NEB decision in favour of Foothills. In September, President Jimmy Carter and Prime Minister Pierre Elliott Trudeau announced they had reached agreement. Two weeks later, a Canada–U.S.A. document on "Principles Applicable to a Northern Natural Gas Pipeline" was signed. This unprecedented international energy agreement was universally heralded as an all-winners, no-losers deal. Capable of handling 3.3 billion cubic feet of gas a day, the energy equivalent of 550,000 barrels of oil a day, this big-inch pipeline was to extend a total of 4,786 miles.

On 2 November, the U.S. Senate and House voted overwhelmingly to approve the president's recommendation. Congressional Joint Resolution No. 621, approving the Alaska Highway pipeline project, was signed by President Carter six days later.

After all the Canadian-American negotiations were completed, there was a symbolic signing ceremony and luncheon hosted by the Canadian government in Ottawa. The senior U.S. dignitary attending was their secretary of energy, Dr. James Schlesinger, a brilliant but dour and humourless gentleman.

I was seated next to Dr. Schlesinger at the luncheon table which was to have included the prime minister. Unfortunately, Mr. Trudeau was detained and we were advised he would try to make it in time for dessert and coffee. When he did put in an appearance it was apparent to me that the honourable secretary of energy was miffed by the prime minister's tardiness.

Trudeau was most cordial to all the guests, and I thought he was suitably gracious to Schlesinger in apologizing for his late arrival. In a very breezy way, with a big smile, the prime minister joked to our table: "I hope you managed to get a decent deal from these Americans." Schlesinger replied, without a smile: "Prime Minister, I'll never understand the suspicions of you Canadians." Trudeau deftly switched the subject from energy to something so vacuous I have no recollection of it at all.

In Canada, another significant date was 3 February 1978, when the Northern Pipeline Agency was established by Act of Parliament. From this point, all the forces of the federal government were aligned with Foothills to face the forbidding array of municipal, county, provincial, state and federal regulatory approvals that would be required in both countries before actual construction could commence.

Mitchell Sharp was appointed chairman of the new pipeline agency. This former cabinet minister was an excellent choice and quickly became the strongest possible advocate for this international endeavour. He had been through the earlier pipeline war in Ottawa in the 1950s. Sharp was frequently in Washington exploiting his considerable diplomatic skill, when it was required, among either the elected representatives or the officials of the department of energy or Federal Energy Regulatory Commission.

The NPA chairman had an ideal teammate in Geoff Edge, who had been chairman of the National Energy Board panel presiding over the lengthy hearings. Edge personally suggested a number of the modifications made to the Foothills project in order for it to be acceptable environmentally and economically. He also spent months in Washington negotiating the approved pipeline's intricate details regarding rate structure and regulation. The unique variable rate of return, suggested by the American energy department negotiators, was largely the outcome of these sessions. The thrust of this tariff regulation was an incentive to keep construction costs as low as possible. A target cost for construction of the pipeline was established. The allowed rate of return to the pipeline would increase to the degree actual costs were below that target, or would be reduced if actual costs were higher. This reward–penalty plan was new to rate regulation.

The mandate of the Northern Pipeline Agency was quite broad. Without much limitation, its officials were to oversee the design and construction of the project, including all environmental considerations, a responsibility of immense scope. Assuming the varied responsibilities of all government agencies normally involved with a venture of this magnitude, the NPA became a one-stop shop for all federal approvals Foothills would require. The NPA was soon staffed with specialists in a number of disciplines, under the direction of Bill Scotland, a former member of the NEB, an engineer well and favourably known to all the Westcoast and AGTL personnel. The NPA people worked smoothly with their counterparts in the growing Foothills organization.

By April 1979, Foothills staff had increased to more than three hundred. In late 1979, Ron Rutherford retired from Foothills, remaining as an oft-summoned consultant. By this time, my fellow directors on the Foothills board included John Anderson, Bob Blair, Jim Byrn, Bill Deyell, Dianne Hall, Bob Pierce, Merrill Rasmussen, Jack Smith and Murray Stewart, executive vice-president, corporate. There was a large group of seventeen officers, which was trimmed a bit because of project delays, headed by chairman Bob Blair and president and CEO Bob Pierce. I served as senior vice-president.

A welcome addition a year later was George Lipsett, as vice-president, engineering and environment. He had been an engineer on the Alyeska oil pipeline. We were just as pleased to recruit Ed Lemieux, as executive vice-president, finance. He formerly had been vice-president of finance with Hydro Quebec. Robin Abercrombie, a senior AGTL executive, joined the board of Foothills about the same time.

One of the first developments requiring the integration of company and governmental efforts was called the Prebuild, yet another idea authored by Ron Rutherford. Simply stated, this was the first phase of the Alaska Highway pipeline project which would ship surplus Alberta gas to the United States as soon as possible. This pre-delivered Alberta gas was to be replaced at a later date by the United States producers when their Alaska gas became available. Obviously, this prebuilding did not include constructing the major portion of the approved pipeline from the Alaska north slope to north of the city of Calgary, which would be 2,082 miles of fifty-six-inch and forty-eight-inch diameter pipeline.

Prebuild involved only the two legs of the pipeline running south from Caroline, Alberta. The eastern leg was 1,512 miles of forty-two-inch diameter pipeline running through Alberta, Saskatchewan and the northern border states to Joliet, near Chicago. Its capacity was 800 mcf per day. The western leg measured 1,192 miles of thirty-six-inch pipeline carrying 240 mcf per day to San Francisco. The estimated cost of both was $3.3 billion.

Walter Mondale, vice-president of the United States, went to Alberta to discuss this subject with Premier Peter Lougheed, with the blessing of the Canadian federal government. This indicated the importance which both administrations conferred on the proposal and the mutual interest in this first phase, involving an international gas-swap agreement.

Two ghosts of the defeated Arctic Gas consortium appeared on the scene to advance a competing proposal to the popular prebuild concept. Vern Horte, former Arctic Gas president, brought together a group of producers and distributors, under the name Pro-Gas. Their plan was to buy surplus gas in Alberta for export to the United States through TransCanada PipeLines' facilities. They were not successful. On 14 October 1980, the Canadian federal cabinet approved the construction of the Prebuild, as the project was officially labelled.

Ian Waddell, New Democratic MP for Vancouver Kingsway, challenged the cabinet's approval, claiming the Northern Pipeline Act had authorized a single pipeline, not a multi-phased project. The lengthy case proceeded through the B.C. Supreme Court, the

Court of Appeal and the Supreme Court of Canada before being dismissed.

The portion of the eastern leg going through Alberta and Saskatchewan would be owned by Alberta Gas Trunk, Westcoast Transmission, TransCanada PipeLines and Consolidated Natural Gas. The U.S. segment from Monchy, at the Saskatchewan border, to Illinois was to be owned and operated by Northern Border Pipeline Co., an assembly of five companies, including Trans-Canada, who had been members of the Arctic Gas consortium.

The Canadian part of the western leg through Alberta and B.C. was to be owned and operated by Alberta Gas Trunk, Westcoast Transmission, Alberta Natural Gas and Alberta and Southern. The U.S. section from Kingsgate, on the border, to San Francisco, was under Pacific Gas Transmission and their parent company, Pacific Gas and Electric.

With that foregoing evolution of corporate structures within the project as a whole, we were now sitting down with a lot of our friends who had been aggressive competitors only months before. Harry Booth of Alberta and Southern, John Sproule of PGE and Harry LePape of Socal Gas joined the board of Foothills (south B.C.). The last mentioned, Harry LePape, holds a distinction no other person can claim. He is reputed to have read every word of the many thousands of pages of testimony in the celebrated and lengthy hearings process in both countries.

Representing TransCanada in the strengthened structure of Foothills (Saskatchewan) were Fred Button, Rad Latimer and George Woods. Individually and collectively they brought a lot of talent to the table.

The participation of our rival, TransCanada, in several sections of the total project evolved in a fascinating way. First, the conditions of the Foothills authorization by the Canadian government demanded a type of melding of the Foothills and Arctic Gas organizations, though the text offered little in the way of specific terms. This required negotiations between TransCanada and Foothills immediately after the latter had been declared winner. To be honest, Foothills was no more magnanimous in victory than TransCanada was gracious in defeat. The strong-willed adversaries on both sides had fought too hard and too long. Not enough time had elapsed for the memory of the personal attacks to evaporate.

Not all the companies who engaged in the contest carried grudges. As somewhat of an anomaly, Imperial Oil exhibited some bitterness but their parent company in New York, Exxon, was quite cooperative in later negotiations. In a disappointing way, Trans-Canada PipeLines in Canada and Michigan Wisconsin Pipe Line Company in the U.S. seemed to lead the disgruntled forces in opposition to the later plans of Foothills in Canada and our associated project Alcan in the U.S.

One prominent member of Arctic Gas showed real class. Shortly after the NEB decision, Shell Canada held a board of directors' meeting in Vancouver. I was invited to their luncheon, where Bill Daniel introduced me as one of the partners of the victorious Foothills group. In a good-natured way he said the NEB decision had been a mistake, in his opinion, but that was the final word and he now wanted to congratulate Foothills and offer the full cooperation of the Shell organization in future developments. This pledge was supported by the applause of the directors. I was proud to tell my colleagues later about this thoughtful action by Daniel.

Tension was inevitable in the first meetings between Arctic Gas and Foothills to determine what could be done to satisfy the wishes of the National Energy Board that there should be some joining of forces to build the pipeline along the route approved. I can readily recall the attitudes of the principal personalities involved. This aspect is clear because I found myself in the role of a peacemaker, although it is admittedly vain to claim that distinction and to suggest it was constructive.

The first formal meeting was held in the Hotel Vancouver on 26 July 1977. It was a very chilly event largely because Foothills expected Arctic Gas to come to this armistice as an enemy defeated. Instead, they came as a consortium which considered it had been anointed by the National Energy Board for an equal share in the Foothills project. Bill Wilder, chairman of Arctic Gas, seemed arrogant in his effort to establish a strong negotiating base. George Woods, president of TransCanada, supported him aggressively but with more detailed knowledge of the project and the NEB decision.

On the Foothills side, Bob Pierce and I had little to say. Actually, Bob Blair and Kelly Gibson only said enough to implant a tough message that Arctic Gas would have to get off their high horse or they wouldn't be in the project at all. Bill Wilder seemed to be their target, which may explain why he soon dropped out of the negotiations.

The next significant meeting was in Toronto at TransCanada's elaborate offices on 12 December 1977. Foothills disclosed the entry fee TransCanada would have to pay to be a part of the Canadian portion of the Alaska Highway pipeline, in the neighbourhood of $50 million. I expressed concern about the amount before the meeting, suggesting that it would clearly be a deal stopper. By simple arithmetic, the entry fee, added to their pro-rata share of the construction costs, would reduce TransCanada's return on rate base to about two full percentage points lower than the return AGTL and Westcoast would enjoy for the life of the project. I was correct; the offer was rejected out of hand and we even had difficulty agreeing to have another meeting.

Eventually, another meeting was held during which Trans-Canada offered to pay $6 million for a 20-percent share of the Foothills project and two seats for their directors on the board. This proposition was rejected by Foothills. The resulting stalemate influenced TransCanada to launch a lobbying effort, a skill they had developed to an art form. They succeeded in having a host of influential people intercede with requests to Foothills that TransCanada be given a fifth of the deal for a reasonable figure. Some of the polite entreaties I recall came from the NEB's Marshall Crowe and Jack Stabback, Ian Sinclair of Canadian Pacific Railway, federal energy minister Alastair Gillespie and Michael Pitfield from the prime minister's office. I specifically remember Geoff Edge telling us that he was concerned about the relationship between Trans-Canada and Foothills. He felt that something must be decidedly wrong when one party is holding fast at $6 million and the other is firm at $50 million. That gaping gulf could hardly indicate a meeting of the minds was being achieved.

It was in July 1978 that Jim Kerr, TransCanada's chairman, formally declined the 20-percent equity that had been reserved for them. He publicly stated that his company supported the concept of the Alaska Highway project but did not feel it was necessary to participate because they considered the two other partners to be capable of financing the project on their own. A more candid explanation would have been that TransCanada was in a competitive struggle with Alberta Gas Trunk Line on a pipeline expansion through Quebec and the Maritimes, making the prospects for an amicable partnership in Foothills doubtful.

At the next meeting of the Westcoast board, it was agreed to raise our company's equity in Foothills from 40 to 50 percent. The reason was TransCanada's decision not to buy into Foothills. Ideally, we had been contemplating a 40-40-20 allocation among AGTL, Westcoast and TransCanada.

I informed the Westcoast board that TransCanada would have been an ideal partner, simply because they would have added a great deal of financial integrity to the project. I explained that Alberta Gas Trunk did not particularly agree and a significant difference of opinion could develop between us regarding TransCanada. Fortunately, as in similar situations with our remarkable partner, a satisfactory environment developed with our 50/50 deal and events moved ahead smoothly.

Sequentially over the next eighteen months, TransCanada secured an amazing collection of equity positions in the project both in Canada and in the United States. They were small individually but quite significant in aggregate. Much of that acquisition success can be attributed to later cooperation and assistance from Foothills.

TransCanada acquired 44 percent of the 160 miles of the Prebuild pipeline through Saskatchewan; 30 percent of the 1,117 miles from Monchy, Saskatchewan, to Joliet, Illinois; and 7 percent of the 731 miles in Alaska which was still on hold. TransCanada was sponsoring at least two other pioneer pipeline proposals at the same time. They were the operating partner of Polar Gas, a consortium planning to bring high-arctic natural gas into Canada, passing west of Hudson's Bay. They were also proposing a line through the Atlantic provinces and Quebec from the new discoveries off the east coast.

As tough and independent-minded as Kelly was, he engaged in selective hero worship which emerged in the affairs of Foothills. One
of his heroes was Fred Mannix, chairman of the respected and successful Mannix organization in multi-construction businesses. He
admired Mannix's obvious entrepreneurial success and they became
very close as fellow directors of the Royal Bank. He told me a number of times that he would like to do a big deal some time with Mr.
Mannix as a partner. This would have been acceptable to all of us.

At a Foothills executive committee meeting in Calgary in early
1978, shortly before the fateful Westcoast board meeting, I was informed that Kelly and Bob Blair had agreed that the Mannix organization should be hired as project manager of the Alaska Highway
pipeline project, involving something like $10 billion to be ex-
pended in Canada. I asked if there had been any competitive bidding for this massive contract. Kelly impatiently informed me that
other quotes were not necessary because Mannix had a superb organization and he was a good friend of all of us. Bob did not seem concerned about the absence of competitive bidding, so I assumed he
was being typically cooperative with Kelly, as he had been with all
of us at Westcoast. Similarly, the fact that Mannix had a pipeline-
construction division looking for work did not seem to ring any
conflict-of-interest bells. There was no satisfactory answer to my
question whether Mannix as the project manager would also hire
Mannix as the pipeline construction firm. My concern had nothing
to do with the capability of the renowned Mannix organization. I
was disturbed by the optics in the forthcoming rate hearing for this
federally-regulated enterprise.

I still could not accept this arrangement and argued that the National Energy Board would challenge this considerable expenditure
being undertaken without competitive bidding. Under the applicable regulation, an agreed rate of return on all capital costs would
have to be approved for passing on to the gas consumers. Thus, to
protect the public interest, the regulator would insist on a competitive bidding process. Bob Pierce, the fourth member of the executive committee, did not participate in this debate in any way I can
recall. The bitter argument continued between Kelly and me, to

Bob Blair's embarrassment. It all ended when Bob agreed with my request to delay this type of decision. Actually, we were a long way from the time a project management firm would definitely be required.

Kelly never forgave me for opposing him in front of our partners. It was not a good scene, but I explained that if he objected to being blind-sided, he should not trap me in a meeting where such an important item was to be rammed through. I could not let it pass unchallenged. A few weeks later he told me that Fred Mannix was threatening to sue us because he had spent about $500,000 gearing up his organization for this assignment. He had assumed he was certain to get the contract, on the basis of a promise from Kelly Gibson. I can understand how confident Fred would feel after a session with Kelly.

This regrettable incident did produce a bit of history I did not know. As another justification for awarding this project to Mannix, Kelly had explained that the "Foothills" name came from one of the inactive companies of Mannix. Apparently, it had been cleared by them for Bob Blair's use. But did that justify the generosity of an uncontested management contract for a $10 billion project? Foothills went on to build its own operating organization and the subject of a project-management company never arose again.

Prebuild did not happen overnight. In 1978, Pan-Alberta, under their aggressive president Scotty Cameron, had accumulated 1.04 billion cubic feet a day for Prebuild export for which regulatory approvals were required in both Canada and the United States. It was not until July 1980 that the Canadian federal cabinet conditionally approved construction of Prebuild. Shipment of Alberta gas to the U.S. started first on the western leg in late 1981. In the interval, approval had been granted to increase the diameter of that pipeline from thirty-six inches to forty-two inches.

The eastern leg commenced shipments almost a year later and that was only to Ventura, Iowa, some 809 miles from the Saskatchewan border crossing. In any case, both legs were now transporting Alberta gas, which volumes were to be replaced by Alaska gas when the northern portion of the pipeline was put into service; that is, from Prudhoe Bay, Alaska, to Caroline, Alberta, north of Calgary.

It is worthy of note that Northern Border Pipeline experienced some interference on the eastern leg of Prebuild from some of their former colleagues in disconsolate Arctic Gas. Midwestern Gas Transmission Company and Michigan Wisconsin Pipe Line Company both attempted to frustrate the construction of Prebuild by resorting to U.S. court appeals. They were no more successful in this effort than Vern Horte and TransCanada had been at the same game. The latter, however, was eventually astute enough to get pieces of Foothills, the partnership they couldn't beat.

In September 1980, a colourful commemorative outing was held on the beautiful rolling prairie near Burton Creek, Alberta. Over three hundred dignitaries attended from Canada and the U.S.A. It marked the initial construction for the dramatic Alaska Highway pipeline. It was an impressive event, well-staged and memorable. A similar celebration that drew a large crowd of politicians, regulators and pipeliners took place near Spokane, Washington, in February 1981, to commemorate the start of construction for the western leg to San Francisco. Possibly the biggest crowd of all assembled in October 1982, near Bismarck, North Dakota, for Northern Border Pipelines' celebration of the completion of the eastern leg. Gas flow had commenced on 1 September.

Putting a group together to finance and build the internationally approved pipeline through Alaska was even more difficult than completing Prebuild. In fact, it didn't happen. John McMillian, chairman of Northwest Pipeline Corporation, formed a new company called Northwest Alaska Pipeline Company to undertake the construction. With this new company as operator, a consortium was organized called Alaska Northwest Natural Gas Transportation Company. In addition to the original Alcan company, there were five former Arctic Gas members in the new consortium. They were Pacific Gas and Electric, Northern Natural Gas, Pacific Lighting Corporation, Panhandle Eastern Pipe Line and United Gas Pipe Line. This original group was later augmented by the addition of new subsidiaries of American Natural Resources, Texas Gas Transmission, Texas Eastern, TransCanada PipeLines and Columbia Gas System.

This Alaskan consortium of eleven companies had a rocky time under the leadership of John McMillian, who had not gathered many admirers during the adversarial hearings. John was not gifted with diplomacy nor was he particularly energetic in repairing fractured relationships. He merely made it clear to the new recruits that his company held the exclusive franchise for a big-inch pipeline through Alaska and they were privileged to be offered a piece of the action. He was just as abrasive with the three major producers on the north slope, Exxon, Arco and Sohio. Northwest Pipeline, as a company, was a pygmy compared to the giants to whom he allotted minority positions in the gas pipeline to traverse Alaska.

The small size of the operating company was only one part of the problem. The other was John McMillian himself. He was not truly a pipeliner and was regarded by his Alaskan partners as a maverick oilman, with a lot of political influence in Washington. Foothills received complaints from some of his new partners, with the warning that we must intercede or the Alcan project would fall apart.

Foothills could have been compromised by this delicate situation, so we were compelled to act. To his credit, John McMillian was quite understanding about our concern and cooperated willingly despite a degree of embarrassment he must have suffered. He welcomed our assistance and provided his clearance to hold meetings with the principals involved. We went first to Exxon, the unofficial representative of the three north-slope gas producers. Bob Pierce led our team which met with them in Houston on several occasions. My recollection is that Exxon were cordial and helpful. They and the other two producers agreed to provide some of the financing for the Alaska pipeline. However, they were adamant when they felt they had reached a maximum investment exposure. This was the question that generated the animosity between their group and John McMillian. He definitely needed the financial support they were inclined to give, but they objected to the way he was trying to pressure them politically to put up even more money.

Bob Pierce continued to meet with Exxon and I accompanied

him on at least one meeting with Sohio in Cleveland. I attribute a good part of the final arrangement with the three producers to his work. Exxon, Arco and Sohio agreed to take 30 percent of the debt and equity of the Alaskan pipeline, to a maximum of $9 billion. McMillian claimed this was not enough. He said the only way the pipeline could be positioned to justify governmental backstopping was at least a 40-percent participation by the three Prudhoe Bay producers. This was in clear contradiction to his evidence during the hearings that government assistance would not be necessary, testimony which had troubled Foothills at the time.

In early 1982, Northwest unashamedly applied to the State of Alaska for financial assistance. The governor appointed a task force to examine the request for public participation in the Alaska Natural Gas Transportation System. The task force members eventually reported support for the general concept; however, they advised against financial participation based on ". . . the magnitude of the contingencies and the lack of a firm financing plan." Possible cost overruns were a phobia with everyone involved in this Alaskan venture. The Trans-Alaska Pipeline System (TAPS) oil pipeline running across the state from Prudhoe Bay to Valdez was estimated to cost $900 million. It finally cost about $10 billion for this 800-mile, forty-eight-inch-diameter pipeline to carry 1.2 million barrels of crude oil per day. Understandably, the public did not trust pipeliners' cost estimates.

Foothills did a circuit of meetings with the utility distribution members of the Alaskan consortium. Personality problems existed galore, McMillian not being the only one at fault. We became involved in many technical discussions regarding tariffs, cost estimates and rates of return. I believe we were helpful. Many complaints had to do with the budget of the consortium. They were disturbed about the expenses incurred by Northwest as the operator and we heard much about personal excesses. We were able to make some discreet observations to John McMillian which were well received and definitely helped ease the situation. Regardless, attrition set in as members started refusing to pay their budget allotments. American Natural Resources was the first to resign. By the time the project was put on hold due to a significant collapse of the gas market in the United States, the consortium had become a very small contingent.

Finally, we spent time with both the elected and appointed officials in Alaska. We discovered a lot of residual affection for El Paso and dissatisfaction with Northwest. They made it clear that they preferred the plan of pipeline transmission along the Alaska Highway rather than across the environmentally sensitive north slope, where they knew the costs would be outrageous. However, they drew a big distinction between El Paso and Northwest as operators. They wanted El Paso to be the pipeline operator in Alaska, along the highway route. We made some delicate inquiries into the possibility of Northwest accepting El Paso for this purpose. It was not possible. Now that John McMillian had the permit in his possession, he was unwilling to accept El Paso, even though he had agreed to do so in our secret pact during the competitive hearings, when his success was most uncertain.

Disenchantment with Northwest persisted. In June 1982, Governor Jay Hammond, a former supporter, named a committee to study alternate methods of moving Prudhoe Bay gas to market. In 1983, the committee, co-chaired by former governors Walter Hickel and William Egan, recommended abandoning the Washington-approved Alaska Highway pipeline project. They suggested a number of alternatives. Similarly, a group of Alaskan businessmen formed a company called Yukon Pacific Corporation for the purpose of constructing a competitive alternative. This concerted opposition indicated that most Alaskans thought almost anything would be preferable to a Northwest-led organization, despite the very acceptable Foothills connection.

Almost inevitably, there arose public statements that our Alaska Highway project had been abandoned by Northwest. Our opponents in Alaska extended this false premise to claim that the federal permit was thus nullified and the U.S. Federal Energy Regulatory Commission had no continuing jurisdiction. The heat finally was taken off Mr. McMillian dramatically. His company was sold in October 1983, and he went on to other, more successful endeavours.

After some unpleasant litigation, The Williams Companies had purchased 71 percent of the shares of Northwest and elected a new board of directors. The new chairman was Joseph H. Williams and the new president and chief executive officer was Vernon T. Jones. On 16 November 1983, Jones formally advised Congress that The Williams Companies remain fully committed to the completion of the Alaska Natural Gas Transportation System.

In addition to the imprecise suggestion by the National Energy Board that Foothills and Arctic Gas should join forces in some fashion, their July 1977 decision outlined the Dempster Connection as a definite condition of approval. This referred to a thirty-four-inch-diameter pipeline running 747 miles south from the Mackenzie delta, near Inuvik, along the Dempster and Klondike highways to Whitehorse in the Yukon. Foothills was required to apply to the NEB by 1 July 1979 for authority to build this pipeline solely for Canadian gas. It was to have an initial capacity of 800 mcf per day, being capable of future expansion to 1.2 billion cubic feet per day.

Foothills established an office in Whitehorse and managed a large pipeline research project from this location, concerning frost heave, crack propagation and other technical problems associated with natural-gas pipelines operating in permafrost. This agenda of experiments was all done under the watchful eye of the National Energy Board and the Northern Pipeline Agency, particularly the latter. The documentation of that work will be of immense benefit when actual construction commences. In fact, it has already produced evidence that some of the large engineering contingency costs in the original estimates can safely be reduced.

In the meantime, Foothills executives were maintaining a close liaison with the native-peoples' groups in the Yukon. Employment for those residents during construction and in normal operations was assured. The Council for Yukon Indians was informed they would be asked to designate two of their native leaders to be represented on the board of directors of the Foothills subsidiary in charge of the pipeline running through that territory, an opportunity they welcomed enthusiastically.

Westcoast, as a partner in Foothills, was particularly keen about the Dempster Connection, sometimes called the Dempster Highway Lateral. It would be an important factor in supporting

Westcoast's philosophy regarding northern pipeline extensions. In our view, it was environmentally superior to any other practical means of moving Canadian natural gas from the Mackenzie delta to southern markets; it would eliminate any need for the costly and objectionable north-slope crossing to reach the Alaskan gas reserves in Prudhoe Bay; and it was a project generally acceptable to the native peoples of the Yukon.

In the midst of our efforts to consolidate the Foothills project, another major opportunity presented itself which required swift and concerted response. Under the U.S. Public Utility Regulatory Policies Act of 1978, a mandate was established for expedited procedures for a pipeline to deliver Alaska oil to Juan de Fuca Strait in Washington State and to the other northern border states of Montana, North Dakota and Minnesota. Simply stated, the president was required to request competing proposals and make a recommendation to Congress for one of them within a prescribed deadline.

Within eleven months of the U.S. president's kick-start, Foothills had designed two different oil-pipeline proposals, proceeded through the regulatory processes, very successfully lobbied in both the United States and Canada, only to withdraw, because of a sudden change in oil markets. Whereas Bob Blair headed the gas venture, I was assigned that role for the oil proposal. Federal support for the former had been non-existent but it was overwhelming for the latter. Ultimately, however, Bob Blair's Foothills Gas was a winner; Ed Phillips's Foothills Oil was a dropout.

President Carter's invitation produced three other serious contenders and a fifth which was little more than a nuisance. The contending companies were Foothills Oil Pipe Line Ltd., Kitimat Oil Pipeline, Trans Mountain Pipe Line, Northern Tier Pipeline and Northern Pipeline Company. Only three, Foothills, Trans Mountain and Northern Tier, lasted long enough to participate in any regulatory hearings.

Kitimat Oil Pipeline was an assembly of companies headed by Edgar Kaiser, Jr. It proposed a new ocean port at Kitimat, on the central coast of British Columbia, to receive crude-oil tankers which would supply a new oil pipeline running from Kitimat to Edmonton, joining the existing Trans Mountain system for shipment of the crude south to Puget Sound at the northwest tip of Washington State. The fishery and other interests near Kitimat unleashed an attack on the environmental consequences of an oil port at that location. The political opposition was immediate and open. Liberal environment minister Len Marchand declared the federal government's opposition to the Kitimat route. Liberal energy minister Alastair Gillespie emphasized the same official rejection. The Canadian department of external affairs notified the U.S. state department that the government was opposed to the Kitimat plan of bringing oil tankers into that region of British Columbia.

Premier Bennett favoured the Foothills all-land route instead of the idea of an oil port at Kitimat. The B.C. government established an environmental inquiry under the chairmanship of law professor Dr. Andrew Thompson from U.B.C. The ensuing report was negative. If that formidable opposition was not enough to submerge Kitimat, internal dissension became a critical problem. The major partners became dissatisfied with Edgar Kaiser's management and the heavy expenses being incurred. After about six months, Kitimat gave up and their consortium disbanded.

The other virtual non-starter was Northern Pipeline Company. This contestant included a few of the original Kaiser group headed by some politically astute B.C. businessmen. They advanced the same idea of an oil port at Kitimat with a pipeline going just to Valemont in the interior of B.C., joining the Trans Mountain pipeline at that point. Having the same environmental obstacles, it did not gain adequate financing and never advanced to the formal application stage.

In a remarkably short time, Foothills designed, costed and prepared regulatory applications for two alternatives that would satisfy President Carter's requirements. One was called the Skagway alternative. It contemplated oil tankers plying from Valdez to supply the new pipeline at the nearby Alaskan port of Skagway, the oil tankers remaining entirely in U.S. waters for that short trip. From this point, the crude would be moved by pipeline climbing along the right-of-way of the historic White Pass and Yukon Railway to Whitehorse. From there, the oil pipeline would be in the same right-of-way as the Alaska Highway gas pipeline, terminating in Edmonton. A quantity of the oil would be carried from Edmonton to the Puget Sound refineries by the existing Trans Mountain pipeline; the balance would move south to Montana, also through a network of existing oil pipelines in Alberta which were capable of economic expansion and connection.

The Skagway alternative would have included Federal Industries Ltd. as a Foothills partner. Their president, Jack Fraser, had conditionally agreed to sell White Pass and Yukon Railway to Foothills, investing the proceeds as his firm's share of the equity in Foothills Oil. This would have been a happy partnership had the Skagway alternative survived because we would have gained the support and advice of an outstanding businessman and his corporation.

The second Foothills alternative was called the Delta Junction proposal. It was an all-land oil transportation project, hooking up with the existing TAPS oil pipeline at Delta Junction in Alaska, proceeding to the nearby Alaska Highway gas pipeline right-of-way and thence to Edmonton.

Despite the helpful cooperation of the White Pass and Yukon Railway, the Skagway idea was soon dropped. Public and political support was overwhelming for the all-land route from Delta Junction, instead of the combined oil-tanker and oil-pipeline proposition via Skagway.

The Trans Mountain Pipe Line scheme was to construct a new oil superport in the Strait of Juan de Fuca, building an island-hopping pipeline from there to the mainland. Their idea would seriously increase the number of supertankers sailing along the west coast of British Columbia. Because this disadvantage contrasted so markedly with the Foothills all-land route, virtually all environmental and political spokesmen favoured Foothills.

The third competitor who at least survived the initial regulatory phase was Northern Tier Pipeline Company. This was an impressive group of U.S. oil companies and a U.S. pipeline contractor, headed by the Burlington Northern Railway. They also counted on a new oil superport in the Strait of Juan de Fuca and an oil pipeline running from there to the U.S. mainland and easterly across the northern-border states. The Northern Tier proposal enjoyed impressive political support in the United States. Indeed, both the U.S. department of the interior and department of energy found Northern Tier to be the best in terms of economics. This was to be expected, considering the spin-off benefits to the United States from this totally American-owned project. Obviously, this assessment displayed little concern about the environmental impact of increased oil-tanker traffic along Canada's west coast. Accordingly, President Carter selected Northern Tier in January 1980. His endorsement was good for only one year, the length of time Northern Tier was given to secure their financing. The project died in that period for lack of financing and a final blow from the State of Washington. On the recommendation of that state's Energy Facility Site Evaluation Committee, Governor John Spellman denied Northern Tier access through Washington.

I made several appearances before the Evaluation Committee in their hearings in Olympia, Washington. On my first day, opposing counsel heatedly attempted to have me disqualified as a witness before the hearing officially commenced. They presented an objection and requested a delay of the opening while the board considered it. The objection, in effect, demanded my disqualification because I was not a university graduate and therefore lacked the professional status essential in these technical hearings.

The chairman refused the requested delay and observed, with obvious disdain for counsel, that a person who had been in the business since 1947, and had become president of the pipeline serving the Pacific Northwest with most of its gas supply, should have something to say of value to the proceedings, with or without college degrees. Under subsequent examination by counsel for Washington State, I presented the toughest testimony I could generate under oath. I had been mightily stimulated for that task. Counsel for Northern Tier declined to cross-examine me, still smarting from the chairman's rebuke. That was the only time in my career that environmentalists and public-interest activists crowded in the corridor to shake my hand. They had sought me out on other occasions in Canada, but with something other than shaking my hand in mind.

There was also a remarkable display of support in Canada for the

Foothills oil pipeline idea. Setting aside the innumerable sessions in regulatory hearings, our lobbying effect required fifteen meetings in Alaska, six trips to Washington, D.C., regional meetings in Chicago, Seattle, Portland and countless sessions with environmental groups in the San Juan Islands. American environmental activists in the Puget Sound area, mobilized by Brian McGavin of Westcoast, eagerly jumped to support our cause because it would remove much of the existing oil-tanker traffic in their sensitive waters, whereas the Trans Mountain plan would have built a new oil superport and boosted tanker traffic. A few of their leaders took up temporary residence in Vancouver to work voluntarily with Foothills on a daily basis. Some stayed in McGavin's home. They were convinced that we had the proper proposal to defeat both Trans Mountain and Northern Tier, and remove oil tankers from their waters.

David Anderson, a former leader of the B.C. Liberal party (and more recently chairman of a government task force investigating oil-tanker safety and emergency response to oil spills), voluntarily coordinated a great deal of public activity on Vancouver Island and in the San Juan Islands to assist us.

Problems developed in the Foothills family, but they only caused a civilized separation, without damage to the project. We had invited John McMillian of Northwest Pipeline to be our associate for the very small portion of the oil line that would pass through Alaska. He was not enthusiastic but agreed to accommodate us because his responsibility would not be onerous. Foothills undertook to do all the engineering and regulatory work on his behalf, merely using the name of his U.S. company. Midway through the hearings, we were notified by Northwest that they did not care to make any more investment in the speculative oil pipeline. We replied immediately, accepting their resignation and assuring them that there would be no further charges from that date. A significant amount owing to Foothills for the engineering previously done on Northwest's behalf was not paid. Foothills, as a company, decided not to press the issue. At the meeting where that decision was made, Kelly Gibson, likely recalling earlier feuds, uttered the philosophy: "If he is too small to pay his bills, we will be too big to ask him."

Federal political support for Foothills appeared almost immediately. Our representative in Ottawa, Jamie Deacey, was doing a good job. Environment minister Len Marchand and energy minister Alastair Gillespie both declared the government's preference for the Foothills all-land route. Prime Minister Trudeau also made a speech in Calgary declaring the government would support the Foothills all-land oil pipeline. Within a week of that speech, an aide-mémoire from the department of external affairs was sent to the U.S. state department confirming Canada's preference for Foothills. The B.C. government filed a formal intervention with the NEB, supporting Foothills and rejecting Trans Mountain.

When the Conservatives under Prime Minister Joe Clark took power in Ottawa, Foothills' position faltered, but only fleetingly and by accident. After the election, I made three trips to Ottawa, personally discussing the oil pipeline with at least ten of the newly appointed cabinet ministers, before I was able to see the most important one, energy minister Ray Hnatyshyn. I recall with gratitude the thoughtfulness of Senator Robert DeCotret having his cabinet colleagues Don Mazankowski and Michael Wilson meet in his office so I could pitch all three at once. Because my eventual department of energy meeting was arranged through the prime minister's office by Jamie Deacey, I did not expect a hearty reception. However, the minister was cordial, but ill-informed and appeared somewhat ambivalent about the tanker-versus-pipeline debate.

I recall this Ottawa meeting with the new energy minister vividly because I had to report it to my colleagues as a rating of one on a scale of ten, with respect to how well I had done my job. Mr. Hnatyshyn did not respond to the various points we made during the visit, causing some awkward gaps in the dialogue. However, his helpful staff people, Harry Near and Pat Howe, diplomatically asked some penetrating questions. I suspect their queries were more intended to make me feel that I had not travelled all across the country for a futile twenty-minute session than to elicit information. Before we departed, I thought I would leave something more memorable than a business card in order to be recognized if I ever appeared again. I volunteered some personal predictions on significant actions the U.S. energy department would soon take that would have ramifications in Canada. Most, if not all, developed as suggested, but I never had an opportunity to return and determine if the minister remembered me as the fearless forecaster of U.S. energy policy.

A few weeks later, following a speech in Saskatoon, Hnatyshyn answered a question on the subject of the oil pipeline in a manner which suggested a bit less resolve on the contentious tanker traffic than the previous Liberal government had displayed. Contrary to that mistaken impression, the Conservatives' new environment minister John Fraser publicly declared "oil tankers will only come into Kitimat waters over my dead body."

For several weeks, question period in the House of Commons was highlighted by accusations from the Opposition that the Tories had lost the strong bargaining position on this international issue that the Liberals had gained with the United States. This was inaccurately extended to suggest that the new government did not agree with the Liberal aide-mémoire previously sent to Washington, and was therefore indifferent to the U.S. threat of more oil-tanker traffic along Canada's west coast. Frankly, the government spokesman did not handle the Opposition's questions well and the media made hay with that hint of ineptitude. At one stage, a personal friend and veteran Tory MP called to accuse me of "hanging us out to dry."

As he was with the Foothills gas pipeline, Premier Bill Bennett was a tireless and effective advocate for our oil pipeline. He worked hard to correct what he regarded as indecisiveness among the Conservatives in Ottawa, and succeeded. Following a think-tank session of the Tory cabinet in Jasper, Prime Minister Clark visited Vancouver. From a meeting in the Villa Hotel in Burnaby, Clark emerged with a smiling Bill Bennett. The prime minister replied to the assembled media that his government did indeed prefer an all-land pipeline over allowing more oil tankers on B.C.'s coast. If the premier's hand had been up the back of the prime minister's jacket, the manipulation could not have been more obvious. There was a knowing smile on the face of Clark's top adviser, Bill Neville. By telephone calls to Jasper and a meeting in the Hotel Vancouver, I had previously approached Neville to brief him on this issue and ask for his assistance. He merely said: "If you can get the media to ask the PM the right questions, you will get the right answers." It worked.

Later, Canada's new prime minister personally contacted President Carter to express his concern about oil tankers along the western coast, referring to the Foothills alternative which would reduce the number of tankers required. President Carter obviously was not persuaded. He selected the proposal of Northern Tier for ocean tankers and a new oil superport, just six weeks after that specific highest-level Canadian intervention.

Frank McMahon had asserted in 1968 that oil and gas from Prudhoe Bay, Alaska, should be transported to the lower forty-eight states by pipelines, rather than by ocean in oil or LNG tankers. During the regulatory hearings for the Foothills oil pipeline, we acknowledged that oil tankers were safely plying the oceans of the world. We asserted that the oil companies and shippers were taking every known precaution for safety the current technology for ocean transport could provide. However, we testified that accidents could happen in the best of operations, and the safety of ocean tankers could not possibly be designed, at any cost, to compare with the solid integrity of an oil pipeline, underground, unseen, unheard and unequalled environmentally. The despoliation resulting from the 1989 grounding of the *Exxon Valdez* has tragically proven us to be prophetic.

Had the first oil pipeline proposed by Frank McMahon been built in 1968, it would have carried the full production from Prudhoe Bay and this calamitous oil spill would not have happened. Had the later 1978 Foothills oil-pipeline project been successful, the accident still could have occurred, because that new pipeline would have eliminated only those ocean tankers sailing down the west coast bound for the Strait of Juan de Fuca, not all the others headed for the U.S. west coast and the Panama Canal.

When the federal government reverted in March 1980 to the Liberals, Foothills truly re-established its unquestioned position as Ottawa's favourite. Energy minister Marc Lalonde reaffirmed the Liberal government's support for Foothills. On the same day, Brit-

ish Columbia energy minister Bob McClelland said that his government was pushing for reduced tanker traffic and the Foothills all-
land pipeline route. The next week, Lalonde was in Washington,
D.C. pressing the Foothills case with U.S. energy secretary Charles
Duncan.

Federal finance minister Allan MacEachen announced on CBC-
TV that Canada would try to revive the Foothills all-land route with
the Americans. Liberal Senate Leader Ray Perrault said studies
could be compiled to show a strong case for Foothills rather than
the ocean-tanker selection made by the president of the United
States.

Finally, on 20 June 1980, Prime Minister Trudeau replied to a
question in the House of Commons saying, "This government has
always expressed the hope that Trans Mountain would not be the
preferred route, but a parallel line along the Foothills right-of-way
for gas would be built to transmit oil from Prudhoe Bay to the U.S.
This is still our preferred course."

With all that support, how could Foothills lose? We didn't lose;
we made a strategic retreat. It is a pipeliner's fondest dream to be
advocating a mega-project that enjoys overwhelming support of the
activists, politicians and environmentalists, without even a single
church group protesting. How sad we could not continue in that
unreal spell of being loved by everyone.

Near the climax of the National Energy Board oil hearings featuring Foothills and Trans Mountain debating each other, two significant developments persuaded us that it would be unwise to continue. First, intervening activist groups, supposedly representing
the interests of the native peoples, were clearly attempting to hold
the oil pipeline development hostage in order to influence the native land claims settlement. Foothills' relations with the executive
of the Council for Yukon Indians had been so satisfactory to date
that we did not want anything to imperil the far more important
Alaska Highway gas pipeline project. Further, and more important
from the standpoint of economics, oil marketing conditions had
commenced a decidedly negative swing. Our studies revealed that
there soon would be insufficient demand from the refineries in Puget Sound and the northern border states to justify building a new

transportation system for crude supplies. Accordingly, financing would have been next to impossible to obtain. We were absolutely correct, yet it was a heartbreak to give up a struggle, to the dismay of such an imposing body of encouragement and support, and to the disappointment of the Foothills professionals who had produced a quality proposal in such a short time.

Ken Hall, president of Trans Mountain, had a personal passion for this challenge that prohibited him from taking a walk and cutting his losses. He was a good friend and we had come to know each other well years earlier when I had attempted to buy his company for Westcoast. He was as resolute in refusing those offers as he was about spending millions on his ill-fated and hotly contested oil pipeline project. Because Ken thought Foothills had merely been a spoiler and he was glad to be rid of us, he continued to spend a great deal of money as the unopposed applicant through the National Energy Board hearings. Trans Mountain did eventually receive approval from the NEB, subject to later satisfaction of marine and coastal environmental questions in the Strait of Juan de Fuca. Within a month, Trans Mountain withdrew from the companion regulatory hearings in Washington State. Thus ended President Carter's unsuccessful attempt at an expedited approval for a new oil-transmission system serving refineries in the Puget Sound and across the northern border states. The White House had a good idea, but a decade too late.

The Foothills oil pipeline idea succumbed as a result of a negative turn in energy markets. It may be resurrected in the future, but only if a significant economic penalty could be justified in replacing the existing transportation system as a trade-off for obvious environmental benefits from a pipeline. In fact, Dick Stokes, president and CEO of Trans Mountain, announced in 1990 that they were reviving a portion of their old proposal. Locating a large off-shore oil terminal in Juan de Fuca Strait, near Port Angeles, Washington, would eliminate the need for oil tankers and barges sailing farther inland through the environmentally sensitive waters of the Strait of Georgia, Haro Strait and Juan de Fuca Strait. Their crude oil cargoes would instead be taken to the three refineries in northwest Washington by an island-hopping pipeline. The port of Vancouver would also benefit environmentally by the present oil-tanker traffic being replaced by a new pipeline from Burnaby to northwest Washington. This Alberta crude would be piped out to the new oil terminal near Port Angeles and transferred to oil tankers for the trip down the U.S. west coast.

Some environmentalists applaud this new plan because it moves the spill hazard from the more sensitive waters in the three straits out closer to open seas. Others complain it only moves the problem without eliminating it and is a poor trade-off for two undesirable pipelines traversing the populated San Juan Islands.

Cost estimates have not been released to the public. It is assumed this environmental initiative by Trans Mountain would significantly increase the landed cost of crude oil at the three large Washington refineries. The refinery at Cherry Point is operated by Arco; the one at Ferndale, by BP; and that at Anacortes by Texaco. In the current atmosphere of oil-spill trauma, the oil companies may agree to pay that economic penalty.

···· 8 ····

ISLAND
PIPELINE

Vancouver Island is one of the most enticing energy markets in Canada still not being served by natural gas. This market has been the subject of spicy politics for at least thirty years, largely because it is a prime example of oil dominating the scene by its advantage of mobility. Modest amounts of liquefied petroleum gases are sold on Vancouver Island, but their share of the total energy use is small. The cement industry and the major forest companies, on the other hand, consume immense quantities of oil. Most of this oil is offered to this market at distress prices, and much of it has a sulphur content that prohibits its use in the state of California where it is produced and refined. Stated bluntly, what Californians will not accept in their environment is dumped on British Columbians.

At least five unsuccessful attempts have been made to construct a natural-gas pipeline from various locations on the mainland to Vancouver Island. The first was in 1961. It was named Magnum, promoted largely by Cascade Natural Gas of Seattle and Northern and Central Gas from Toronto. They proposed a low-pressure, flexible pipeline designed to function in the depths and tides of the waters of the San Juan Islands.

There was some political support for this project and little environmental obstruction. On actual tests, however, the technology failed. The flexible pipeline was to be provided by British Callander Cable Company. Unfortunately, their couplings would not function at the channel depths and the entire concept was abandoned. The manufacturer paid several million dollars in damages to the sponsors of that aborted venture.

The second effort occurred in 1964, as an idea Ron Rutherford, then with the Bechtel Corporation, had taken to Frank McMahon at Westcoast Transmission. Under the name Island and Coastal Pipeline, they proposed a lateral from Westcoast's mainline at Williams Lake, running west to the mainland coast and across the strait to Vancouver Island north of Campbell River. This proposed crossing was openly supported by Premier W.A.C. Bennett. Sufficient market could not be guaranteed on the Island to justify the capital expenditure, so this attempt failed on the basis of economics. Another blow was the murder of Island and Coastal's president, Fred Diettrich. He was shot during an office dispute.

The third effort was called the western loop, largely the idea of Westcoast's Charles Hetherington. Its takeoff point would similarly be at Williams Lake. That line would split in two, one leg going to Powell River and the other to the Howe Sound region, then to the B.C. Hydro system distributing natural gas to Vancouver consumers. It would provide a second feed at the western end of their system. Thus the first objective of this plan was to provide a needed security link for Vancouver in case of any interruption in supply from the vulnerable single line entering that important market through the Coquihalla Pass and the Fraser Valley. That single pipeline was also the sole carrier for all Westcoast's gas to the United States. The secondary purpose was to provide a less-costly crossing to Vancouver Island. In 1969 Dr. Gordon Shrum, chairman of B.C. Hydro, opposed this plan on the advice of his marketing chief, Phil Barchard, because it traversed what he thought was a part of their exclusive gas marketing area. Without Hydro's cooperation it was futile to proceed with the Island crossing as a single-purpose venture.

In 1970, a fourth attempt was made. This application was by Pacific Northern Gas, supported by its parent, Westcoast Transmission. It was similar to the Island and Coastal idea of 1964, except that the crossing was between Powell River on the mainland and Comox on Vancouver Island. Market conditions on the Island had improved somewhat by this time. Other proponents emerged for a pipeline crossing, which resulted in a competitive hearing being called by the provincial government.

Hearings by the B.C. Utilities Commission concluded in 1972, just before the Social Credit government was defeated by the New Democrats. A decision was never rendered and the subject of a Vancouver Island pipeline was given low priority by the NDP. This contrasted with their later aggressive and successful attempts to improve the total economic outlook for the natural-gas industry in British Columbia.

The fifth proposal for a Vancouver Island gas pipeline came about in a threatening way. It was mandated in 1981 by the premier of British Columbia as a project to be designed and completed by the B.C. Hydro and Power Authority without any hearings or competition. In the press announcement for this unconventional procedure, Premier Bill Bennett emphasized that his strategy was to preclude any participation by the federal government in a plan that involved a pipeline crossing waters that were under B.C. jurisdiction, in the opinion of the province. He mentioned the National Energy Board as the federal agency he intended to bypass and, by implication, made it clear that any influence of Petro-Canada in the province was to be avoided.

Bennett's anointment of Hydro as Island pipeline builder involved several critical irregularities. First, it was contrary to the accepted practice of inviting competing proposals and interventions by other parties to regulatory hearings for the purpose of safeguarding the public interest in energy supply. Second, the agency selected for this task was primarily an electric utility. It also functioned as a natural-gas distributor, without any technical experience in big-inch, high-pressure transmission pipelines, let alone underwater pipelines. Further, it was a crown corporation whose gas tariffs had never been regulated and tested by public hearings.

This inflammatory slighting of Westcoast by Premier Bennett was considered to have sufficient negative implications to warrant a

decision by our full board of directors. As a result, the board authorized management to oppose the premier publicly on this matter in
any appropriate fashion. An intense public-relations battle commenced with Westcoast's provocative press release: "Blackballed by
the premier."

The reason for Bill Bennett's exclusion of Westcoast from any
planning for a pipeline to Vancouver Island was perfectly clear, and
we were convinced that it was a misguided decision. Its roots lay in
the acquisition of 32 percent of the common shares of Westcoast
Transmission by a federal crown corporation, when Petro-Canada
took over Pacific Petroleums on 10 November 1978 by the initial
step of buying the Pacific shares owned by Phillips Petroleum of
Oklahoma. Owning a natural-gas pipeline was not part of the federal government's announced public role for Petro-Canada. The acquisition was more of an accident than a plan. Westcoast simply
was part of the package of assets acquired from Pacific. The premier's advisers convinced him that was a bad thing for the province. He did not need much persuasion, given British Columbia's
favourite sport of fed-bashing. Bennett immediately invited me to a
session with him in Fort St. John, where he was attending a conference. I was told that Westcoast would have to separate itself in
some way from Petro-Canada, or lose the support of the province
for anything we expected to do in British Columbia. The premier
emphasized that this was a corporate matter and it would not affect
the personal relationship between us. Intentionally or not, his unreasonable posture did damage the final years of my career at
Westcoast.

There were a number of meetings on the subject of Petro-Canada
with the premier, some of his ministers, advisers and government
lawyers. Our position was that it was legally impossible to separate
ourselves from Petro-Canada as long as the NEB controlled our export licences, the only profitable part of Westcoast's business. Furthermore, we used every opportunity to explain that the provincial
fear of federal domination was unfounded. The premier was most
persistent in his opinion that no other province in Canada had suffered the imposition of a federal presence to equal Petro-Canada
controlling the only natural-gas pipeline in the province, being the

largest land holder, producing the most gas and oil, dominating re-
fining operations, controlling one of the natural-gas utility distributors and negatively influencing the destiny of petrochemical development. He forcefully declared that the situation was intolerable
and he felt compelled to rid B.C. of that federal intrusion.

In 1980 Premier Bennett had provided three government lawyers
to meet with the lawyers of Westcoast and the B.C. Petroleum Corporation. His impatient instruction was to devise a legal plan
within three days to free Westcoast from Petro-Canada. At the prescribed deadline, this hastily assembled group confirmed what
Westcoast had claimed from the beginning. A forced separation
was not possible; thus, federal consent was required. Consequently,
the premier decided to pursue the political option. On different occasions he saw Prime Minister Trudeau and energy ministers Gillespie and Lalonde on this subject. While the Conservatives were in
power, he personally approached Prime Minister Joe Clark. Bennett's unwavering demand was that Petro-Canada must sell their
shareholding in Westcoast to private interests. The replies he received were similarly consistent. He was told, in each instance,
that the matter was for the Petro-Canada board of directors to decide. Bill Bennett asked me to follow up his approach to the prime
minister by seeing Clark's top adviser, Jim Gillies. At that time, the
thrust of the Tories was to bust up Petro-Canada altogether. I offered the unsolicited opinion to Gillies that the Canadian public
did not want Petro-Canada eliminated. My advice was to perform
some cosmetic surgery to calm the natives: merely sell off their interest in Westcoast. He obviously was not persuaded.

I do not know whether Bill Bennett or any of his ministers approached Petro-Canada directly on this subject. However, it is a
reasonably well established fact that anyone who made that request
of chairman Bill Hopper or the board of Petro-Canada was told that
the Westcoast shares were not for sale. Under the urging of the premier, I raised the same subject with Alastair Gillespie and later
with Marc Lalonde. They were both courteous and understanding
but still referred me to Hopper. This recommended approach was
not difficult because he was a friend and a colleague on the board at
Westcoast and well aware of the pressure being applied. Bill's an-

swer to me was the same as to everyone else: "I like Westcoast; it's a good investment and I will be a buyer of more stock, not a seller."

While Westcoast management considered that Petro-Canada's public mandate did not include the control of a natural-gas pipeline, we soon realized that if we had to have a major shareholder, Petro-Canada was clearly preferable to Pacific Petroleums. Both of these major shareholders were in unavoidable conflict with some of our operations, but Petro-Canada managed that circumstance more equitably and with more sensitivity and finesse than Pacific Petroleums had. After the change of control to Petro-Canada, Westcoast had considerably more freedom in its oil-and-gas exploration and development, and in its dealings with the gas producers who were competitors of our major shareholder. It always astonished friends in the industry when we confirmed that morale was better at Westcoast and our fortunes appeared brighter with a crown corporation as the major shareholder instead of Pacific. Unfortunately, the punishment meted out by Premier Bennett because of Westcoast's involvement with Petro-Canada was still to come.

Bill Bennett suffered another ill-founded obsession about Westcoast Transmission which he felt had been exacerbated by the Petro-Canada connection. He could not understand why we were not growing into a petrochemical giant like NOVA in Alberta. He had to be reminded that his government's opposition to Westcoast's plans, contrasted to the Alberta government's support for NOVA, was a big reason. However, other hindrances were even more formidable. Alberta's natural-gas reserves were ten times greater than B.C.'s, and located in more hospitable geography for adjoining petrochemical operations. Some Alberta plants were still enjoying old gas-purchase contracts at 20 cents per mcf, most were about 80 cents; while in B.C., that feed-stock price was in the three-dollar range. Also, the Alberta plants were as much as 800 miles closer to the main petrochemical markets in eastern Canada and the U.S. midwest and northeast.

Just prior to the premier's bombshell, in the form of a mandate to B.C. Hydro to build the Island pipeline, I had agreed to serve on the board of directors for Expo '86. Around town, this was considered a prestigious appointment by the premier. However, having undertaken a political battle with Bill Bennett, whom I considered a friend, I decided with regret that it would be awkward to work for him, as exciting as that Expo assignment would have been. Accordingly, I withdrew by telephoning one of my favourite cabinet ministers, Evan Wolfe. He attempted to dissuade me, but finally accepted my resignation with regret, suggesting that he would explain my decision to the premier with a little more delicacy than I had used with him.

Westcoast's and my own reaction to the premier's announcement was particularly spirited because we had recently been denied approval for a mega-project that would have been a credit to both the company and the province. The ever-resourceful Ron Rutherford had been inspired to develop an idea that would have made possible a northern gas pipeline route to Vancouver Island, clearly superior to Hydro's southern crossing in terms of economic benefit to British Columbia. After a thorough study of world supply and demand, in cooperation with Union Oil of California, he determined that a window of opportunity existed at this time to build a fertilizer mega-plant. Its location would be Powell River; its cost, $750 million. The siting was perfect, on a large piece of land on deep water made available by MacMillan Bloedel. Powell River in those years was economically depressed and suffering the hardship typical of a one-industry town during a recession. That is why MacMillan Bloedel and all the elements of the community were so supportive and accommodating.

Our proposed joint venture for the fertilizer plant was to be led by Westcoast as the major shareholder, with Union Oil, Chieftain Developments and B.C. Resources as partners. This was a formidable group from the standpoint of financial resources, technical know-how and feed-stock supply. The addition of B.C. Resources was essentially a political move on the assumption that Bill Bennett would be anxious to assist the company he had formed in a bold privatization strategy. Another of my ideas that didn't work.

The Powell River fertilizer plant would not have required government subsidy of any kind. Its total output was to be purchased by one of the partners, Union Oil. As a hedge against any future deterioration in world markets for fertilizer, Union Oil contractually agreed to reduce the production of its other three world-scale plants to the same degree production had to be lowered in Powell River. In other words, Union Oil was willing to suffer the same cut in production in three other installations they owned outright to ease an output drop in a plant where they had only 25-percent ownership. This was a unique marketing contract which we described to Victoria to support our proposition. They were unresponsive; Union Oil was incredulous. This capricious rejection of a marketing concession more generous than any offered in Union's worldwide operations was beyond their comprehension.

The fertilizer plant would be the economic linchpin for Westcoast's proposal for a pipeline to Vancouver Island; the one feature that could make both projects patently viable. That line would run from Westcoast's mainline at Williams Lake directly to Powell River. At that point it would sell as much gas as all of the customers on Vancouver Island would consume, 20 billion cubic feet a year at a load factor of 95 percent. Obviously, this was a prize any pipeline would covet. Having the first customer along the line take half the total capacity significantly reduces the transmission cost to every customer downstream. While this happy circumstance was a delight to everyone involved, it was not acceptable to the government of B.C. simply because it would easily defeat the southern pipeline crossing they were attempting to grant to B.C. Hydro without competition.

Even as I dictate, ten years later, it is incomprehensible that political entanglements could so short circuit the judgement of a premier and his senior ministers. With the top executives of all the companies involved, including huge Union Oil, we visited Victoria several times to implore the ministers and officials to consider the economic benefits of this enterprise financed totally by private funds. There was not a technical nor an environmental question we could not answer effectively, and the Powell River community was clamouring for us to locate there. The one phantom complication we could not neutralize was the indirect participation of our parent, Petro-Canada. At one formal meeting with the cabinet economic committee, Stephen Rogers was less than civil to John Anderson concerning that association. He asked John about the extent of

Petro-Canada's investment in Westcoast. After John replied, Rogers accused him of misleading the meeting by neglecting to disclose Petro-Canada's very small holding in PNG, Westcoast's subsidiary. This was an inconsequential oversight. The minister's overreaction revealed how the dice were loaded in this set-up situation. It was not characteristic of Stephen Rogers, so we assumed he had been programmed.

One minister at that same meeting was sympathetic. After the criticism by Stephen Rogers, Bill Vander Zalm calmly interjected that he thought the objective of the government was to encourage private enterprise to undertake developments that would contribute to the economic growth of the province. That bit of gratuitous philosophy earned him indignant and disapproving stares from all his colleagues around the table. It was a shocking display and not at all alleviated when chairman Bob McClelland terminated the meeting abruptly without extending the scheduled time to compensate for starting us twenty minutes late. Our representatives had travelled from Los Angeles, Edmonton and Vancouver for that brief session.

After that unpleasant meeting, I decided not to return to Vancouver with the others. I took a room in The Empress hotel and telephoned Bill Vander Zalm's office to attempt to make a dinner appointment. Within ten minutes, the reply was that he would come over right away, mid-afternoon, and stay for dinner. We were together at least four hours. The minister was most candid in describing the problems he was having in the Socred cabinet. More than candid; this was our first meeting and he was somewhat reckless because he knew I was fairly close to the premier. I never embarrassed him; this is my first open reference to that hotel-room meeting.

Vander Zalm insisted the problem was more than our Petro-Canada association; it was a don't-get-cosy-with-business attitude pervading the cabinet. He then told me that his executive assistant had gone into private law practice and one of his new clients was the municipality of Powell River. He pledged to help the cause of the fertilizer plant in any proper way. I assume he tried, but he could not have had much influence in cabinet.

Despite the political hurdles we faced, a formal application for the fertilizer plant was filed with the B.C. government in November 1979, largely in response to the entire community of Powell River rallying to our cause in such an outstanding way. When we could not even get official acknowledgement of that application, the officials of Union Oil were more than disillusioned; they were offended. Fred Hartley, the colourful chairman of Union Oil, was particularly disappointed. As a graduate of the University of British Columbia, he was emotionally linked with this province. He simply could not understand the obstinacy of Victoria when all the technical or economic questions were satisfactorily answered. Union had hosted B.C. government non-elected representatives at their large fertilizer plant in California which is surrounded by luxury homes and a golf course. This trip was to demonstrate the environmental acceptability of such an operation. They were especially upset to be accused of using pressure tactics when they explained the window of opportunity for a new world-scale plant in British Columbia would exist for only two years. They were patient in explaining how these large plants are located around the world, with each following more or less in turn as the world market increases. Unfortunately, rational discussion was impossible in such an atmosphere of wilful obstruction.

The battle of principles in the Vancouver Island pipeline dispute between the premier and Westcoast, visibly Ed Phillips, became very intense throughout 1981 and 1982. Editorial positions across the country almost unanimously supported the company, simply because the use of public hearings was so clearly the established norm in these matters. Talk shows and television appearances were universally supportive of Westcoast. Objective news reports generally portrayed the physical aspects of our plan for the pipeline crossing to Vancouver Island as superior to B.C. Hydro's. The fervent backing of all segments of the Powell River community was a demonstration of organized advocacy beyond anything I had ever experienced.

Mayor Derry Simpson of Powell River led the team that distinguished itself magnificently in the struggle to have the proposed Westcoast fertilizer plant approved for their city, as a key to the economics of a gas pipeline to run from that area's coastline, underwater to Comox on Vancouver Island. As far as I could determine, every recognizable association, lodge, businessman, professional, union official, school principal and local politician joined the campaign. I spent a lot of time with these good people. That was a decade ago but I still recall, with great gratitude, the support of Powell River backers such as Harold Long, Arnold Carlson, Jim Price, Ron Seeley, Don Lidstone, John Murray, Ron Moss, Peter Toigo and so many more.

A lobbyist's handbook could be written on the effective way they used every promotional tool to influence Victoria. That they failed is an exposure of the sad situation in the Socred administration's approach to energy projects, not the slightest evidence that the citizens overlooked any possible strategy or hesitated to make any personal sacrifice in the effort. The local MLA was supportive but without any influence. Don Lockstead was an NDP!

This remarkable powerhouse of public-spirited people accomplished something I would have judged impossible. Bill Bennett wanted B.C. Hydro's Island pipeline to go through the community of Delta in the south. The Powell River alliance persuaded Delta officials to tell the premier that they didn't want it. They did just that with good reason. The pipeline would have been a boost for Powell River, but a bust for Delta. The ground in Delta is acknowledged as a seismic trap for sensitive underground structures. With earthquake disturbance, the soil would liquefy, making a high-pressure pipeline vulnerable to rupture. Incredibly, the government remained adamant in their insistence on this technically hazardous route. They denied the community that begged for it and attempted to force it on the community that didn't want it.

A provincial election occurred at the peak of this aggressive advocacy. We commissioned a Goldfarb public-opinion poll to determine the prospects in the Mackenzie riding which included Powell River. At a cost of $7,000, it indicated that a Socred candidate could capture that constituency, so firmly held by the NDP, with a campaign based on opportunities for economic improvement in the region. We succeeded in having popular hotelier and businessman Jim Price run against incumbent Don Lockstead.

I spent time in that constituency assisting the Social Credit candidate. Premier Bennett refused to appear in Powell River, although I had unofficially been pointed toward that riding by Mike Burns as one of the premier's "group of twenty." That undercover designation meant it was a seat that could be taken from the NDP with extra attention. Energy minister Bob McClelland finally agreed to make a campaign speech in Powell River. My wife and I were in attendance. After a vacuous speech, McClelland refused to answer any of the barrage of questions on the fertilizer plant and the Vancouver Island pipeline. Finally, two men went onto the stage, grabbed the microphone and angrily demanded the minister state his position for or against the fertilizer plant. A mild scuffle started, whereupon one of the organizers hustled Betty and me out of the hall. We didn't see the ending but Bob McClelland joined all of the campaign committee later for a drink, apparently unfazed by the experience. He deserves some credit for taking on a task the premier had ducked. The Socred candidate for that constituency was defeated in the election, possibly because the electorate felt that the pipeline and plant would only be built in their community if the NDP formed the government. Lockstead won 11,000 votes; Price, 8,000; and Liberal George Shaw, only 1,000.

The fair-play question in the public debate about the Island pipeline generated so much support for Westcoast that we were able to concentrate in our public campaign on the physical advantages of the crossing route we had proposed back in 1970, compared to the route mandated eleven years later for B.C. Hydro.

B.C. Hydro claimed their project with a 33-mile-long southern crossing from Delta to the Lower Mainland to a point near Nanaimo would cost only $125 million. Few believed them except the politicians, who appeared to accept that low-ball estimate. Westcoast acknowledged the cost for its project from Williams Lake to a 19-mile-long northern crossing from Powell River to Comox would be about $350 million. We countered that B.C. Hydro's estimate should be at least $250 million, double their claimed cost. A larger capital cost for the northern crossing was manageable on the basis of the proposed new fertilizer plant in Powell River. This huge gas consumer would provide revenue to support almost half of the northern route's $350 million capital cost. B.C. Hydro did not have a single new major gas user on its route that would reduce the cost burden of all the other customers downstream.

Bennett's incredible reaction to that undeniable economic advantage of the northern crossing was simply not to authorize the fertilizer plant being built. The application to construct this $750 million plant had been filed with the B.C. government in November 1979. It died because the province never granted a formal departmental review.

Energy minister Bob McClelland was in the forefront for the government in this pipeline contest. In television interviews he was pressed pointedly on the question of Hydro's low capital cost estimate. He resorted to the ultimate assurance: "I guarantee the pipeline will not cost a nickel more than $125 million." When reminded that experienced pipeliners at Westcoast said Hydro's cost would be over $250 million, McClelland once replied: "That's because Ed Phillips uses a $10 calculator to produce his estimates." That was a catchy one-liner, but he would live to regret those remarks, and feel almost betrayed by B.C. Hydro who provided him with such wildly inaccurate estimates.

Ultimately, the heat got to the premier and he made a surprise announcement in Kelowna that there would be a public hearing to determine the better project between Westcoast's northern route and Hydro's southern crossing. Bob McClelland had not been informed of this unexpected policy reversal. In talking to the media in Victoria the same day, he unavoidably confused the situation totally by declaring that there never would be a hearing because the government had mandated the southern crossing by B.C. Hydro. When I met Bob McClelland on the street a few days later, all he said was: "So you wanted a hearing, you'll get a hearing." His tone was ominous and the message very clear.

The Westcoast board was informed that we would be going into a hearing in which we would be a sure loser. The directors agreed we had to participate, having objected on the basis of principle in the first place. The hearings were held; to no one's surprise, the B.C. Hydro southern crossing was declared the winner. The tragedy to report is that the economics of that southern crossing were so atrocious, B.C. Hydro was never able to take advantage of their victory. The province sought a federal subsidy of $500 million to make the project viable. We had not asked for a dime, assuming the fertilizer plant would be approved. Later, the provincial government lowered the subsidy request, but nothing could convince the federal government to participate. The incredible irony is that Bill Bennett started this fight telling the feds to butt-out and lost it while begging Ottawa for a hand-out.

The public hearing commenced on 27 September 1983. From the massive amount of material required in submission to the hearing, together with skilled cross-examination by Westcoast counsel on that evidence, it was revealed that B.C. Hydro's costs would indeed be more than Bob McClelland's nickel above the $125 million estimate. They would be more like $300 million. Cross-examination also drew the admission that B.C. Hydro had spent $32 million just to prepare their application, mainly in fees to consultants to design the pipeline for which Hydro had no in-house expertise. A $32 million submission for a project they originally costed at $125 million seemed out of whack. Westcoast's costs for the same purpose were about $2 million. Hydro's inability to estimate accurately should really have been no surprise: the same thing will happen every time you hire a plumber to paint your house.

The economics of the northern crossing became similarly poor, having been destroyed when the government blocked the building of the fertilizer plant in Powell River. That one customer on the mainland coast could have borne something approaching half the cost of the pipeline for the benefit of all the potential gas consumers on Vancouver Island.

The word "punishment" was never used by provincial politicians in discussing their opposition to Petro-Canada's influence in British Columbia. They were more subtle in saying they could not support Westcoast as an affiliate of a federal crown corporation, but that lack of support from a government that can largely influence the company's destiny truly equated to punishment.

By a strange turn of fate, Petro-Canada entered the debate at one point supporting the government and criticizing Westcoast's northern crossing. Without the knowledge of senior management, Petro-Canada engaged a consultant to make an independent comparison of the northern and southern crossings. Unluckily for us, they commissioned this task to a former employee of Westcoast who obtained all his research from Hydro without as much as a telephone call to our engineers. His report to Petro-Canada lauded Hydro's southern crossing and condemned Westcoast's northern crossing. This confidential document was presumably leaked by someone in Petro-Canada to the energy ministry in Victoria and it was soon in the hands of the press. Damaging publicity, particularly in the *Vancouver Sun* headlines, was soon on the streets and Westcoast was presented with the delicate problem of its major shareholder maligning its proposal. Chairman Bill Hopper was out of the country at the time. On his return he swiftly determined that this was an accidental and not intentional intrusion into the debate.

Victoria officials enjoyed our embarrassment for a few weeks. Westcoast did not suffer too much because the media gave us generous space and time for rebuttal. This was easy, given the lack of depth and objectivity in the study bought by Petro-Canada. I must ask Bill Hopper some day what he paid for it. Or, maybe I should ask Auditor-General Kenneth Dye, who appears to have a keen interest in Petro-Canada's expenses. I suspect my mischief would fail on a test of materiality.

We rationalized Petro-Canada's criticism of our northern crossing as an accident involving one individual's engineering advice that was not objective. We couldn't be that generous with the B.C. government. They were capricious in blackballing that northern crossing, because their energy department's files were replete with documentation from Westcoast, and at least two other very qualified firms, about that route's technical, economic and environmental superiority. In the 1972 B.C. Utilities Commission public hearings, two firms had presented months of evidence assembled at great expense, in competition with Westcoast for the permit to build the natural-gas pipeline to Vancouver Island.

One of those companies was Malaspina Gas Pipeline Ltd., sponsored by Canadian Utilities Ltd. of Edmonton. In addition to their own expertise, they employed consultants formerly with the Bechtel Corporation in San Francisco. Their credentials could not be challenged. Their testimony was valid and persuasive.

Malaspina's principal objective was to obtain the franchise for distribution of natural gas for all of Vancouver Island. To be certain that distribution franchise would be viable and advantageous to the gas consumers, they first had to assure the least-cost delivery system of that gas from the mainland to the Island. That explains their selection of the northern crossing as the better route, and their willingness to invest in a big-inch pipeline to guarantee that final choice.

The other authoritative group stressing the superiority of the northern crossing was Centennial Pipelines. It had notable engineering prestige, being sponsored by H.A. Simons, consultants, and also employing pipeline veterans from Bechtel. Brian Bentz represented Simons; Charlie Bailley was the former Bechtel engineer. They testified they would not participate in any underwater pipeline crossing other than the northern route which was determined to be the best of all they had studied.

Although with the confusion of the change of government to the NDP the BCUC had never rendered a decision on that earlier 1972 hearing, the government in 1981 had available to it a vast amount of testimony by the most-qualified people in the business that the northern crossing was the better route. All three groups proposed the identical crossing from Powell River to Comox. Our contest only concerned which of us could complete the project in the best manner. In the face of that overwhelming expert evidence, the B.C. government later mandated the inferior southern crossing.

Later vindication is insufficient compensation for the millions wasted by the proponents of the fertilizer plant mega-project, but at least the record can be made clear by reporting some future events. About six years later, Stephen Rogers, who had become B.C.'s energy minister, actually approached John Anderson about reopening the idea of the fertilizer plant. John obviously had not forgotten the altercation with this minister, yet he was totally willing to see what could be done for the benefit of Westcoast and the province. Accordingly, he persuaded Union Oil and Chieftain to join Westcoast in another market study. After the additional expenditure of almost $250,000, the conclusion was inevitable; the project simply could not be revived because two world-scale plants had been built in Indonesia in the interval. The minister was so advised and, although I did not hear the conversation, I imagine John Anderson reminded Stephen about his government accusing Union Oil of pressure tactics in the reference to a limited window of opportunity.

Little is known publicly about this performance of the B.C. government and possibly it will not even receive an asterisk in the history of industrial development in this province. That does not mean it was not a staggering loss. One eruption of obstinacy killed two projects at the same time, the fertilizer plant and the Island pipeline, neither of which required a dime of government assistance, and would have contributed a banker's ransom in tax revenues.

With an admission of bias, I still maintain the Bennett government's strategy was irrational. They not only wounded Westcoast; in the process, they sacrificed a mega-project fertilizer plant that would have been an economic boost for the depressed region of Powell River and for the province as a whole. In the end, their unwise strategy failed dismally. Their chosen Hydro pipeline proposal disintegrated after a huge expenditure in planning reports. And Ottawa's Petro-Canada is even more involved in British Columbia than it was then.

In 1981, the political duo of Premier Bill Bennett and energy minister Bob McClelland had blackballed Westcoast by naming B.C. Hydro to build the Island pipeline on the southern crossing without competition. Ironically, seven years later, in 1988, the combination of Premier Bill Vander Zalm and energy minister Jack Davis, also Socreds, similarly blackballed B.C. Hydro by excluding them when inviting Westcoast and others to join forces to build the elusive and oft-promised Island pipeline. If any further evidence of the unpredictability of politics in B.C. was necessary, this was it. Both extremes in this remarkable reversal are discriminatory, but there was a weighty difference in the motivation for the two.

In the first instance, the Bennett government was phobia-driven to obstruct Westcoast because of federal government participation in the form of the National Energy Board and Petro-Canada. In 1989 a different approach was employed. The Vander Zalm government selected a compromise route designed by Ron Rutherford for the energy ministry. Rutherford offered pieces of the action to Inland Natural Gas, Chieftain Developments and Westcoast Energy Inc. Only Chieftain declared any real interest in that preliminary search. Then Victoria actually sought federal government participation. Same province, same party, different premiers.

This is not meant to be a defence of the Vander Zalm government's policy of singling out B.C. Hydro for exclusion; discrimination is discrimination irrespective of the target. However, it can at least be affirmed that the motives of Vander Zalm and Davis were not vindictive but, rather, were based on practical considerations. They wanted the most economical pipeline crossing. They insisted it be constructed by acknowledged pipeline experts, not by an electric utility. And they recognized that federal-government participation would be essential. Their plan of action may have been controversial but it was determined, direct and entirely above-board.

The energy minister's first step in the more recent proposal was that assignment to Rutherford. Ron had retired from Westcoast and Foothills and was then alone in Pacific Coast Energy, backed by Chieftain Developments. He was commissioned to select a route for the most viable Vancouver Island pipeline without any predilection for northern or southern crossings. He was successful in producing a compromise but not optimum route, initially estimated to cost a low $250 million including distribution on the Island.

The government's ultimate call for bids on a pipeline to the Island drew response from Inland Natural Gas, Inter-City Gas, Pacific Coast Energy, Island Gas Transmission and Northwest Pipeline. Some offered considerable variation from the Rutherford route. After departmental review, as opposed to yet another public hearing, Pacific Coast Energy was awarded the permit.

Westcoast had joined Pacific Coast Energy Corporation for this project. That firm now comprised Alberta Energy Corp., Chieftain's parent, and Westcoast Energy Inc., the latter being the operator and 50-percent shareholder, and still effectively controlled by a federal crown corporation. Vander Zalm's pragmatism permitted him to dilute selfish provincial interests further by accepting an Alberta company as a partner with Westcoast.

One of the provisions of the Liberal government's ill-fated National Energy Program was an undertaking to provide $500 million for natural-gas pipeline extensions in the eastern provinces and in British Columbia. This was an effort to reduce the consumption of oil by providing natural gas in areas not served by that superior fuel. Westcoast urged the provincial government to take advantage of this offer in a number of ways. With what we regarded as misguided provincialism, Victoria refused to make an application of any sort for this assistance. When the NEP was later modified, there was pointed mention that the eastern provinces were benefiting from that federal assistance but British Columbia had not shown any interest in the money offered. We renewed our efforts to have B.C. pick up this offer, suggesting that this published announcement could be a warning the generous accommodation was about to expire. The government remained adamant about refusing its share of this federal largesse. Commendable, in a sense, but not consistent with its happy acceptance of all other federal transfer payments.

The new Socred administration, featuring Bill Vander Zalm and Jack Davis on this issue, was quite the opposite. With superb timing, they aggressively requested Ottawa to make good on its old promise of financial assistance. The B.C. Tory caucus joined in the quest for help from their fellow members in Ottawa. B.C. made their request quite public in the weeks of heavy campaigning by the Conservatives for re-election in 1988. Consequently, among the pre-election handouts distributed by the government across Canada was a subsidy for the celebrated Vancouver Island pipeline, making a total federal and provincial contribution of $300 million. This total included a bundle of grants, loans, price back-stopping and conversion assistance. Despite federal budget limitations, the promise was reaffirmed after the election.

Construction has started on this latest proposal to build a pipeline to serve Vancouver Island with natural gas after five expensive and unsuccessful attempts over 29 years. It is not because the economics are better than the earlier attempts; they are worse than Westcoast's 1979 recommendation. Its success is the result of the B.C. government sensibly cooperating with their federal counterparts instead of engaging in Ottawa bashing.

·····9·····

WESTCOAST
TO WESTAR

The late 1970s in British Columbia saw a parade of mega-projects, with breathless political announcements in riding after riding, most with propitious electoral timing. Reviewing the results, the box score is tragic, mainly because some of the mega-projects that went ahead were little more than government make-work schemes and political fantasies unsupported by economic due diligence. Others with some substance didn't survive the planning stage, but they consumed taxpayers' money. It seemed that the intellectual thrust in Victoria was "thinking big beats thinking smart." In a quick summary, the Northeast Coal mega-project was scandalous with the established southeast coal region being damaged and the taxpayers being burned more viciously than the fifty-six banks involved; Kitimat Methanol embarrassed the government and disappointed the shareholders but will survive after restructuring; Powell River Fertilizer was simply a shame the way it was scuttled by the government; the Vancouver Island pipeline sank in the strait with the fertilizer plant; the Kitimat LNG, which the government wanted, failed because of their fumbling; the Coquihalla Highway was a mess in cost overruns; Expo '86 was a triumph for the government despite the budgeted net loss of $350 million.

Before detailing the mega-projects in which Westcoast was involved, it may be helpful to explore a feature of my business background which is relevant. In 1945, I became advertising manager for Canada and Dominion Sugar Company Limited. This title was not descriptive of my actual function, which was lobbying, in the proper sense of that term. My responsibility was to monitor political developments affecting the intricate sugar business and to advise politicians and officials with respect to legislation and regulations involving the industry generally. Politics and sugar were always stirred together. One critical issue was the tariff protection on imported raw cane sugar. Just as important were provincial subsidies on which the sugar-beet industry depended for survival. My most interesting assignment was to secure all the political clearances for the permanent move and lodging of scores of families from Belgium and Holland to work in the sugar-beet fields of Ontario after the Second World War. This task involved negotiations at federal, provincial, county and municipal levels. Just as challenging was the need to contract farmers to grow 30,000 acres of sugar beets, the minimum amount necessary to reopen a sugar refinery that had been closed during the war.

I was not a lobbyist-for-hire, as the professional term implies today. I was on the permanent staff of a single employer and designated to lobby that company's interests where politics were involved. I enjoyed the opportunity immensely. Starting at the age of twenty-eight, it was a valuable learning experience to have face-to-face meetings with powerful politicians and officials including Ottawa's C.D. Howe and Sugar Administrator S.R. Noble and Ontario's Premier George Drew and ministers Tom Kennedy and Tod Daley.

When I moved to Consumers' Gas in 1947, most of my time was spent with both elected and appointed authorities in the federal government and in Ontario. A new dimension was added because of Consumers' official connection with the city of Toronto and thirteen other municipalities. Consumers' distribution pipelines were anything but big-inch. Intriguingly, there were remnants of replaced wooden gas pipes under the streets of Toronto. These were hand-bored cedar logs sealed at their fitted joints with pitch. They had been cut from the forest around what is now Bloor and Yonge Streets.

All of this is meant to say that I was not a pipeliner, but I had considerable exposure to politicians and bureaucrats before joining Westcoast in 1968. At Westcoast my responsibilities demanded a level of lobbying activity exceeding all I had done previously. For fourteen years, I was constantly in contact with senior officials in Ottawa and Washington. Specific trips with important missions took me to the capitals of twelve states in the U.S., with many repeat visits. In Canada, I had formal appearances with various ministries, officials and hearings in six provinces and both territories. As much time as possible was devoted to attending conventions, conferences, inquiries, political meetings and generally gumshoeing the corridors of political power bases. I describe all of this with pride because of the positive and essential nature of that lobbying.

Without apologizing for the vanity of the foregoing recitation, it was necessary in order to authenticate my personal conclusion about the quality of various political administrations. There are good politicians and superb officials in every administration, but some are clearly better endowed than others. On a test of enlightened response to the legitimate needs of the business fraternity, after many years' exposure, I would say that the government of Ontario was consistently the best. Alberta was close; Ottawa was better than Washington, D.C.; Washington State, better than California, just as examples. But, I am truly distressed to say that the province of British Columbia does not have a distinguished reputation on the test of sensitivity and responsiveness to business. My opinion is shared by some businessmen and even more bureaucrats in other jurisdictions. Admittedly, my assessment of the situation in B.C. is a sweeping generalization; also, it does not include an analysis of the room the bureaucracy has to move or the quality of direction provided by the elected officials; and, finally, it makes no allowance for two turbulent government changes in the 1970s that induced the bureaucracy to hunker down.

All the civil servants can't be a Jim Matkin, who had many roles leading to the pinnacle of deputy minister of intergovernmental affairs before he moved to the private sector. Nor can all of them be expected to be a Larry Bell, who serves the province with distinction as chairman of B.C. Hydro. But hundreds of decision-making bureaucrats must be doing their very best, consistent with the tone of the elected administration. If the premier and the energy minister order an electric utility to build a gas pipeline to Vancouver Island without a public hearing, what are the deputy minister and his staff supposed to do? All walk off the job? The same with building a railroad and instant townsite in the boonies.

Perceptions are not always accurate, yet they are inclined to feed on themselves. An MLA friend, concerned about some perceived anti-business decisions, rationalized the hazard by saying, "This province has so much going for it, even we can't blow it."

Having no stomach for the political alternative of the NDP, business in B.C. has traditionally supported the Social Credit party and any of its candidates. There was always a feverish courtship at election time, and business responded with generous contributions. After each election, however, the Socreds' ardour for business was not so evident. Even the NDP appeared acceptable to some businessmen during the between-election chill; but that accommodation always evaporated at election time.

Although elected for only one term in B.C., the NDP has secured a high percentage of the popular vote in every campaign. In the 1970s this was attributed to the populist Dave Barrett and his dynamic style as their leader. In my opinion, his popularity spooked the Socreds, and Barrett's 1972 victory influenced them more than ever to attempt to build a populist image.

If multi-millionaire Bill Bennett could pose as a populist, devout Bill Vander Zalm should claim to be Mother Teresa's son. But, unfortunately, the desire for that image required the Socreds to keep big business somewhat at a distance in order to hoodwink the populace. In this operating mode, the government fostered projects that would give solace to the voting masses; for example, the Coquihalla Highway, Expo '86, a frontier railroad, a new remote townsite and make-work projects disguised as mega-projects. On the back burner went any deferrable program that was not highly rated as voter-friendly, such as higher education, research or reforestation. Stated another way, the Socreds mastered the technique of keeping business at arm's length between elections, but extending the reach of those arms enough to get into the pockets of big business for large campaign contributions come election time.

Additionally, attitudinal changes were attempted. Apparently to gain the applause of that abstract and undefinable voting mass, the government appeared prone to picking chippy disputes with the province's doctors, landlords, developers or teachers, all of whom represented only powder-puff voting muscle. Premier Bill Bennett was different from his premier father in some ways, but in this strategy of populist pretence he unleashed his predecessor's Ottawa-bashing passion. And that hurt Westcoast directly.

In my view, the long series of earlier Social Credit governments had been reasonably accommodating to the justifiable needs of business. Certainly their record was worthy of that imprecise description of free-enterprise, and praise was deservedly heaped on Bill Bennett for his restraint program when that unpopular business-like stance was so necessary and unmatched by any other administration in Canada. The puzzle to me is why the phantom threat of Dave Barrett and the "socialist hordes" could dupe more recent Socred caucuses into formulating policies that were not helpful to business.

Bill Bennett could not have received the let's-play-populist advice from Austin Taylor, his close friend, confidant and chief fundraiser. Austin was a founding director of Foothills, a close personal friend and my fox-hunting mentor. Nor does that strategy sound like political advisers Michael Burns or Patrick Kinsella, both of whom had Bennett's ear. And it defies the test of reasonableness to assume that any thrust in this direction came from fair-minded and veteran cabinet ministers such as Grace McCarthy, Evan Wolfe, Alan Williams, Stephen Rogers, Garde Gardom, James Chabot, Hugh Curtis, Peter Hyndman, Pat McGeer and others. Further, it was not the style of Leslie Peterson, who retained his influence after leaving cabinet. There is evidence that even Bill Vander Zalm was not in step with some policies, and letters to the editor from demoted backbencher Jack Davis made his concern about the thrust of Socred policy abundantly clear.

Whatever its origin, the Social Credit government's anti-big-business stance frustrated Westcoast's ability to make a positive contribution to the province's economy many times during my tenure with that company. Some examples will demonstrate that my opinions are not based on simple paranoia.

In 1972, Ron Rutherford had been planning to establish a methanol plant in Kitimat, the feed-stock to be supplied by Westcoast's subsidiary Pacific Northern Gas. This was a modest proposal for which a small, idle plant would be purchased in the United States and dismantled for re-erection in Kitimat. The economics were sound but the supply of gas suddenly became non-existent. As recorded earlier, the gas fields in Beaver River and Pointed Mountain had gone to water and Westcoast lost 30 percent of its total supply. It was thus impossible to use gas for a new enterprise while the American export customers were being seriously curtailed.

In 1979, when the gas supply was more secure, the idea was resurrected. This time, however, it was to be a world-scale methanol plant costing about $275 million. The partners were Westcoast, Chieftain and two Japanese companies. Of the plant's total capacity, 70 percent was to be sold to Japan on a firm-price contract, the balance going to the variable spot market. The economics were sound, but not rich, if the feed-stock could be purchased at no more than $3 per mcf. This price for feed-stock compared to the low 80 cents per mcf generally being paid by the large methanol operations in Alberta. Nevertheless, Westcoast was willing to proceed despite that cost burden. Unfortunately, the B.C. government insisted that the natural gas had to be purchased through the B.C. Petroleum Corporation at $3.35 per mcf. Westcoast attempted to negotiate a higher contract price for the finished product from Japan. They agreed to some increase but not enough to justify paying $3.35 for the natural-gas feed-stock. The government hold-out for that high feed-stock price killed the project for Westcoast. None of the Victoria officials went into mourning, because they had lined up another potential investor for a methanol plant. Some of them like Doug Horswell and Harry Swain in the energy ministry appeared to understand the damage the pricing policy could do to our project and were sympathetic to our objections. Regardless, we still lost the game.

Ocelot Industries of Alberta entered the scene with an offer to build a methanol plant of the same size and to pay the inflated $3.35 per mcf for the natural-gas feed-stock. They convinced the government that they could do this deal, despite Westcoast's withdrawal, because their plant would only cost $175 million and 70 percent of their output would go to the spot market at expected higher selling prices. We knew this was impossible but the provincial government officially approved the project. During my next conversation with the minister in charge of industrial development, Don Phillips, he said: "Westcoast is too cautious. Vern Lyons of Ocelot is more my kind of people."

When Vern Lyons requested Westcoast's John Anderson to build a costly pipeline to deliver gas to the new methanol plant, he was told that there would have to be a take-or-pay contract for the sale of gas to justify that heavy capital expenditure for a single customer. That message was taken to Victoria as a complaint and the government officials quickly castigated John for attempting to kill the Ocelot project in a display of sour grapes. John explained his reasoning and then offered a shrewd compromise. He said if the government was so certain about Ocelot's credit, he would sell the gas to the government on a take-or-pay basis, and they could make their own deal on the resale to Ocelot. They did just that.

To jump to the end of this tale, John's assessment was correct. Ocelot could not pay its gas bills and had to make an arrangement with the Royal Bank to assign its mortgage on the plant to the B.C. government as a guarantee of gas payments in the future. As a director of the Royal Bank, Anderson must have been intrigued by that event from a different perspective. The gas bills were unpaid for years, but that's the kind of customer Don Phillips apparently preferred to Ottawa-tainted Westcoast.

The reasons for Ocelot's credit problem were obvious. Their methanol plant actually cost $320 million, instead of the $175 million they had estimated. Compounding that extremely faulty estimate, the spot market for methanol slipped badly and only 30 percent of their output was on contract sales at firm prices. This was all a sorry result for Ocelot and an embarrassment to the government. Eventually, however, there was a financial restructuring and diversification into other products, making the operation viable and a good gas customer for Pacific Northern Gas, controlled by Westcoast.

If Ocelot is paying anything like the $3.35 per mcf the government demanded from Westcoast, I will eat my pipeliner's hard hat. The point remains, nevertheless, that if the government had not been so obstructive in its dealings with Westcoast, the methanol project would have proceeded smoothly and been a profitable venture for all concerned from the day it commenced production.

Another B.C. mega-project involving Westcoast was the generally popular idea and practical desire in 1980 to locate a $2 billion liquefied natural-gas plant on the coast of B.C. By a process I will describe simply as deep refrigeration, natural gas could be reduced to one-six-hundredth of its volume and transported to markets in that form by specially designed ocean vessels. The technology was not at all new; it was being exploited by installations all around the world. It was an LNG system that El Paso entered into the contest for the transportation of natural gas from Alaska. At this same time, there were very imaginative plans to move natural gas from the high arctic to Europe and other destinations in the form of LNG.

The LNG opportunity on the coast of B.C. attracted two competitors, Dome Petroleum and Rim Gas, which was a partnership of Westcoast Transmission and Petro-Canada. An astonishing aspect of this situation was that Dome Petroleum was generally acknowledged as being essentially bankrupt at this time. Nevertheless, they threw tremendous financial resources and a large number of personnel into the fray. I recall one particular session in which Dome was represented by seventeen people, compared to our modest contingent of three and another three or four from Petro-Canada. This was typical of Dome, and their celebrated excesses had more than a little to do with their eventual financial collapse. But on this mega-project they persevered, lobbied ferociously in Victoria and Tokyo and eventually were given the permit to proceed by the B.C. government.

Both the competing LNG plants were to be located in the Kitimat area. Oddly enough, Dome selected a site Westcoast had abandoned because of soil instability. The output capacity of each was to be virtually the same. The sales arrangement was somewhat different. Dome planned to purchase its own fleet of LNG ocean vessels to deliver their product to Japan. Our arrangement was to sell the LNG at dockside with transportation to Asia being the responsibility of the users. Obviously, both plans would depend on relatively the same sources of natural gas for conversion to LNG, and the processes were identical.

As on earlier undertakings, political hostility was repeatedly directed against Westcoast and Petro-Canada. During preliminary negotiations with government officials, scarcely one of the features of our plan was accepted as having any validity; whereas the sales pitch by Dome received full credibility.

Bill Bennett was always generous in giving me time to discuss any energy matters involving British Columbia. He was not devious in his opposition to Petro-Canada and constantly emphasized that this was not a grievance directly with Westcoast or with me personally. Rather, his hang-up was the federal government. On one such visit, he confided in me about an overwhelming reason for his preference for Dome that had nothing to do with politics. He explained he had been guaranteed by Bill Richards of Dome that they would build at least three huge LNG ocean vessels in the port of Vancouver. I was aghast, exclaiming that not even Japan could be sure of building its own LNG vessels, considering the competition from Korea. The premier did not seem concerned, so I asked him if he truly believed that the port of Vancouver, with its reputation for high cost, could possibly compete in this sophisticated type of shipbuilding. He calmly replied that was not his problem because it was a definite undertaking from Dome.

When I returned to Vancouver, I telephoned Travis Petty at El Paso, asking him to send me photos of their LNG vessels that were idle and tied up at docks around the world. He sent me three eight-by-ten glossies of surplus LNG ships; one was available at the price of scrap, one was being converted for coal and the other for grain. I sent these photographs to Victoria, merely as a test of reasonableness of the claim by anyone that they would build three new LNG tankers in Vancouver while surplus vessels were on the open market for purchase or charter. There was no reply and Dome was awarded the big prize.

It is not much of an overstatement to say that the entire energy industry in Canada was stunned with the announcement that Dome had been selected by B.C. to complete what had grown to a $4 billion mega-project. In July 1982 I was at a bank board meeting in Toronto when the news came over the Dow about energy minister Bob McClelland's announcement. My bank colleagues were incredulous because Dome's incipient financial collapse had been public knowledge for months. The president of one of the major oil companies asked me: "How could Dome win this job when they can't finance 75 cents?" If I could have answered that question, I could have unravelled the perplexing mystery of why the B.C. government continued to be so determined to bypass Westcoast and Petro-Canada.

Similarly, the National Energy Board was supportive, in the absence of any other B.C.-approved contender. However, Dome's NEB export permit granted in January 1983 was made conditional on final gas-supply arrangements with the producers. This requirement was never met. Dome wanted a guaranteed return on their investment. The producers, conscious of the financial problems of Dome, could not accept purchase contracts that did not provide them with minimum net-back gas prices at the wellhead. They understandably reasoned that any cost problems in the Dome operation, particularly high-financing costs, would result in discounting the price to be paid for their natural gas. Consequently, this dramatic project slowly died on the drafting tables. Producer interest waned as the LNG markets softened. The chosen builder could not perform, and the window of opportunity closed for British Columbia.

Reflecting on the Dome problem, *Vancouver Sun* business columnist Rod Nutt wrote on 19 January 1984: "Two years ago, then energy minister Bob McClelland astounded the business world by choosing financially shattered Dome Petroleum Ltd. to build a $3.5 billion liquefied natural gas plant in B.C. The decision also shocked Dome's main rival bidding for the LNG plant, a consortium of Westcoast Transmission Co. Ltd., Petro-Canada Ltd. and Mitsui

& Co. The reasons for McClelland's decision to go with Dome may never be known, but there was a strong indication at the time that Premier Bill Bennett vetoed the Petro-Canada consortium because of the federal government connection through Petro-Canada."

Should I appear to be exaggerating the irony of Stephen Rogers approaching John Anderson to resurrect the fertilizer plant, after having thwarted it when it made economic sense, let me complete the saga about this LNG scenario. About the same time as the fertilizer plant episode, the new energy minister similarly appealed to Westcoast to reopen the LNG study because the province was now desperate for valid projects to stimulate the economy. As an incentive, he said they would remove some previous prohibitions and permit Westcoast to build an LNG plant in the Lower Mainland, even on the Fraser River if a suitable location was available. As with the previous request, John was most accommodating and had the support of Westcoast's partners in taking another look. It did not take long because two new LNG projects had been announced in Indonesia and another in Australia. The world energy scene had changed so dramatically in the interval that there was absolutely no opportunity to breathe life into this mega-project again. Erect a huge cross on the coast of B.C. to mark the demise of another economic venture.

A post mortem is illuminating because it can show how the world could have turned for B.C., but for government pettiness. My picture of what might have been is the LNG plant in Australia that captured enough of the Japanese market to prevent a second attempt by Westcoast and Petro-Canada. In the industry's vernacular, the Aussies closed the window. Their plant went on stream in July 1989, programmed to build a complex capable of shipping 3.4 billion gallons of LNG per year to eight utilities in Japan.

The location is the northwest shelf of Australia, near a town called Karratha. This area of rocks and scrubgrass was formerly populated by lizards and a few hardy pioneers. That barren region now has 13,000 residents and is referred to as "LNG City." By 1994, the dollar value of LNG exports will rival that of the nation's income from wheat and iron ore. The LNG plant was the largest construction project in Australia's history, costing $3.5 million per day at the peak. Total expenditures in the Karratha region were $9 billion. This includes the cost of the full infrastructure of plant, off-shore natural-gas platforms, pipeline and tankers.

It hurts to recall how close we came to a somewhat smaller but still spectacular boost to British Columbia's economy.

The last in this awkward parade of mega-projects marching to the tune of the Social Credit government was Northeast Coal. From the very start, it was always out of step. No matter how long it survives, it will never properly fall into formation.

The Northeast Coal mega-project was parented by the minister in charge of industrial development, Don Phillips, a good friend but not a relative as he hastily reminds everyone. Its touted noble purpose was to open up the interior of B.C. for more employment and the proper exploitation of an abundant natural resource in the form of coal. The deposits involved are in a location known as Tumbler Ridge, south of Dawson Creek. This is a remote, forbidding, mountainous region with coal as its only exploitable resource. The views are spectacular and the challenge to explorers is enormous. But a preferred place to live and raise a family it isn't. Its greatest attribute as the site for a mega-project was the good fortune of being in the riding of Don Phillips, an imaginative and aggressive minister of the Crown. Another contributing feature was the influence this minister had with Premier Bill Bennett, whose father had a passion for extending railroads into remote regions during his administration, leading to the Dease Lake extension fiasco.

Not all the influences were internal. Japan is always on the search for energy supplies of all types. They are masters at developing competition among energy-rich nations so they would never be captive to an OPEC-type situation. The Japanese steel mills had been purchasing a reasonable proportion of their metallurgical coal requirements from the established and fully integrated coal industry in the southeast corner of British Columbia. During his many trips to Japan seeking business for the province, the minister described the undeveloped coal deposits in his riding. The Japanese saw an opportunity to establish a competitive source of supply, including a second coal port on the B.C. coast, as insurance against labour disputes at the southeast mines and the existing port at Roberts Bank near Vancouver. This time, the competition would not be between two nations; it would be unique in pitting two regions in a single province against each other. This is a cute concept for the buyer; a dumb deal for the seller.

This particular scheme distinguished itself immediately by generating negative public outcry. The tone and amount of criticism from expert sources were evidence the multi-billion-dollar project should not be undertaken. Jack Davis, then a back-bench MLA Socred, went public on the subject. His courageous and erudite letters-to-the-editor exposed the hazardous economics of this particular coal development. The media were generally critical. Columnist Marjorie Nichols exhaustively and negatively reported this subject. Her material was considered valid enough to be the thrust of a one-hour CBC-TV special. This presentation also featured mining experts, union leaders, town officials and displaced miners who were all opposed. It was not balanced reporting, for the simple reason that there was a lack of supporters other than the involved government officials and appointees. The most enthusiastic supporters, the Japanese steel mills, were not represented on the program. Nevertheless, the need for the provincial and federal governments to provide enormous subsidies manifestly demonstrated that the whole idea was economically unsound.

This scheme was offensive to the business community. Its basic concept was indefensible, considering that the government was subsidizing an uneconomic and unnecessary coal operation in one corner of British Columbia that would compete with the established, efficient and investor-owned coal industry in the southeast of the same province. But the government was not to be deterred. The time seemed perfect to garner some of the federal money the Trudeau government was generously sprinkling around B.C., under the encouragement of Senator Jack Austin who was doing a great job for his home province in that respect. In total, I believe the government subsidies could develop into something like $1.5 billion as underpinning for an unpopular mega-project in an uninhabited and remote area.

The existing, mature coal industry in southeastern B.C. featured several non-subsidized, self-sustaining coal mines, a railroad to the coast with Canadian Pacific Railway unit trains dedicated to this service, a coastal coal port capable of loading 20 million tons a year into the largest coal tankers in the world, and a string of well-settled cities and towns offering a superb standard of living for the thousands of coal miners and their families residing in a geographically ideal valley location. This remarkable assortment of self-sufficient facilities had to be duplicated, if not matched in quality, for the new mega-project touted by the government. The general public, and clearly the editorial writers, questioned the wisdom of building a new townsite isolated in the far-away mountains in order to serve two new coal mines, which would require more than 60 miles of new railroad passing through two mountain tunnels to get their product to the mainline. It all seemed patently bizarre, coming so soon after the findings of the Mackenzie Commission concerning B.C. Rail and the cost of building railroads for political purposes.

The Mackenzie Commission was a B.C. royal commission, chaired by Supreme Court Justice Lloyd Mackenzie. The labour nominee appointed to the inquiry was Dave Chapman of the Machinist's Union. The business nominee was prominent financier Syd Welsh. The financial advisor to the board was David Sinclair, senior partner of Coopers and Lybrand.

The terms of reference included an examination of the finances of B.C. Rail. The timing suggests that the serious cost overruns of the Dease Lake railway extension, that had added dangerously to the debt burden of B.C. Rail, could have precipitated the study. The government responded to most of the commission's recommendations, most notably the forgiving of something like $300 million of B.C. Rail debt.

The thrust of the commission's advice had to do with subsidies. Their point was that any railroad extension should be recognized for what it truly is. Is the purpose a sound, economic development for the system, or, is it a project of political motivation with some alleged global advantage for the citizenry? If it is the latter, the railway should not be saddled with the operating losses or the required subsidy. The B.C. government seems to have acknowledged that their Northeast Coal project fits the label of political motivation because the taxpayers, not the coal mines nor B.C. Rail, will be paying the big difference between high costs and low revenues.

The complaint that this initiative would seriously compete with the existing coal business in the province was brushed off by government spokesmen and by Ron Basford, a former federal minister, who had been appointed coal administrator by the province. The indisputable facts are, however, that the day coal shipments commenced from the northeast, the Japanese purchases from the southeast started dwindling as a percentage of their total requirements, and that trend never stopped.

In early 1981, multi-millionaire businessman Jimmy Pattison and I were invited to join the board of the beleaguered British Columbia Resources Investment Corporation, at the suggestion of the premier, I was told. BCRIC owned two-thirds of Westar Mining, the largest and lowest-cost coal producer in the southeast area. During the public debate on the northeast-coal scheme, I openly stated that the government plan would unavoidably affect the viability of our operating mines in southeast B.C. This statement was used by the NDP to challenge the Socreds during question period in the legislature. I suspect the premier was displeased and mentioned his annoyance to Bruce Howe, BCRIC's president, because the latter made it clear to me that my comments had been unwelcome, in the context of referring to one of his conversations with Bill Bennett.

Several times, the board of directors of BCRIC discussed the advisability of taking a public position on this issue, given its impact on the coal industry. Bruce Howe demurred on each occasion. My suspicions were aroused that he was intimidated by the government when what had the appearance of a phoney question was planted at a BCRIC annual meeting, asking if Northeast Coal would harm Westar Mining in any way. I felt sorry for the chairman and esteemed coal expert, Walter Riva, when he offered an apparently orchestrated reply, something like: "No, because we would have faced the same competition from other sources in any case." It was not a proud moment.

Also, Gary Livingstone, the Westar Mining president, blew it all at a convention in Calgary just days later. He criticized Northeast

Coal and claimed that real damage would result. The media gave this unrehearsed and more candid declaration considerable coverage.

I am admittedly vulnerable in the tone of my suspicion about Bruce Howe's timidity in this matter. He could challenge me about the crusade I waged against Premier Bennett concerning government policy on the Vancouver Island pipeline, and then demand to know what actual benefit my effort was to Westcoast's shareholders. That potentially damaging retort is something for me to think about, in case I am mistakenly reincarnated as a lobbyist and not as an astronaut or publisher of *The Globe and Mail*, my recurring dreams.

Another feature of the questionable Northeast Coal venture that attracted vigorous objection was the structure of the sales contracts with the Japanese. They were described by Don Phillips as take-or-pay contracts. Perhaps they were, as far as I know. However, the unreal pricing regime enshrining a coal levy so much higher than the prevailing world price was certain to erupt violently at some future date. The rationalization was that new mines require higher sales prices than old mines. Someone forgot that new mines inevitably become old mines just as cute kittens become cats. That maturing situation boiled over in 1988.

After a few years of paying the new-mine premium prices, the Japanese steel mills requested renegotiation of the purchase contract. Following months of unsuccessful talks with Quintette Coal Limited, the dispute was submitted to international arbitration. Norman Anderson, formerly chairman of Cominco Limited, was nominated to the arbitration panel by the Japanese steel mills. Chester Johnson, former chairman of B.C. Hydro, was designated by Quintette. When Anderson and Johnson could not agree on a chairman, the court appointed highly regarded former B.C. Chief Justice Nathan Nemetz. This high profile arbitration team travelled between Canada and Japan, casting a wide net for witnesses. One expert appearing was none other than James Schlesinger, former U.S. energy secretary. This international arbitration process consumed an incredible two years at a rumoured cost of $15 million.

The lengthy deliberations produced an award in May 1990. The original price of $110 per ton was to be reduced in stages to $82.40 by the end of 1990, with the next review of prices being scheduled for 1 April 1991. Additionally, Quintette was directed to refund $46 million to the Japanese steel mills for overpayments that had been made in the meantime.

In his report, Justice Nemetz makes reference to the extraordinary obstacles which faced the Northeast Coal project from the outset:

> both parties . . . in effect agreed that the northeast project was sui generis because the opening of this remote wilderness area in northeastern British Columbia required an expenditure by the Canadian and British Columbian governments of over $1 billion to put in the railway and new port at Prince Rupert, not to mention the establishment of the town of Tumbler Ridge. While the evidence shows that expenditures for infrastructures have been made in other countries, there can be little doubt that the Canadian expenditure was immense even by today's inflated standards. The exclusionary clause in the Gregg and Line Creek contracts reinforces my conclusion that the Quintette mine and its contract possess unique characteristics because of its geographical location and the large capital investment for infrastructure provided by both government and the private sector.

Quintette's nominee, Chester Johnson, in his supplementary comments to the award, summed up the basis of objection to the Japanese call for retroactive renegotiation in this way:

> I would have come to [a] different conclusion because of my determination, upon the evidence, that the JSI [the Japanese corporations involved] were well-informed on their own about the technical aspects of this mine when they entered into the agreement. Despite that knowledge, which testimony showed convinced at least some of the members of the JSI that the project was risky, they persisted in pushing this project not only with Quintette Coal, but with the federal and provincial governments and the railways. In my view, the evidence discloses that they wanted a completely independent

source of coal, with a shorter sea route to Japan, and were prepared to pay a higher price than they were paying for southeast coal to obtain this separate source. There can be no doubt that they knew that Quintette was one of the higher cost potential new projects.

The Japanese steel mills accepted the arbitration decision immediately. Quintette launched an appeal to the B.C. Supreme Court which was not successful. Then they applied for and received from the court a type of suspended bankruptcy under the Companies' Creditors Arrangement Act. This equivalent of the U.S. Chapter 11 provided Quintette with breathing room for six months in order to restructure its financing. The unsuccessful Supreme Court approach was then submitted to the B.C. Court of Appeal, where it was dismissed by Chief Justice William Esson. Those of us in the business have to ponder the consequences, had the courts overturned a binding, unanimous, international arbitration decision reached after such lengthy and costly deliberations.

The arbitrated Northeast Coal price of $82.40 effective year-end 1990 is in sharp contrast to the $61 (Cdn.) world price currently paid for the same quality coal to the southeastern B.C. mines. Thus, Quintette suffered a reduction of 25 percent from its original coal price, but will still enjoy a premium of 35 percent over the world price recieved by Westar. That quite remarkable anomaly and refinancing may temporarily save the mine and the instant village of Tumbler Ridge, but it unmasks the artificiality of the economic underpinning of this B.C. government mega-project.

Ultimately, the decision may come down to what has to be saved—the bankers or the jobs.

The birth of British Columbia's Northeast Coal venture had the legitimacy of the rabbit delivered from the magician's hat; the politician's hand was faster than the taxpayer's eyes.

Incidentally, it should be made clear that the two coal companies did not initiate this controversial mega-venture. They merely accommodated the government by developing their properties as part of a total enterprise the economics of which would be protected by a number of considerations, including government assistance and subsidized freight rates. Quintette was a consortium including Denison Mines, several Japanese companies and over fifty banks around the world. That mine had problems from the start, only to find its operating location unsuited to the actual geology discovered. Denison has written off its total investment in Quintette but remains the mine's operator. Quite the opposite, the smaller mine known as Bullmoose was first class. It is operated by Teck Corporation with Rio Algom as a major participant. This mine came into production under budget, on a site perfectly suited to its coal deposits. Unfortunately, its planned production is only about 2 million tons a year, compared to troubled Quintette's 5-million designed capacity.

The public could not be the best judge of the intricate economics concerning coal production and functioning of the new coastal coal port, but they could instinctively sense the high cost of running a new railroad many miles through the mountains and two expensive tunnels in order to fetch this new supply of coal. They had taken a licking on the Dease Lake railway extension. Their questions were simple. Why reach out this far into nowhere to dig more coal when there are many decades of proven coal reserves still to be mined in southeastern B.C. by the existing, efficient infrastructure in an area relying on that economic activity to sustain its standard of living?

Jack Davis, as a backbencher, made several public statements in 1980 concerning the new railroad. His calculations were that the railroad would have to carry about 20 million tons of coal a year just to break even. The government's response was evasive, claiming that level of shipments would be attained eventually, although the two mines planned annual production of only 7 million tons total to start. The government would not admit that the break-even point of 20 million tons from the north could only be reached if the existing southeast mines virtually shut down. Subsequent events illustrate how damaging was that flawed judgement of coal volumes.

As chairman of Westar Group Ltd., the two-thirds owner of Westar Mining in southeast B.C., and as a director of Westcoast, an energy transporter monitoring the transportation aspect of this mega-project, I have retained a special interest in watching its development.

During Westcoast's search for diversification opportunities in the 1980s, pipeline transportation of coal received a lot of attention.

Several existing U.S. pipelines carrying a mixture of finely ground coal and water were studied. This coal-slurry transportation method had some applications, but its primitive form was not generally attractive and it was being successfully blocked by the powerful railway lobby. The technical problems of freezing and water disposal forced Ron Rutherford to look for a solution. Some experimentation by the Colorado School of Mines led to Ron's next resourceful proposal. With the government of Alberta and Chieftain Development as partners, Westcoast put together a coal-slurry deal that would feature methanol as the fluid agent, rather than water. The government of Alberta was most cooperative. They invested in this company because it would economically develop coal reserves that would otherwise remain in the ground, in an accessible and populated northwest region of that province. The coal would be finely ground to flow in the pipeline in suspension with methanol. The required methanol would be processed in a plant at the mine site as a derivative of coal. The smooth flowing properties of this blend had been established by experimentation. The burning qualities had similarly been proven by actual combustion tests in Japan. Through the duration of the test tanker trip to Japan the coal particles stayed in suspension. On arrival, the slurry could be used as it had been blended, or separated and burned as either pure methanol or pure coal, whichever the particular energy application required. This simplification of energy inventories was particularly attractive to the Japanese users.

It was hoped that the facilities of the Trans Mountain pipeline could be used in the initial stages to move this produce from Edmonton to the coast, expecting that there would eventually be a large-diameter, dedicated slurry pipeline running directly from Alberta to a suitable port farther north on the west coast. As with so many other creative energy projects designed in those years, this one was put on the shelf as the world price of oil started to fall. It, and such others as coal liquefaction into oil, will be revived one day, but it was this special expertise in coal movement that attracted Westcoast's attention with respect to the Northeast Coal project.

When it became apparent that this project was going to proceed, despite its faulty economics, I casually asked Don Phillips if he had examined the use of a coal-conveyor line instead of rail, the principal advantage being the greater flexibility in grades up and down mountains. This idea had come to me through Rutherford from John Southworth, a well-known consultant to Japanese trading companies. Clearly, a conveyor line would also reduce the length and size of any necessary tunnels and thus cut the expense of construction where the risk of cost overrun was the greatest. I referred to Japanese technology that had been used for a long-distance rock conveyor in South America. At a later meeting, in the presence of Ron Basford, Phillips asked me if Westcoast would undertake a conveyor study on a speculative basis and provide a cost estimate in thirty days. I accepted the challenge.

Ron Rutherford set everything aside for this task. The Japanese conveyor manufacturer was most cooperative and competent, under the urging of Southworth. They rapidly dispatched a team of engineers who worked on the site with Ron, covering every foot of the route. Within the time limit prescribed, an acceptable route was chosen and surveyed. For the 100 km route, a twelve-section conveyor was designed with a takeoff of materials complete enough for estimating the costs. Swan Wooster engineers estimated the total construction costs for this fully enclosed conveyor system. It appeared that the cost saving could be in the area of $150 million from the railroad estimate of $550 million for the rail line only. The saving in the cost of rolling stock would be additive. Because this lateral conveyor was to connect with an existing Canadian National Railway line, I reviewed the concept with their president, Ron Lawless. He was impressed enough to agree conditionally to join Westcoast in building this unique transportation system for coal and operating it if necessary.

The conveyor cost estimates were supplied to Don Phillips's staff, who expressed immediate enthusiasm. This emotional high disappeared in a few days when the minister called me to request that our proposal be put under wraps. He explained that the premier preferred a multi-purpose railroad to a single-use conveyor. I reminded Don of the considerable expense Westcoast and the Japanese had undertaken on a speculative basis, but with the expectation of some business if a significant cost reduction could be assured. Further, I advised him that officials and engineers of a French conveyor company were en route to Vancouver, at our request, to prepare a competitive bid on their slightly different design. He expressed sympathy but said that Bill Bennett's position was final, even though the premier had been informed that there would be no substantial cargo other than coal to be shipped from that region. News leaked out about the conveyor cost saving. The premier gave the same reply to the media about the benefit of a multi-cargo railway. The media did not challenge him to identify the type and quantity of the other products to be transported. In question period in the legislature, the responses merely explained that a conveyor system had been investigated and was not found acceptable. Westcoast still has some expensive conveyor drawings tucked away in the files. Why did I keep trying?

To date, nearly a decade later, nothing but coal has been carried on this railroad, supposedly a multi-purpose transportation facility.

As reported earlier, I became a director of BCRIC while still employed by Westcoast. As one of my retirement activities, I later became chairman of that corporation, now called Westar Group Ltd. In that capacity, my personal discomfort is very pronounced concerning the desperate struggle against bankruptcy by Westar Mining, with its two coal properties, Balmer and Greenhills. Its Balmer mine is the largest and most efficient operation in that southeast region featuring several superb mines. One of the reasons for bankruptcy exposure is the coal-mining overcapacity in British Columbia subsidized by the government. As some of the Japanese tonnage was shifted from the southeast to the new northeast complex, Westar was compelled to keep its operation going by chasing around the world for sales volume to fill that void. Distress sales were found and the two mines operate at capacity, but the net revenue from these long-distance shipments is less than the return per ton sold to Japan. To be accurate, however, the principal cause of Westar's financial problem is the triple punch of the low world-price for coal, the exchange rate with the U.S. dollar and high interest rates. Nevertheless, the subsidized competition is a substantial factor and Westar Mining has written down the asset value of

$650 million on its books to zero, just as Denison did with its share of Quintette. That twin circumstance has to have some meaning.

The progressive planning and expansion of the coal operations in southeastern B.C. have been retarded as a result of the competitive impact from the northeast. Once-thriving communities in the region now feature unemployment, some boarded-up houses, some abandoned shops and motel units, some schools with partly filled classrooms. Sixty thousand square feet of Westar Mining's office space stand totally vacant. At one time, Westar employed 2,800 people at its Balmer and Greenhills mines. The total today is only 1,900—a loss of 900 jobs by just one company in the area.

The record worsens every year. In my opinion, Northeast Coal will eventually be regarded as the worst commercial initiative of that particular administration of the B.C. government. History will not be kind to their record in energy mega-projects generally. The record will scarcely notice the fertilizer plant fiasco, which was largely unknown outside of Powell River; it may recognize the LNG boondoggle with an asterisk simply because of its size; and it will display only for entertainment value the five futile attempts at building the Vancouver Island pipeline. However, history may not be that charitable on the folly of spending an enormous amount of money to develop a remote, uninhabited, tiny piece of this province. Whatever the ultimate outcome, Bill Bennett and Don Phillips will be able to watch the show from front row centre: Bennett as a director of Teck, the operator of Bullmoose; Phillips as a member of the board of Quintette.

The closing years of my career at Westcoast have been marred by energy mega-project failures. However valid as emotional compensation, my acceptance and success in other political jurisdictions in both Canada and the United States have served to maintain a good balance and a reasonable batting average. The experience in British Columbia engendered disillusionment and frustration; never despair and rage. I maintained my enthusiasm and patience which produced happy years at Westcoast and demonstrably sustained me in a varied business life after a phantom retirement in 1982, at the mandatory age of sixty-five.

My last close encounter with Bill Bennett as premier of B.C. and Stephen Rogers as the energy minister was a stimulating and rewarding finale. After my illusory retirement, I was approached in 1985 by an agency of the French government, the Bureau de Recherches Géologiques et Minières, called BRGM for short. They invited me to join a team intending to develop the best of the mineral prospects they had gradually discovered in Canada through $25 million in exploration. The corporate name eventually became Cheni Gold Mines Inc., with me being the only non-French-speaking member of the board. That shortcoming may have been a handicap, yet I was able to persuade Cheni to develop as its first priority a gold-mine property in my home province, north of Smithers. I became central in its promotion and financing.

For the intended Cheni gold mine to be viable, a $10 million access road had to be constructed to the remote site of the proven gold reserves. I was designated to enlist the support of the provincial government for that road. Undaunted by my dismal batting average in B.C., I approached energy minister Stephen Rogers with the enthusiasm of a novice lobbyist.

Cheni's geologist had obviously briefed the minister's technical staff so convincingly that Rogers actually hinted, during that first meeting, that they had already endorsed the idea. After a few good-natured jibes about what could an old pipeliner know about a gold mine, Rogers invited my French colleagues and me to outline the economic benefits for British Columbia. We promised to move the Cheni head office from Montreal to Vancouver, conveniently omitting the fact the permanent staff was only three persons. Other benefits were stated with more substantial validity, I must affirm. Subsequently, the request was made for the government to build the road on the basis of a future payback by the company after profitable production had commenced and the combined price of gold and silver reached a certain index figure. The meeting concluded with more jovial banter about a pipeliner's second coming as a gold miner, all of which was thoroughly puzzling to the French witnesses.

Within a matter of weeks, the next bit of information on the access-road request came from the premier himself. He momentarily slowed a receiving line at a Government House function to take me aside for the good news that the cabinet had given approval that afternoon. This was anything but a mega-project, but that took nothing away from the exultant feeling of a triumph. Had there ever been a fear I was possessed by a government curse, that episode exorcized it for keeps. Cheni Gold Mines started production in March 1989 and has been profitable every month since. I was named chairman of the board in mid-1990.

These reminiscences are scarcely worthy of a lofty term like memoirs but, whatever they are, they would be incomplete without reference to the management team at Westcoast and how it fared in producing rewards for the shareholders. This story started in 1968, the year I joined Westcoast. Net income that year was $8.8 million, a good portion of that merely being phantom profits in the form of interest accumulated during construction of the YoYo gathering pipeline. The next year, it dropped to $2.4 million, a mere 2.7 percent return on equity.

Kelly Gibson took over in 1970, quickly appointing me vice-president of administration. This marked the initiation of a harsh cost-reduction program. Not a corner of the operation escaped our scrutiny. Westcoast Transmission had never been fat, but we made rapid improvement by picking the bones even cleaner. In the first year of that program, profits rose to $9.2 million from $5.3 million in 1970. I was made executive vice-president that year, which I suspect was the chairman's way of approving the tough decisions concerning cost control. Jack Smith told me later the staff ran a pool on how long I would last at Westcoast as a result of my new cost-control edicts. The longest tenure anyone bet on was six months. The winner was paid off when I passed that milestone, being the closest guess to my actual survival term of about fourteen years to retirement.

In 1972, the full revenue benefits were accruing from the Fourth Service Agreement which Charles Hetherington, D.P. McDonald and Peter Kutney had negotiated with the U.S. customers. That year's net profit rose to $20.8 million. Following that impressive result, there was a sequence of seven consecutive years of increases in net profit after tax. The string was only broken in 1980, the figure falling slightly to $45.6 million, compared to $46.5 million the year before. In 1982, the year of my retirement, the company reported a net income available to shareholders of $66.9 million, $1.65 per share, a record that has not been matched since, at least by 1989.

Westcoast has always been noted for its competent, efficient, professional management. One small example of our ability to make accurate cost projects and stick to them is shown in our distinguished role in an undertaking otherwise so bitterly criticized for huge cost overruns and spending irregularities. To accommodate the Coquihalla superhighway, Westcoast had to move some of its high-pressure mainline from level spots in the valleys needed for the roadway. Several sections, totalling twenty-four miles of pipeline, had to be relocated. In 1979, the NEB authorized a budget of $19.8 million for this work. When it was completed in 1984, the actual cost was $21.7 million. This was a 9-percent overrun; not up to Westcoast's standards, but commendable in view of the confusion during the five years since the original estimate, and unanticipated changes during construction. As far as I know, this good performance was not mentioned during the official inquiry into the runaway costs of the total Coquihalla project.

The Westcoast team was well respected in the industry and by the regulators. It was known as sufficiently talented but undermanned. That portrayal would be just as accurate for middle management, supervisors and all staff. The imposing statistical collection of staffing and expense ratios maintained by the National Energy Board in Canada and the Federal Power Commission in the United States depicted Westcoast as the leanest of all major pipelines. This is not to suggest that record was a distinguished attainment. It was a flinty culture naturally created over the years by the exigencies of a pipeline company operating in a geographical region with more physical handicaps and political interference than any other. Consequently, I hesitate to refer to the good old days; I say it's good the old days have passed.

As much as I would like to take the space to describe all phases of the Westcoast operation I admired so much, that would be impractical. However, I feel compelled to pay a tribute to the key players during my final years. Under Kelly as chairman, I was president and CEO, and John Anderson was executive vice-president and chief operating officer. John and I worked very much as partners. On the administrative side, financial matters were in the capable hands of Jack Smith. His reputation in the investment fraternity was superb, just as it was with the regulatory bodies. Legal matters were the responsibility of Dick Williams, Q.C., as general counsel. He was a distinguished lawyer, obviously comfortable in the constant pressure of regulatory hearings. Dick took early retirement for health reasons and he was succeeded by Gordon Lade, formerly of Pacific Pete and Petro-Canada.

Guiding the important function of gas supply and sales was Art Willms. He was originally an academic economist but quickly attained respectful recognition in the intricate maze of regulatory affairs. Art similarly developed an international reputation for his skill and fairness in dealing with the important gas producers and, of course, the essential gas users, particularly the large export customers in the U.S.

The engineering required by Westcoast, and the amazing amount of design work and estimating for mega-projects, were supervised by Jack Kavanagh. Like the others, Jack was highly respected in the trade and by the regulatory agencies before whom he presented a great amount of technical testimony. The quality of the work of his staff and the speed of their output astonished many experts, and that included Bob Blair, a man of remarkable personal experience in that same direction.

Operations were handled competently by Ed Johnson, a professional in every respect who had been with the company from the year the pipeline opened in 1957. A blunt and stolid person who shunned the limelight, this man knew every nut and bolt on the system. He was often described as a pipeliner's pipeliner, very demanding in the performance of others but admired greatly by every employee on the vast network of pipelines and compressor stations in remote locations.

Al Green served in a special classification because of his wide experience. In his professional career, he had acted as a designer, builder or executive for virtually every oil or gas pipeline in Canada. At Westcoast, Al had been chief engineer, later in charge of gas supply and sales. Prior to his early retirement, he was a director of the company and impressively handled the important role of liaison with our partner in Foothills.

The most recent executive addition during my tenure was Bill Caswell, who was assigned all the gas-processing plants and the responsibility for diversification into projects for liquids extraction. His previous experience had been with major petro-chemical companies. His beneficial contribution was becoming most evident at the time of my retirement.

Sheila Iverach was Doug Owen's secretary, a great help to me from my first day. When Doug resigned, Sheila became my secretary. Later she was promoted to administrative assistant, in which role she was thoroughly competent and displayed impeccable judgement in the many tasks which required the utmost in confidentiality.

Many worthy executives have been unnamed in these reminiscences, but they all contributed, with the foregoing list, to a force of people who met every challenge along the way. It is amazing to me how their understandable disappointments did not deteriorate into utter discouragement as the energy mega-projects, on which they devoted extraordinary effort, were postponed, defeated or simply died. It is not unreasonable to expect that this type of dedication will eventually garner its reward.

I was proud to serve on the Westcoast board from 1969 to 1989, after which my colleagues favoured me with the honourary appointment of director emeritus. At the presentation I joked that this was my second such award. The company Social Club had named me Santa Claus emeritus for the many years I played that role at the Christmas party for the employees' children. They fired me because they wanted someone older-looking and fatter.

During my twenty years on the Westcoast board I shared the table at directors' meetings with Frank McMahon, Doug Owen, Kelly Gibson, D.P. McDonald, John Houchin, Charles Hetherington, Arthur Mayne, Frank Ross, Bob Stewart, Bill Tye, Norman Whittall, Len Youell, John Anderson, Chunky Woodward, Ernie Richardson, Bob Roberts, Taylor Kennedy, Merrill Rasmussen, Al

Green, Jim Byrn, David Helliwell, Bill Hopper, Andy Janisch, Joel Bell, Ed Lakusta, Wendy McDonald, David O'Brien, Derek Parkinson, Mike Phelps, Art Willms and Bill Neville.

Recalling each of those names stirs a warm feeling of friendship and reminds me of an abundance of wise counsel, friendly advice, comforting assurance, helpful criticism, frequent encouragement and a general feeling of a supportive group all working together. The breadth of education, training and experience in that directors' roll call was truly outstanding. All Westcoast shareholders benefited from the dedicated service of the directors they voted to represent them.

My last direct responsibility with Westcoast was the one that afforded me no pleasure at all. It was an honour to be asked to offer the eulogy at John Anderson's funeral, but it was most difficult due to the shock of this sudden passing of my best business friend. John died from cancer in August 1987, just eight weeks after the first sign of any illness. The business community and all his colleagues at Westcoast sadly shared this loss with his family.

Westcoast's succession plan was not geared up for this eventuality, despite its sophistication. Because of John's apparent good health and vigour, it was assumed that there would still be a number of years in which to select and groom a successor from several young and capable executives in the company. Fortunately, Derek Parkinson stepped into the breach as interim president, serving admirably with the resourcefulness and dedication of a career financial executive. However, he would not agree to accept the position on a permanent basis, and set a deadline for his early retirement. I shared a little in the limelight of Derek's performance by boasting to all who would listen that I had persuaded him to join Westcoast just a few years earlier. Derek had been vice-president and chief financial officer of MacMillan Bloedel when I was on their executive committee. Following the Noranda takeover of MB, John Anderson and I were fortunate to recruit him.

During that interval of Derek's interim appointment, the directors chose Mike Phelps to be president and chief executive officer, and promoted Art Willms as executive vice-president and chief operating officer. Art had been a career executive with Westcoast;

Mike joined more recently, having been recruited from the federal government. A bilingual lawyer with a graduate degree from the London School of Economics, he practised law briefly before serving as executive assistant successively to Otto Lang in justice and Marc Lalonde in energy. It was in this latter role Mike caught our attention, and John Anderson heartily agreed with my suggestion he should be a target for recruitment.

Westcoast has new leadership; it will have new ideas and new directions; but it will never change from its dedication to community, provincial and national service, consistent with the supremacy of its principal product, Canadian natural gas. A constant reminder of its corporate presence in Vancouver will be the handsome Westcoast Energy Hall, a three-storey, lobby addition to the classic Orpheum Theatre made possible by a donation from Westcoast. Originally known as the Westcoast Hall, the word Energy was added at the insistence of Vancouver Mayor Gordon Campbell. He said the further description was necessary to illustrate a new vitality Westcoast had added to the cultural quality of the city and the province.

Neither Mike Phelps nor Bill Hopper has explained what their new director emeritus is expected to do. Not much, I expect. Nevertheless, the respite may not be for long. With great restraint, I may muzzle myself when the Vancouver Island pipeline goes into service; but I will make no such commitment concerning the Alaska Highway pipeline. I have lots more to say about that.

····10·····

THE FUTURE OF
ARCTIC GAS

The Foothills Alaska Highway natural gas pipeline, put on hold for market reasons, will eventually be revived. It does not replace an existing gas-delivery system, and it will feature favourable economics, coupled with environmental advantages. Explicitly, it is not a trade-off deal—it's win-win.

It is not difficult to accept and understand the failure of an oil-pipeline proposal when world oil prices fail. However, why a natural-gas pipeline plan should be delayed for the same reason requires some explanation. According to Ron Rutherford, the innovative incentive rate of return provisions damaged the project. He argued that it added to the cost of wheeling gas to the lower forty-eight states and thus contributed in some degree to the whole scheme being postponed. World energy economics is a complex subject. I will not attempt a full discourse in this record because that depth is not necessary and it is beyond this writer's competence in any case. Some elementary facts will have to suffice.

Old king coal retains it crown as the predominant energy resource in North America, simply because of its vast and accessible proven reserves. Its use and impact on energy pricing, however, are restricted by the associated environmental problems. Trendy nu-

clear power is also an energy supply of significance with limited impact on pricing levels. It is costly and has to contend with wide
public concern about safety. Both fuels could very well stage a
comeback by reason of technological advances, but, in the meantime, the powerful influence on world energy economics comes
from oil. Not much effort is put into developing coal, nuclear energy, electricity, natural gas, hydrogen, synthetic fuels or solar generation without the basic consideration of what the cost of energy
produced by any of those sources or methods would compare to the
cost of an equivalent BTU derived from oil.

Natural gas has innumerable advantages over oil with respect to
safety, convenience, cleanliness, versatility and environmental
considerations. The long list of benefits is known as the "form
value" of natural gas. It even includes, as a very minor example,
consideration that users pay for gas weeks after they use it; and for
oil, before they use it. Nevertheless, oil controls natural-gas pricing
largely due to the one advantage it does enjoy; that is mobility. The
various grades of oil that compete with natural gas can move from
refineries by pipeline, highway, rail and water, an extremely flexible delivery system in containers large and small. It is even flown
to remote locations in tanks aboard aircraft.

That energy source is totally fickle in its dedication to any market. When economic circumstances dictate, oil can abandon its attention to any market and move elsewhere without any substantial
capital cost. Sharply contrasted to that mobility, the network of
underground gas pipelines is the only means of delivering natural
gas. That structure represents a large capital investment and, more
importantly, it is dug in and can't pick up and move. Its capacity
can be juggled up or down, but the system's economics are extremely sensitive to load factor. Consequently, it becomes dedicated to a specific market and is not able to adjust easily when that
market changes, certainly not able to flit to a new region where
there is less competition.

The derivatives of natural gas, liquefied petroleum gas, liquefied
natural gas and compressed natural gas, have some flexibility as to
delivery systems, but there is a penalty in cost. The final result is
that natural gas enjoys a modest price premium over oil because of

form value, but it is never free from the competition of oil at spot prices, distress prices or term contracts.

When crude-oil prices were in the $40 US range per barrel, the demand for natural gas skyrocketed because it was a bargain, even at the regulated tariff increases. New delivery systems, in the way of transmission and distribution pipelines, were proposed for almost every region of North America. Similarly, other energy alternatives to oil were sought, the most impressive example being the dedication of $9 billion by the U.S. government for research in synthetic fuels. When world oil prices collapsed, virtually all of the activity in seeking alternatives also fell apart. The price of natural gas fell in the United States, demand faltered and a surplus supply developed which was named the "gas bubble." Accordingly, the market in the lower forty-eight states simply was not able to absorb natural gas at the cost required to produce, process and deliver it all the way from Alaska. Thus, it was the declining world oil price that put the Alaska Highway natural gas pipeline on hold.

I am constantly amazed how quickly this continent, particularly the United States, lets down its guard when the threat of an oil dearth or an OPEC price squeeze slackens. Our impassioned and subsidized energy-conversation programs simply lose their punch; and the breathless, scientific rush for synthetic fuel substitutes is quietly suspended, some of the allocated budgets being redirected to other items, such as higher compensation for congressmen and parliamentarians.

The chairman of the U.S. government's synthetic fuels administration resigned and wasn't replaced. The multi-billion-dollar budget was unspent and programs that had been started merely languished and died. The private sector also lost its sense of urgency, letting research programs drift. "Nothing will work without $40 oil," they complained. Energy security and self-sufficiency obviously aren't worth a dime. Arco, who had developed a most impressive accumulation of solar-heating knowledge, sold that operation to a British firm. Westcoast shut down its coal-liquefaction and coal-methanol slurry studies. The Hibernia show dimmed its lights, and the zeal for oil and gas exploration in the Beaufort Sea faded. I was a director of DynCorp in the U.S. who abandoned their acclaimed Hydrocarbon Research Inc., but, to Canada's good fortune, it was bought at a bargain by Art Price, president of Husky Oil. That purchase gave Husky proprietary rights to impressive technology, particularly in heavy-oil upgrading and coal liquefaction.

When OPEC was putting it to us, President Jimmy Carter trumpeted with great gusto: "The energy crisis is the moral equivalent of war!" He rallied the troops and promised that salvos of U.S. greenbacks would be volleyed at the enemy. Sadly, when OPEC merely called time out, we in North America quit the war, saved our money and decided the whole effort wasn't worth the sacrifice, promptly resuming our energy binge with imported oil.

It seems that as long as we North Americans can drive our Cadillacs to the gasoline pump for a fill-up without a lineup, we are oblivious to how much of that gasoline was produced from imported oil and how easily that vital flow can be stopped. At least forty of the U.S. states have abandoned the 55 mph gas-conservation speed limit and permit racing along at 65. In the others there is little risk in getting a ticket between 55 and 65. All's well and there's no need to panic—until the next oil embargo or price explosion. Where would we be today if Old Testament Noah had quit building his gopher-wood ark every time that the clouds parted in the sky above?

More than a decade has passed since U.S. President Jimmy Carter wrote to Prime Minister Pierre Trudeau on 17 July 1980:

> Because I remain steadfastly of the view that the expeditious construction of the [Alaska Natural Gas Transportation System] project remains in the mutual interests of both our countries, I would be prepared at the appropriate time to initiate action before the U.S. Congress to remove any impediment as may exist under present law to providing that desired confidence [to commence building] the Canadian portion of the line.
>
> Our government also appreciates the timely way in which you and Canada have taken steps to advance your side of this vital energy project. In view of this progress, I can assure you that the U.S. government not only remains committed to the project; I am able to

state with confidence that the U.S. government is now satisfied that the entire Alaska Natural Gas Transportation System will be completed. The United States' energy requirements and the current unacceptable level of dependence on oil imports require that the project be completed without delay. . . .

In this time of growing uncertainty over energy supplies, the U.S. must tap its substantial Alaskan gas reserves as soon as possible. . . .

The need for action expressed in this prescient letter remains relevant today. Carter's clearsighted sense of urgency, when their dependency was on 30-percent oil imports compared to today's 50-percent, stands as a condemnation of the inaction of successive administrations on both sides of the border.

Assuming the next inevitable energy crunch will not be wisely anticipated and neutralized in advance by the governments involved, the critical necessity of the Alaska gas pipeline will be evident only as soon as the world oil price escalates again. The large reserve of natural gas in that state is the sole untapped major source of energy on U.S. soil. Thus, it is inevitable it will one day be supplied to the lower forty-eight states. In the meantime, everything to make that happen is in a state of readiness, as far as the private sector is concerned. Foothills' thorough engineering and cost estimates are constantly updated; and they have purchased a 22-percent position in the consortium authorized to build the portion of the pipeline running through Alaska. Some agencies concerned in the governments of both Canada and the United States are constantly examining the project, in preparation for its inevitable start-up at an unknown date. I feel that there is a case to be made for starting construction now.

Foothills and its partners are managing the Prebuild portion of this project on a profitable basis during this waiting period by exporting Canadian natural gas with a short haul to the United States, as opposed to the long haul it would be to move that amount of energy all the way from the north slope of Alaska. The operation of the eastern and western legs into the United States has been successful in all respects. Actually, the eastern leg is in the process of being expanded.

The National Energy Board has authorized export to the United States of 9.2 trillion cubic feet of Canadian Mackenzie delta gas, over a period of twenty years beginning no later than the year 2000. The major gas producers in this arrangement, Esso, Gulf and Shell, are acknowledged experts concerning the potential natural-gas reserves in the Mackenzie delta. They have the skill and the resources to develop those energy supplies to the degree that Canada's domestic requirements will not be imperilled. Moreover, their compliance with this country's regulatory processes will be exemplary, particularly with respect to the environment, in my opinion. My confidence is just as high regarding the total revenue to flow back to the Canadian petroleum industry infrastructure and to the many Canadian taxing jurisdictions involved. Similarly, the native peoples of the Canadian arctic are certain to be the beneficiaries of increased economic heft.

In my view, the NEB's export authorization is a good step forward. I hope the same quality of regulatory judgement will be evident when the next two strides are taken; first, the approval of the actual export-sales contracts with the American gas buyers; second, the all-important selection of the pipeline route and the company to build and operate the required transmission system.

There is no apprehension in my mind concerning the eventual terms and conditions of the firm sales contracts. There is an abundance of precedence in this area from which the respective sellers and buyers will be able to design agreements that will satisfy all the normal commercial requirements and will gain regulatory approvals in both countries. In other words, most of the tests can be reduced to mathematical precision and there is a minimum need for judgement of the abstract. Additionally, the principal source of my personal comfort is the statutory thrust of all NEB decisions. Without minimizing the relevance of the myriad of factors this regulatory body must face, their final, heavily weighted test comes down to Canada's public interest.

The final and most important decision in this grand scheme will be the selection of the pipeline route and choice of the company to build and operate the transmission system. This will not be nearly as straightforward as granting the export permits and approving the sales contracts. Accordingly, Canada's public interest will have to bear mightily on the deliberations and final decision. Innumerable technical factors could be black and white, with simple comparisons. Initial capital costs and immediate ripple economic benefits are definable and will not generate much counterattack among the pipeline competitors. However, long-term benefits and future cost-of-service will be unavoidably obscure, considering the puzzling future impact of the construction of the large-diameter pipeline for Alaska gas from the north slope along the Alaska Highway, whether it precedes, follows, or is built at the same time as the pipeline for Canadian delta gas. Even more complex is the colossal judgement that will have to be applied in comparing all the social and environmental opportunities and hazards of the alternative routes. With that heavy proportion of considerations in the abstract, it is evident why I am not as sanguine about the route decision and timing as I am with the first and second steps in this challenging international project.

Over the years before I retired, I depended on pipeline advice from a host of experts like Charles Hetherington, Ron Rutherford, Bob Blair, Al Green, Bill Deyell, Ray Mordan and Jack Kavanagh. Consequently, I feel stripped at least to my shorts in this articulation of my route selection. Where are you guys when I need you?

Few will argue that the route selection is not loaded with the almost imponderable environmental question. Nor will anyone challenge my view of the pipeline's national importance. This is a huge international transaction involving the route selection and the choice of a pipeline builder and operator to move a tremendous amount of energy 1,400 miles at a minimum, possibly as many as 1,700. This new transmission system to be connected to existing prebuild pipelines presents the most stringent test of satisfying my personal vision of the perfect arctic pipeline; that is, one being controlled in Canada but serving a noble international purpose. If we get it right, this can be a win-win project for both Canada and the United States, without any rationalized or abstract trade-offs being required to balance the teeter-totter with equal satisfaction for both countries.

Two good route choices are immediately apparent, merely by

eye-balling the map of the north. The more obvious one is along the Mackenzie River, across the northeast corner of B.C. and then through Alberta. It would clearly be less costly to build and to oper-ate, simply because it is shorter. A pipeliner is always attracted to the perfection of a route as straight as the crow flies, due to the cost of gas transmission being so sensitive to distance.

The second good possibility is to carry the Canadian gas along the Dempster Highway south to Whitehorse, then along the Alaska Highway through the Yukon and B.C. into Alberta. The distance would be greater than along the Mackenzie River, and hence the cost of both construction and future operation would be higher. However, it is my opinion that a pipeline through the Yukon would have fewer environmental vulnerabilities. After all, locating a pipeline along a straight highway should pose less risk than tracking a rambling river and crossing some of its zigs and zags. This circum-stance should be carefully evaluated and credited against the route's higher cost.

Let me be clear. Both of these routes have been studied exten-sively, especially the valley of the Mackenzie River. Either can be constructed satisfactorily by the industry for the benefit of the local populations. Fortunately, both could be good systems. But one will be better than the other. There's the rub! Better for whom? Cana-dians or Americans?

If this project had the ideal status of moving only Canadian gas that would be produced only by Canadian oil companies, for sale only to Canadian consumers, even a desk-bound pipeliner could make the right decision. I would nominate the less-costly route along the Mackenzie River, hoping to maximize national benefits for Canadians.

That spontaneous conclusion could be valid, but certainly not without risk. Environmental disturbances can be reasonably man-aged by the pipeline industry and the resulting use of natural gas to replace other fuels is a plus for the environment. Nevertheless, the gamble is that Canadians could be exposed to more environmental vulnerability along the Mackenzie River than along the Dempster Highway. This would have a substantial cost factor, the actual as-sessment being in part subjective. In the perfect scenario that this project was entirely Canadian, the chance of possibly worse environmental conditions along the Mackenzie River could be justified because any cost benefit from the gamble would flow to Canadians.

Unfortunately, that ideal all-Canadian aspect does not exist. This particular international energy project is attractive to Canada in many respects, but it is pertinent that the plan is largely for the commercial benefit of multinational oil companies and the comfort of American gas consumers. That situation presents the National Energy Board with a unique challenge in making its final determination on the basis of the Canadian public interest.

Toying with Canadian environmental exposures on a project planned for the exclusive benefit of Canadians represents a burden of responsibility. Yet that load is not as threatening as taking any sort of a chance with our environment almost entirely to oblige the Americans. This is not a bogeyman issue, with mindless disregard for the superlative reputation of our industry for protecting the environment. Accidents can happen, as witness the *Exxon Valdez*. Three of the most sophisticated and responsible oil companies in the world gambled on shipping their north-slope oil by ocean tanker, a cheaper method than moving some of it south of Alaska by overland pipeline. As a result of a freak oil-tanker accident, their anticipated transportation cost saving has been eroded seriously by the most expensive oil spill in the continent's history.

At this moment in Canada, environmental issues top the list of items for social, commercial and political debate. Canadians may be in the dark and ambivalent about many public issues and government programs. They may be bitterly divided and opinionated on abortion, bilingualism and gay rights. But the populace is totally united in its impassioned drive for environmental integrity. A green wave is engulfing Canada while it is rather extravagantly proclaimed that the fate of the earth depends on the priority we give environmental issues. When he was federal environment minister, Lucien Bouchard said: "I'm not that concerned about my political career; I care more about the environment." When a politician makes a statement like that, in my mind, that is news!

The minister was tested on his lofty declaration by the 1989 environmental dust-up in Alberta. During a public hearing on the giant Mitsubishi pulp plant on the Athabasca River, Robert Lane, a senior federal environment official, declared the mill would be unacceptable. This damning assessment shocked Mitsubishi executives and Alberta government environmental people alike. They had all thought their extra attention to detail and more than the normal call to compliance with all rules and regulations would have resulted in smooth approval. This led to the Alberta environment minister, Ralph Klein, telephoning frantically to Bouchard with the request that he say it wasn't so. However, the federal minister said that he would support what his official had said. This episode indicates the penetrating examination of environmental integrity is going only in one direction—deeper and deeper. Building a pipeline underground along a river is very different from locating a pulp mill on it. But the message is clear.

In 1988, the report of the federally appointed Energy Options Advisory Committee, headed by Thomas Kierans, hinted at the need for increased government vigilance in social implications of energy decisions. Referring to participants' presentations, the summary noted: "Intervention is appropriate . . . when there are social costs such as environmental damage that prices do not reflect. . . ."

The American gas users and the U.S. regulatory bodies that protect their interests do not need any advice from us on the integrity of the environment in energy projects. They are quite alert to their own exposure and would be sensitive to ours; that is, unless the issue is not raised, which is not very likely. A recent *New York Times* public-opinion poll suggested that 80 percent of Americans believe that protecting the environment is so important that requirements and standards cannot be too high. Nearly 80 percent of the respondents believed that continuing environmental improvements must be made, regardless of cost. I wish these people were making the selection of the pipeline from the Mackenzie delta.

The debate concerning the choice between the two best pipeline routes will be conducted in that atmosphere of national uneasiness. Pipeline companies, regulators and intervenors who downplay the relevance of environmental vulnerabilities, do so at their peril. That is why the Dempster Highway route could eventually be the surprising underdog winner; and I have backed an underdog before.

The U.S. public interest will be well served by a pipeline along either route. It is axiomatic in world energy economics that any country profits handsomely by the affordable use of another nation's energy resources, particularly those of the country next door within easy reach. The advantage to the United States of dipping into our arctic natural-gas reserves for a firm period of twenty years, under protection of the Free Trade Agreement, is substantial. They could reasonably be required to pay the short-term, additional cost-of-service occasioned by some diversion of the straight-line pipeline route as extra precaution for the delicate environmental situation in the Canadian arctic. Our premium fuel, natural gas, is worthy of a premium price.

To use the current jargon, the U.S. will enjoy a later clawback of at least some of the cost differential created by choosing the longer Dempster Highway route, which is not that much greater distance, given the immensity of the entire transportation system through Canada and then into the pipeline network of the United States. A large part of this so-called Dempster Highway proposal would actually be along the Alaska Highway. Conveniently, this is the right-of-way designated for the future Alaska Natural Gas Transportation System by both the Canadian and U.S. governments. Thus, this portion for moving Canadian gas to the states could be considered a type of prebuild for the eventual pipeline that will be built to transport American gas from the north slope of Alaska to the lower forty-eight states. Having a functioning right-of-way in place would be a useful leg-up on the future cost of the ANGTS.

If all the foregoing opinion is criticized as overzealous nationalism, I would reject that accusation and certainly not apologize for having advocated reasonable but determined bargaining with the United States. I heartily favour the gas-export proposition because it can be put in place without our own energy destiny being at risk. It definitely is certifiable that permitting our good neighbours to share a regulated portion of Canada's gas reserves in the arctic, in order to preserve their own dwindling fuels, is an international accommodation of almost incalculable value. In my view, it is a persuasive bargaining position to be exploited for the economic and environmental wellbeing of our fragile arctic northlands and its people. When the world's natural energy resources were shuffled and deposited, Canada was dealt a high-count hand. Why not bid it for the slam?

My opinion concerning the company that should build the pipeline, along whichever route is finally approved by the NEB, is so biased I will not dwell on it at the length I am tempted to do. What can be more compelling than the few arguments to which I will confine this discussion? Foothills is already the largest Canadian operating system in the export of natural gas to the United States. Through its two partners, NOVA and Westcoast, it has more technical expertise and actual operating experience in permafrost and muskeg than any big-inch gas pipeline in North America and holds the exclusive permits for construction along both the Dempster and Alaska highways. It long ago established a training program for native people and employs many today; and it is ready to move off the mark instantly. The federal government's Northern Pipeline Agency can attest to Foothills' competence and state of readiness.

In retrospect, Frank McMahon's first profound statement to me in 1968, that he was going to build gas and oil pipelines to move Alaskan products through British Columbia to the lower forty-eight states, still tingles my bones. More than that, the realization we failed this visionary virtually assaults me. We truly erred in opting for oil tankers instead of pipelines, but it is not too late to move a good deal of that energy safely on land rather than perilously on the ocean.

Considering the long lead time required to complete the pipeline, construction should start right now on the Alaska gas pipeline as approved by both Canada and the United States well over a decade ago. Also, to conform with the original requirement of the National Energy Board, the present intention to move Canadian delta gas up the Mackenzie River valley should be switched to an application by the parties involved for a route along the Dempster Highway, connecting with the ANGTS near Whitehorse.

The only reason this huge, $26 billion Alaska energy project was not started after full regulatory and legislative approval was its failure on a single test—economics. At the time, that immense pipeline cost would have landed the natural gas in Chicago at a price well above the energy equivalent of oil and domestic U.S. gas which existed in temporary abundance.

The evolving justification for reshuffling the deck now is that the enlightenment of the interval has revealed at least four major tests that are mandatory now, not just one. They are economics, the environment, security or self-sufficiency and national interest. Objective examination of each of those tests signals an early start, so the pipeline can be in full operation by the mid-1990s.

Under surveillance of the Northern Pipeline Agency in Canada and the authorities concerned in the United States, the Foothills organization has maintained a state of readiness. Their experts have upgraded the project's engineering and its cost estimates as permitted by technological advances and the results of extensive research and testing by actual gas pipeline operation in permafrost. Over the years, the original construction cost estimate has been slashed progressively. One big cut came ridiculously easily. Simply reducing the pipe diameter to forty-eight inches, as Foothills originally proposed, from the fifty-six inches preferred by the U.S. Federal Power Commission, was a bonanza. Another easy catch was the lower interest rate for the massive borrowings, compared to over 20 percent used in earlier cost estimates.

Another easing of the original cost estimate had to do with the stringent metallurgical specifications for high-quality steel required for gas pipelines. A relatively high proportion of molybdenum is required in the recipe. The price of that critical additive was virtually out of sight when the original pipe quotations were submitted. It had peaked at $28.70 US per pound. Recently, it has averaged about $3.34.

As the Foothills experts rework all their intricate estimates, the original $26 billion has today shrunk to about $15 billion (US), in 1988 dollars. That figure still puts Alaska gas into the lower forty-eight states at a price higher than the currently depressed charges for domestic supplies. Nevertheless, the significant cost reductions put the project economically within reach. The inescapable impact of the law of supply and demand for local energy supplies will inevitably boost the price of oil and gas consumed in the lower forty-eight. Thus, the economic test could be satisfied by the middle of the present decade.

Next, the environmental test, which was prominent in a technical sense but somewhat disregarded ten years ago as to its economic impact, cannot be ignored now. Legislators, regulators, resource executives, industries and even home-makers all have no illusions about the old rationalization that marginal economics necessitate some compromise on environmental standards—quite the reverse. Environmental integrity requires a tipping of the marginal-economics scale to a go signal, despite some cost premium.

This all works in two positive ways for building the Alaskan gas pipeline. First, it supports the Dempster Highway pipeline route as an alternative to the Mackenzie River pipeline for delta gas, earlier described by the NEB as an environmentally unacceptable route. Second, the environmental concerns apply pressure for increased use of natural gas, an energy source that is environmentally "friendly."

Security and self-sufficiency is a test that wafts in the wind, particularly in the breezy speeches in the U.S. Congress. From President Carter's declaration of a state of war on the energy crisis, the United States under succeeding presidents has drifted into lethargy so manifest that it now imports more than half its daily crude oil requirements. That apparent national recklessness may be more a planned occurrence than an unhappy course of events. It is crafty for a nation to hoard its own shrinking energy reserves while gobbling up supplies of others at low prices. To be successful, however, that strategy must have a fail-safe mechanism to flip into action when foreign supplies are suddenly embargoed, or even subjected to slow-downs. I seriously doubt whether President George Bush has a button in the White House which he can push to produce immediate alternate energy supplies, just as he can finger NORAD into action for another type of emergency. The United States embarked on a dramatic program of underground storage for vast quantities of oil during the Mid-East oil crisis of the early 1970s, to be released only in an emergency. Located in salt caverns in Louisiana, this strategic reserve contains only about a couple of months' oil supply. This alleged preparedness draws as many horse laughs in the industry as did the multi-billion dollar synthetic fuels program that was unceremoniously scrapped when the energy fright of the Carter era subsided.

I happen to prefer the concept of self-sufficiency conceived and practised by New Zealand. From total dependence on imported crude oil for its refineries, this relatively small nation now produces more than a third of its gasoline needs. With that remarkable elevation of its energy security, it also achieved a corresponding reduction of oil tanker traffic in its coastal waters and ocean ports. All of this required an immense technological gamble. It also demanded acceptance of unsatisfactory economics, even if the scheme turned out to be technically perfect. In a joint venture with Mobil Oil, New Zealand agreed to employ the untried methanol-to-gasoline process invented by the brilliant chemist Dr. Warren Kaeding at the Central Research Laboratory of Mobil Chemical, coincidentally managed by my brother Donald. This invention allows conversion of natural gas from offshore wells into gasoline. The first commercial attempt is now producing gasoline in quality and volume beyond the designed expectation, and the pioneer plant is being expanded. The product is still more expensive than imported supplies, but New Zealand claims the security and environmental aspects are worth the penalty of that premium.

Japan is another brilliant manager of its energy supplies, possibly because their need for offshore fuel is so immense. They are clever fuel converters but their real skill is in worldwide sourcing of all types of energy in its natural state. That diversification is so complete, they are virtually invulnerable to a total embargo by any nation. Despite Japan's huge energy demand, their sourcing strategy has fostered abundant competition for that large market and prices have behaved to Japan's advantage in that controlled circumstance. Canada suffers from that influence in the way the world price of metallurgical coal is dictated by Japan.

Ponder a few basic figures that illustrate why the U.S. should demand a start on the Alaska Natural Gas Transportation System now. On the basis of my composite of several expert projections, the United States could require about 20 trillion cubic feet of natural gas per year by 1995. They may be able to produce about 15 tcf of that demand from their own reserves in the lower forty-eight states. That leaves a shortfall of about 5 tcf per year to be satisfied by imports. Help from the traditional gas fields in Canada could be about 1.5 tcf, and that's all, until new pipelines can be built to the north slope of Alaska and the Mackenzie delta in Canada. Thus the lower forty-eight states are still lacking about 3.5 tcf per year. Prudhoe Bay gas pools off the north slope of Alaska hold the solution. The proven natural gas reserves there have been technically reduced but there is much more to be discovered. This is the largest untapped natural gas reserve on U.S. territory. It's their own, to use as they wish. The ANGTS could initially deliver 2 billion cubic feet per day, increasing to more than 3 bcf; the equivalent of 400 to 600 thousand barrels of oil every day.

Against the U.S. deficiency of possibly 3.5 tcf per year, expected by the middle of this decade, the daily throughput of the ANGTS would provide only about 0.8 tcf per year south of the border. My argument is that this is the first source that should be tapped to remedy the U.S. problem. The arithmetic is simple. There would still remain a need for 2.7 tcf after Alaska gas is on stream.

Some more imported supplies could arrive in the form of LNG, and another 0.4 tcf of relief could come from the Mackenzie delta, courtesy of Canada. I urge, somewhat rudely, wake up America! With new supplies from all those sources you could still be under water by about 2 tcf per year sometime in the mid-to-late 1990s. Canada can export more natural gas. Both the industry and government have demonstrated a clear willingness to assist, but it would take years to crank up this country's pipeline capacity for a challenge of that magnitude. Foothills estimates that it will take nearly *six years* from the time full go-ahead is given until the arrival of the first arctic gas at Caroline, Alberta, and from there to the United States through the two existing prebuild pipelines.

To be sure, there is an undeniable margin of error in all the foregoing demand and supply projections—they could swing either way. But even reducing the U.S. demand estimate by 10 percent and increasing their domestic supply outlook by 5 percent, Prudhoe Bay gas is still required for the shortfall.

Finally, the matter of national interests may be analyzed. The

United States has the supply problem, so their national interest is admirably served by the ANGTS. Canada has the commercial opportunity, so its national interest could be satisfied in the same transaction. What could be better than that?

Canadian economic benefits clearly are to be derived from the massive material and construction expenditures for the portion of the ANGTS on our soil. With the treaty protection in the pipeline agreement between Canada and the United States, our sovereignty is inviolate and their ownership of the Alaska gas in transit is secure. Similarly, Canadian ownership and operation of the sections of the pipeline in this country will enhance net revenue gains, assure environmental integrity and maximize Canadian dollar content with respect to equipment, supplies and payrolls. The substantial generation of taxes will bring a rosy flush to the cheeks of all the politicians involved.

In my view, the true interests of the native people in the north were not well represented in the frosty arctic pipeline debate of the 1970s. More than the Berger pipeline embargo has elapsed with time. A more enlightened view of the operation of the oil and gas industry in the north has emerged. Similarly, the native peoples have a clearer sense that their social structure and heritage are not threatened by properly conceived and closely regulated pipeline operations. Rather, they now visualize benefits from this activity, along with progress in their land-claims struggles. When construction activity commences, and essential information is circulated among the communities, the native peoples will be supporters, not opponents as they were depicted fourteen years ago.

If I seem to speak passionately about the ANGTS construction schedule, my impatient mood comes from the pipeline's inevitability. Why dawdle and eventually fall all over ourselves building this pipeline in a panic mode when the need for arctic gas becomes desperate? Recent events in the Middle East have demonstrated again how vulnerable is North America's oil supply to the unpredictable actions of a tinpot tyrant. The ultimate should be our objective— an environmentally acceptable arctic gas pipeline of the right size, on the right route, at the right time.

INDEX